Shame and Creativity

Shame and Creativity: From Affect Towards Individuation is about shame and how we can use creative methods to transform shame into a lifelong process of self-development. Using a Jungian understanding of the personal and collective unconscious, shame is described as one of the most central affects in relation to self-worth and a good quality of life. The story of Inanna's descent to the underworld will form the clinical structure of healing shame using creative methods, such as painting, movement and imagination.

The main purpose of the book is to communicate a spiritual potential in working with shame using creative methods. The approach is clinical and has a focus on practical ways to process shame based on mythological guidelines.

The book is divided into three parts: Part One is about shame, based on affect theory, Jungian psychology and psychological creativity; Part Two discusses shame in relation to seven primary affects, introducing the Blue Diamante model to describe how shame is often hidden behind other affects and suggesting that all affects must be involved in processing shame; Part Three identifies the steps in the Blue Diamante model with the ancient myth of Inanna's descent to the underworld, it discusses the development of the original self behind shame and presents a new model for transforming the relationship between the masculine and feminine aspects of the psyche, together with art therapy methods.

The originality of *Shame and Creativity* lies in its combination of affect theory, Jungian psychology and a creative methodology. It aims to inspire clinicians to recognize shame and to work more directly with shame as it appears in the therapy room. The book will be of great interest to art therapists and students of art therapy. It will also appeal to all readers interested in creativity, shame, Jungian analysis and affect theory.

Vibeke Skov, PhD, founded the Institute of Art Therapy, Denmark, based on a Jungian approach to creative development, in 1987, and has educated students in art therapy ever since. She has a private practice in Bredsten, Denmark, and also works as a glass artist and painter. She has published several books, most recently on integrative art therapy and depression.

Shame and Creativity

From Affect Towards Individuation

Vibeke Skov

Routledge
Taylor & Francis Group

LONDON AND NEW YORK

First published 2018
by Routledge
2 Park Square, Milton Park, Abingdon, Oxon OX14 4RN

and by Routledge
711 Third Avenue, New York, NY 10017

Routledge is an imprint of the Taylor & Francis Group, an informa business

© 2018 Vibeke Skov

British Library Cataloguing-in-Publication Data
A catalogue record for this book is available from the British Library

Library of Congress Cataloging-in-Publication Data
A catalog record for this book has been requested

ISBN: 978-1-138-20675-5 (hbk)
ISBN: 978-1-138-20676-2 (pbk)
ISBN: 978-1-315-46413-8 (ebk)

Typeset in Times New Roman
by Apex CoVantage, LLC

Contents

Figures and plates

Figures

Plates

Tables

Introduction

This book is about shame, the experience we can have of wanting to get away from being a failure in the eyes of someone else in order to hide where no one can see us. Shame is a concern for all of us. It does not merely exist in those who suffer from a conscious and daily effect of low self-esteem and self-hate. It is mostly hidden below the threshold of conscious awareness and it affects our lives, relationships, society and spiritual connectedness.

The potential in working with shame is to get to know ourselves better and to ignore that inner judge who tells us that we have no value in being who we are. Living up to outer expectations in order to avoid shame can take us away from this development of our own inner potential. The negotiation between inner and outer demands is a lifelong process, which Jung named 'the process of individuation'. He found that a good quality of life was a result of an inner connection between the conscious ego and the unconscious self in the psyche. The basic thought is that shame is destroying this important connection between who we think we are and who we can become. We lose faith in ourselves when we allow others to define us.

Inspired by the Jungian analyst L. H. Stewart (1986), my approach in this book is that shame is activated through experiences of being rejected by some important other, and later by our own inner judging voices. Healing shame therefore includes working with the outer reality as well as the inner. The outer reality is important because that is the place where shaming others makes us feel small and insignificant. The inner reality is equally relevant, because that is the place where we can re-connect with the 'greatness of the self' that was lost in shame experiences.

Most of these rejections are forgotten or repressed to the unconscious, but they still influence our lives and the way we like or dis-like ourselves. In addition to this, we tend to find partners who continue to shame us when we do not expect to be loved for who we are.

In Western cultures we have tried to solve these psychological signs of emotional unbalance with cognitive approaches reflecting the rational left-brain emphasis we value. During this period the lack of emotional balance within the individual has increased to a level which today is difficult to regulate without medication. The focus has been on fixing the problem more than on finding out the activators and psychology behind the problem. As Wilkinson says, "Psychodynamic psychotherapy stands at the interface of what might be termed the cognitive–affective divide" (2010, p. 186).

This book is a reaction to that divide and suggests an integration of mind and body, cognition and affect, by using creative processes as a tool. In creative processes the affects are experienced as moments of letting go of control and 'something' else taking over. It is referred to as a 'flow' process and is something that feels good (Csikszentmihalyi, 1996). Involvement in creative processes is therefore quite opposite to shame experiences, which seem to hold one in the darkness of invisibility. When using the term 'creativity' I refer to a process of originality based on the expression of something new that touches the soul – an experience of having moved beyond the person we thought we were and the discovery of something we can become. Creativity is therefore more than the process of creating something original. In this book, 'creativity' also refers to the discovery of who we are as individuals by using an expressive tool like painting, modelling, movement or voice. Creative processes are therefore expressive as well as impressive, as we use the artwork as a mirror of the inner life. We can therefore never repeat a creative process even when we wish to do so in order to get back to that condition of joy. It will no longer be original as we try to repeat something instead of letting go of what we already know in order to create something new. This courage of letting go of the known is therefore an important part of original creativity and also what most individuals find most difficult, because we tend to define ourselves from what we know we are. Losing our sense of identity during the creative moment is the challenge we confront when we are working with therapeutic change.

Some think it is a mystery that just cannot be learned and that creative individuals are born with this talent or maybe just crazy enough to dare what most people don't. I propose that the creative process is inhibited by shame in all of us. I also suggest that shame can give access to that lost creativity that we need in order to grow as individuals.

In the clinical field of psychotherapy, there seem to be different views regarding the concept of the unconscious, represented in the Freud–Jung divide. Some clinicians, following Freud, see the unconscious as a personal domain, filled with unwanted experiences from the lived life. Others, following Jung, include an archetypal layer in the psyche. Shame experiences are of course always personal and unwanted and therefore mostly rejected by consciousness. My point of view in this book is that the personal and the archetypal need to interact in order to change the affect of shame. When we use a personal approach we learn to accept the lived reality, while the archetypal orientation can bring us new discoveries that can become part of the future.

I would like to suggest that healing of shame follows an archetypal pattern, grounded in the collective unconscious, because the collective unconscious contains the possibility of imagining a life without humiliation. Imagination is such an important function in the psyche, since it directs us towards the future and towards change.

The archetypal part of the psyche, not yet belonging to personal consciousness, is a never-ending resource that we need in order to develop something original and new in life. In shamed individuals, the resources of dignity, empathy and self-care can become known only when they enter the world where these qualities are hiding, and that is most often outside the personal domain.

Indications of a shift in paradigm in the psychotherapeutic professions are now suggested, mainly due to the findings in neuroscience and newer attachment theories. One of the main speakers for this change is Allan Shore, with his research of the importance of the emotional right-brain communication in early attachment and the consequences in later life, when this attachment fails to be 'good enough'. Schore says, "The highest human functions – stress regulation, intersubjectivity, humour, empathy, compassion, morality, and creativity – are all right brain functions" (2012, p. 7). These higher functions seem to have decreased over time, indicating less and less emphasis on the value that right-brain activity can have in our lives. A shift in paradigm would need to include a different attitude to right-brain processes, as otherwise our therapeutic methods remain dissociated from the nature of the problem itself.

Authentic presence means to stay in the 'here and now' moment, being who we are, which is one of the potentials in healing shame, because shame makes us want to go away from the shaming other as a step out of the moment. Stress also makes us disappear from the moment as we try to speed up our lives towards future accomplishments. Methods like mindfulness have become the modern solution to bring back consciousness from a dissociated other reality, but do not include methods to transform shame.

We value our work to be more important than our relationship to our children, making them believe that they are not worth the same attention, which is the key to activate shame of being a failure. We have lost our sense of humour, empathy, compassion, ethic and creativity in a society where the focus is always somewhere in the future. As such we are living in two realities. One is our physical presence and the other is where our awareness travels. A married couple in therapy were discussing their relationship and while the man was telling his wife how much he wanted to support her, she went shopping in her imagination. What to eat for dinner and what to buy . . . she just disappeared from the moment and no longer heard what her husband said. Later, she explained how she was able to support herself, and felt he diminished her by taking the role of wanting to help her. She did not need his help, but his presence.

The strong individual is viewed as a person who can endure experiences of shame without showing signs of vulnerability. We pretend not to care when someone belittles us and just disappear a little from the world every time. In the clinical field, we are treating the reactions to shame, such as sadness, anger and fear, as more acceptable emotions without connecting those to an underlying shame.

My approach in this book is that shame is always a trauma, no matter how often or how humiliating an experience it is. It is a loss of connection with the greatness of the inner self, our self-value, talents and dignity, which can make us feel good and help us make the right decisions throughout life. Without this compass of the soul, we can feel lost in dependency patterns to others who might lead us into meaningless directions.

One of the old paradigms in therapy has emphasized the transference relationship as the healing agent in therapeutic change. This belief is now questioned by newer research about therapeutic change, and the transformative process of change is considered to go through inner relational dynamics *based* on a supportive outer relationship more than caused by one (Schore, 2012). The shift in understanding of human change still needs to influence the clinical methods we are using in therapy, where the therapist will be important in a more indirect way.

The potential in using projective methods, as suggested in this book, is, to some extent, to replace the therapist's role, as the most important 'other'. The artwork becomes a mirror of the soul instead of the therapist and the voice of the self comes out of the dialogue with the image. Using a projected image as a representation of the unconscious makes it possible to get access to the inner life, as it is no longer as unconscious as it was before the expressive process.

The process of projection and introjection in art therapy corresponds to the human cycle of living. We attach to the outer world through our projections, which are often more subjective than objective. We sometimes see what we want to see or what we expect, more than what is actually there, because we transfer personal experiences from the past to the outer scene in the present.

We do the same in working with images. We pretend that the image has a life of its own as we explore the artwork and while we wait for the client to recognize the projected image as an inner reality as well as being an outer image. In the art therapy process, we learn to complete the cycle of projection and introjection in order to know more about ourselves through the projected image.

In the art therapy profession there has been a divide between those who think the expressive process is the healing agent in therapy, and those who think that it is the dialogue afterwards that transforms us. I like to bring these two approaches together by looking at the expressive process as a *preparation* to the name-giving process that follows, and therefore it is crucial that they are connected and equal.

The approach presented in this book combines Jungian psychology and affect theory with creative methods to heal shame. The 4,000-year-old myth of Inanna's descent to the underworld is used as a story that shows the way back from the underworld experience of shame. I have translated some of the dramatic moments in this story of Inanna's journey into psychological language, in order to use it as a transformative structure in working with shame.

The potential in processing shame from a perspective that is not based on patriarchal values can bring forward a vision of a more creative culture based on equality between man and woman.

I think the myth of Inanna can be deeply inspirational to both women and men today. The pattern described in the story is archetypal, instinctive and powerful in its images of psychic transformation and wholeness between the conscious and the unconscious part of psyche. We get the key to come back to life, even when psychological death seems unavoidable, and we hear about the consequences for men when women find their inner wholeness and use it. It may seem that the sacrifice for men is bigger than it is for women, because the masculine has more value in our society, but I do not think it is so. In the story of Inanna, her husband Dumutzi does not choose his descent when Inanna returns but tries to escape, because he feels more comfortable being a king. The same may be true for society, indicating a reason why the whole subject of shame has been taboo for so long. When enough individuals become aware of their shame, they may challenge society to make changes, even when there is resistance to do so.

It is easy to make this subject a gender issue, but it is also important not to do so, because we need both the masculine and the feminine inside our own psyche in order to develop a new world order where shame is not in charge.

I also think we need some kind of manual or program in order to know what to do, when shame is recognized and brought to awareness. The few programs available have a priority of cognitive processes with a focus on developing empathic skills as a replacement of shame (Dearing and Tangney, 2011).

I think a transformative process needs to include more steps in order to replace shame with empathy. Experiences of being rejected must be healed before compassion can be released.

Using only cognitive methods will not include right-brain activity and the implicit memory system that contains all the repressed shame scenes from life. They will keep having an effect on consciousness and on behaviour tricked by new rejections.

My approach in this book is also more clinical than theoretical. I am interested in theory so far as it supports the understanding of processing shame and I intend to combine different approaches because they all add something to the whole.

The first part of this book is about knowing what shame is, after many years of repression and silence. It is about the inner relationships operating beneath the threshold of awareness within the individual.

I think we need to understand the psychology and development of shame and how the shamed individual is caught in cultural patterns of rejecting original creativity. I see it as important to have some understanding of the *purpose* of processing shame before the actual process takes place.

The bridge between unconscious shame and shame behaviour is being presented as a relational unbalance connected to the inner self. Jung's understanding of the self as a regulative and guiding function in the psyche represents the basic psychological paradigm. Getting familiar with the inner life through creative processes is suggested as a method that also introduces the 'greatness of the self' as a motivational factor in processing shame.

I do not differentiate between grades or intensities of shame, because I think all shame experiences are humiliating to the self.

The second part of this book is related to the way shame is experienced as a living reality. We are often controlled by the affects as patterns of unconscious interactions, leading to a life we grow into, without the possibility to choose. In the chapter, shame is presented in connection with the other primary affects of fear, sadness, anger, surprise, joy and interest. Ego development and the process of individuation is described as movements through the affects and introduced in my 'Blue Diamante model'.

Using the affect theory in therapeutic processes as a practical overview to re-connect mind-body, ego-self, cognition-experience and inner-outer realities can hopefully bring back new understanding of the role that shame and creativity play in the transformation of self.

The central issue in this chapter is to reveal the affective disguises of shame. Fear, anger and sadness can make us overlook shame as a tricking affect to those emotions, because shame is more invisible and dreadful to consciousness. I also hope to show how shame is more connected to the self than any of the other negative affects, because it is a self-related affect, while the others are reactions to a wounded self and therefore considered more superficial.

The affect of shame will be related to four different domains in life; the biological, psychological, social and spiritual aspects of living. This differentiation will lead into different clinical approaches to the healing of shame.

In the last part of this book the focus is on the transformative process of healing shame. When individuals have the courage to know of their shame, I think it is important to have some tools that can be useful as a transformative agent. Art therapeutic methods are recommended to play this role in working practically with shame.

Based on the myth of Inanna's descent to the underworld, the healing of shame is suggested to take place through five steps: 1) preparation, 2) descent, 3) death, 4) return and 5) new world order. These steps are also described as affective experiences of approaching the inner self through creative processes and dialogues with images. Jung's psychology, the affect theory and practical creativity are held within a psychological understanding of the myth of Inanna.

Literature

Csikszentmihalyi, M. (1996). *Creativity*. New York: Harper Perennial Publications.
Dearing, R. L. & Tangney, J. P. (2011). *Shame in the Therapy Hour*. Washington, DC: APA.
Schore, A. (2012). *The Science of the Art of Psychotherapy*. New York: W.W. Norton & Company.
Stewart, L. H. (1986). Affect and Archetype: A Contribution to a Comprehensive Theory of the Structure of the Psyche. (pp. 183–203). In: Schwartz-Salant, N. and Stein, M. (editor). *The Body in Analysis*. Illinois: Chiron Publications.
Wilkinson, M. (2010). *Changing Minds*. New York: W.W. Norton & Company.

Part I

Knowing shame

About shame

Cozolino (2016) differentiates between appropriate shame and core shame and says, "Appropriate shame is an adaptation to social behaviour required by the group. Core shame, on the other hand, is an instinctual judgement about the self, as it results in a sense of worthlessness, a fear of being found out, and a desperate striving for perfection" (p. 10). In this book the word *shame* is synonymous with Cozolino's concept of 'core shame' referring to those experiences from life that destroy the inner connection to the self.

When asked, most individuals do not remember their shame experiences, but they do recognize the effect that shame has on their self-esteem. Nathanson has listed some of the inner self-judgemental voices as: "I am weak, incompetent, stupid . . . I am a loser . . . I am unique only to the extent that I am defective . . . I am ugly or deformed . . . there is something wrong with me sexually . . . the feeling that one is unlovable" (1996, p. 18). The connection between a self-judgemental attitude and earlier experiences of being shamed by another often stays unrecognized as complexes in the psyche.

Since Freud's drive theory dominated the clinical field in most of the last century, shame was not taken seriously in the clinical debate and was often ignored as an affective condition beneath so many other signs of psychological unbalance. Morrison (1989) suggests that Freud's lack of interest in shame was rooted in Freud's own shame sensitivity, and he also thought this was the case with many of Freud's colleagues. The psychodynamic approach based on Freud's psychology has therefore also ignored shame, insisting that guilt is more important.

Shame has been called many names without addressing shame itself. Instead the focus has been on the effect shame has on our lives and society. We have been occupied with depression, eating disorders, emotional regulation, trauma, terror and other dissociated states that threaten our well-being as humans. We have searched for therapeutic ways to understand and treat these signs, but without considering shame as an underlying force. During these years there has been an unspoken rule that traumatic experiences are like explosive complexes in the psyche: we should let them be, because an awareness of these unconscious complexes would create a fragmentation in the psyche. The bottom line was that the unconscious was a dangerous place to go, and so we left shame behind on the island it came from, within the individual.

I think we are now in a transition of looking for methods that include both left- and right-brain processes in order to make a bridge between the conscious and the unconscious part of the psyche (based on a general consensus that unconscious processes affect our conscious life and behaviour). In the contemporary literature about shame, there is an emphasis on using a right-hemispheric communication in therapy as an emphatic quality of the therapist, which will then eventually be modelled by the client, leading to self-care instead of self-hate (DeYoung, 2015; Akhtar, 2016; Sanderson, 2015; Garfield, 2009; Dearing and Tangney, 2011). The emphatic attitude of the therapist has become the healing agent, and with a new focus on the therapist's own shame, an issue in the debate. Considering the fact that most therapists are trained without having processed their own shame, there is a special awareness on the risk of re-traumatizing clients by not paying enough attention to shame vulnerability in their clients as well as in themselves. Dearing and Tangney found that "at present, there exist only a few explicitly shame-focused therapies: Gilbert's compassion focused therapy . . . Rizvi et al.'s shame-enhanced DBT for the treatment of borderline personality disorder . . . and Brown's Connections curriculum for shame resilience" (2011, p. 399).

In this book I would like to combine different approaches to the understanding of shame, with the goal of using shame vulnerability as a key to connect with that inner original part in us, which Jung calls 'the self'. The process of getting to know more and more parts of ourselves, who we are and what we can accomplish, has been described by Jung as the process of individuation. In practical terms it means that we need to pay attention to the inner life as well as to the outer, in order to know how life's experiences affect us and our consciousness about ourselves. In therapeutic processes, we usually have the time and attention to change the conscious attitude to function in a more introverted way, with the purpose of listening to the voice of the self. No matter which method the therapist uses, the focus is on the client's well-being, and through the attention of an empathic other, the client learns to approach the inner life with less judgement and rejection.

We do not know what content is in the unconscious and we therefore need a negotiator between the conscious and the unconscious mind. In this book the image has this function as it is used as a representation of the unconscious. What was unknown to us before the creative process becomes known through the dialogue with the image. It combines the physical reality of the artwork, with the psychic reality of the self, and through this relationship, new understanding can develop.

Shame does not heal by itself, especially because we hardly know of it. It operates beneath the threshold of consciousness in ways that we are now beginning to understand the range of.

What is shame?

Shame is first of all a self-conscious experience of being without power in a relationship, where someone else ridicules us to the degree of humiliation.

Though shame can be experienced on so many levels, from 'small' rejections to 'great' humiliations, shame experiences are always to some extent traumatic. Shame paralyzes us and make us disappear from the actual moment and from our own self in ways that in most instances are not healed. We get lost and eventually we pretend to be someone we no longer recognize as our own self in order to avoid further rejections.

One client, who had a long history of shame from her relationships with her family, friends and colleagues, was living with a dissociative pattern which took her away from the present moment and carried her into a lonely place of being disconnected to those around her. In an art therapy dialogue, she would associate to past experiences, which were familiar to her and where there were no emotions. Just as we were talking about something important related to the image, she would leave the image (and me) as if she did not hear the question and go to a different place that had no connection to the image or to the question asked. Of course we both ended up with some confusion, as the dialogue took us to a place where no meaning was found, until this pattern was discovered. The shame was activated as a fear of being rejected if she stayed with me in the moment. It was also shame that prevented her from connecting with something that was important to her and therefore the dialogue became empty, superficial and with no orientation.

The physical signs of shame are a face that is blushing, head bent down and lack of eye contact. The need to escape the situation is instinctive and maybe not conscious, and so the body will freeze and the mind dissociate in order to survive the humiliation of becoming a nobody in the eyes of another.

One client was brought up in a family that she described as a 'concentration camp'. She had been a servant to others for her whole life as a natural way of living, so part of her access to her own emotional life was frozen. Her sister, four years older, was considered the most beautiful and intelligent in the family and the client was supposed to be like her, but she never felt she could live up to this ideal. She looked for volunteer work where she could repeat the pattern of being used by others, because that was what she thought she deserved.

She never knew that she was caught in a shame pattern, and when finally she was 'set free' in the creative process without orders to follow, she got scared and did not know how to use that freedom. The sudden awareness of shame activated a sadness of having lost so many years in a self-abusive pattern, but also gave her a new motivation to change her life.

In spite of the view that shame is a reaction to being rejected by someone else, I think that the transformation of shame is first of all an *inner* transformative process. We don't have the power to stop someone from shaming us, but we do have the capacity to change ourselves.

Approaches to shame

The wish to gain better self-esteem is usually a topic in most psychotherapy, and therefore negative self-evaluation is an important issue in therapy. Nathanson (1992) describes the polarity between shame and pride, and sees the pattern as a three-step process: a) shame activation, b) cognitive process and c) reactive behaviour. The thoughts we have after a physiological experience of shame are based on earlier experiences of a similar nature. The relationship between experience, cognition and reaction takes place as an unconscious chain of action – reaction patterns involving both right- and left-brain functioning. Negative thoughts like "I am weak, incompetent, stupid, helpless, ugly, unlovable," become the activator to behavioural patterns of withdrawal from social interaction (ibid, p. 317). This might explain the interest in the cognitive therapies for working with mental aspects of shame patterns: attempting to change the inner voices with more positive ones based on an expectation of new behavioural patterns. The problem in using a cognitive method only is that the activation from the implicit memory system and all the shame scenes that are stored there are ignored and not included in the transformative process of change. The integrative interaction between cognition, emotion and affect as a process of lasting change can therefore not take place in this paradigm. The cognitive approach to the healing of shame behaviour can in worst cases introduce new ideals for how we should think of ourselves, and when this does not work or hold for a longer time, the individual can instead re-activate the old shame pattern by not being able to live up to the outer expectations. When we take research from different paradigms into consideration related to the transformation of shame, I think we end up with a general consensus of the need to involve a) affect, emotion and cognition, b) imaginative processes and c) sharing and processing shame scenes. To this understanding I would like to add a need to involve the creative expression of original self-parts.

The question we should ask with all of these approaches is, when do we use which paradigm in the overall process of change? If we use Rosen's model of change as a movement through ego-cide (letting go of an old pattern), initiation (symbolic interaction with self) and return (living a new self-part), we might see that different therapeutic methods are preferred during the three phases of change (Skov, 2015). Every part of the transformative process is a creative process of movement from one place to another, as opposed to being stuck in a rigid pattern of behaviour. Often the small steps in such a movement from one place to another do not make rational sense to us while we are experiencing the process. Often we feel lost, confused, unsure and emotionally vulnerable, until we reach some understanding of what is going on. Trusting the process means trusting that there is a meaning ahead in time. As one student asked in the middle of a two-week course: "Can you explain what you are doing, because I don't know what is happening?" She was sure that I had a plan and knew where we were heading, without realizing that she was guided by her own self and that I simply created the environment for her to be creative. Of course it is always a dialogue, where we both create the moment together, but the inner experience of that moment depends on how each of us are able to let go of the past in creating a new moment of reflection and novelty. The letting go of a familiar way to reflect when we explore something new, like an image, is the basic challenge in every creative process. To trust that vulnerable position in consciousness where we do not know what surprises the next moment will bring is really the creative initiator to change. My student did so by trusting that I had a plan that would hold her through those moments of not-knowing, and of course it was her own self transferred onto me that made her complete this journey without too much fear.

The paradigm behind shame

One unspoken rule that we are living by in a society based on the laws of patri-archal domination is that the feminine principle of relationships is secondary to rational reason. There is an increasing tendency to allow only well-documented research to enter the clinical field of psychology as an attempt to control thera-peutic processes assuming that the therapist's own original creativity cannot be trusted for its empathic quality. According to Shepherd (1993) the split between science and therapy is also a split between thinking and sensation on the side of science, and feeling and intuition on the side of therapy. The tendency today is to add more thinking and sensation into clinical work and to reduce the use of feel-ing and intuition, which shows in the preference of cognitive therapeutic methods. There seems to be a collective fear of stimulating the unconscious and the solution is to take more control through rationalization. When we assume that the building block to original creativity is based on the interaction between control and chaos, or between the conscious and the unconscious, we are losing our connection with original creativity because we don't trust the outcome of this interaction to be good for either the individual or our culture. Therefore it is important to get back to a basic understanding of how we as individuals change and develop in the best possible environment.

With an increasing emphasis on the relational psychology in research, there seems to be a new or stronger emphasis on the relationship between the client and therapist as a healing agent in therapy. I think we may overlook the importance of creativity as a transformative process *within* the client while we focus on re-doing the developmental process. Neuropsychological research (Schore, 1994; Cozolino, 2010; Grawe, 2007) points in both directions. The researchers empha-size the lack of 'good enough' parenting as a foundation for shame, but they also emphasize that therapeutic change is an internal process that involves imagination and activation of different functions in the brain. My emphasis in this book is that the emphatic relationship is a pre-condition for therapeutic change and not the cure in itself. We still need to include psychological creativity as a key to lasting change, but since there is very little research to confirm this, it is still not part of the paradigm behind therapeutic change. To activate imagination and play, the client must be able to follow a curiosity that is free from outer expectations and therefore free in the relation to the therapist. This change of focus is one of the cornerstones in art therapy, because both client and therapist are discussing the artwork as an image of the inner life in the client.

One client came with a lot of anger inside that was activated by rejections from her ex-husband. She was on the edge of being overwhelmed and afraid of having a psychotic breakdown, because she felt that a lot of inner voices were talking to her at the same time in her head making her confused about right and wrong. In the therapy, she was invited to find an object in the room for each voice in her head, and she chose two staplers as her anger, a brush as her shamed part, a black plastic cover as her shame refuge, a tape roll as her analytical voice, a scissor as her perfect side, and a used cloth as her imperfect side. During the discussion of the different voices it turned out that it was the imperfect part that was activating anger. When she was criticized for not being perfect, there was no inner voice taking her side to support her, and the shame pattern took control and made her hide under the black plastic cover. Realizing this pattern made her create a connection between her conscious part and the isolated, shamed part, and gradually she came to remember two men whom she felt could support her in the present crises by actively confronting her ex-husband, arguing her case in order to set her free in her economic dependency on him. By projecting the inner voices, she was able to find new solutions that she could not see as long as her anger and shame overwhelmed her from the inside. It exemplifies the importance of making a separation between the affect of anger and ego consciousness, in order to look at the pattern from a different perspective.

Unconscious shame

There seems to be a general agreement among neuropsychologists that most shame experiences are held in the implicit memory system in the personal unconscious, depending on the intensity and humiliation of the self (Schore, 1994; Cozolino, 2016). This is mainly due to Schore's research on the early mother-child relationship and the consequences of a mis-attunement leading to the child's experience of being a failure.

Akhtar (2016) suggests three reasons for the emerging interest in shame today, where the first is related to the growing need for self-exposure as a narcissistic trend in our culture. The need to be seen and mirrored by others can be a way to avoid the experience of shame and function as a compensative behavioural pattern, where shame remains hidden in the unconscious as a controlling factor. Another suggestion, he says, is a need to understand where (especially in eastern cultures), shame communication is used as a power to control the population. The third reason comes from psychoanalysis itself, due to the increase in childhood abuse and other humiliating parental behaviour, which cannot be related to guilt alone.

A further reflection on the increasing attention on affect-regulation is that more and more individuals lose control of their lives. They want to feel better, lose weight, get out of addictions, bad relationships, stress, depression, meaninglessness, loneliness and so on, and they experience that they cannot use their conscious will to do so. This leaves the control to the unconscious and the affects. The collective and personal ideals about being perfect and in control have created a shadow in the unconscious that is less perfect and not controllable through negotiation and cognitive therapy.

In art therapy I often meet this ego ideal in clients who wish to create the perfect painting. One client started a painting process full of enthusiasm, but within the first ten minutes she lost all her energy, felt tired and just wanted to go to sleep. When we discussed what happened to her during these first ten minutes, she said: "I found an image in the colours I expressed, but then I knew that I could never make that image as perfect as I wanted it to be, so I gave up". The shame of not being able to make the 'perfect' painting was not a conscious experience as much as a bodily reaction to shame. Years of experiencing shame without naming it is a challenge in our time and many individuals say, "I have felt it all my life but I did not know it was shame until now". Shame is something we all have and when we learn to name it for what it is, we can do something about it.

Because shame is often not made conscious, we have to look at the reactions to shame as a way to understand the connection between shame and shame-related behaviour.

The behavioural patterns that follow shame have been studied by Stewart (2008), who described the destructive power of shame. When it gains control of consciousness it can cause murder, suicide, terror and depression (depending on the introvert or extrovert attitude).

The different layers in shame, being both a traumatic experience and a cultural condition for all of us, make the subject complicated and lead to different clinical orientations.

Understanding shame as a parental humiliation of a child with damaging consequences seems to be a general opinion amongst clinicians who listen to the stories of their clients in the therapy room. To stop the spiral from repeating itself through generations, the knowledge we have of shame must be passed on to all of us, parents, teachers, therapists, children and adults who are willing to know their own shame.

I think it is important to understand the cultural background for shame as each social system has a way to use shame as a regulator for social behaviour. The way we are controlled by the social system can be a shame activator that we do not question, because the power of the system is so much stronger than the power of the individual. Reactions to shame experiences caused by the social system are therefore more often made conscious as anger reactions due to the restrictions felt by the individual. It can later be compensated for in situations where the power balance is reversed and the connection to the first experience is lost.

Shame has many grades of intensity, and some experiences are more acceptable to consciousness while others create dissociation in the psyche due to the degree of humiliation. Knowing when to differentiate shame as a socializing experience or as a humiliation of the self is complicated by the fact that shame is seldom shared with others. The lack of self-regulation in many individuals today indicates that shame, as a self-conscious experience, is avoided by consciousness, so individuals are not able to 'see' themselves from an outside perspective, and therefore not able to change their behaviour. One of the goals in processing shame is that we can endure looking at ourselves without shame of what we see, because then we can also make different choices.

In an article by Hooge from 2014 a new approach to shame is suggested, which he calls "positive interpersonal consequences of an ugly emotion" (p. 95). Hooge suggests that we should look at shame as a positive experience, because "shame would motivate behaviors that are aimed at protecting the threatened self from further damage and at restoring the threatened self if possible" (p. 102). This approach is opposite to that of Kalsched (2013), who has found that individuals create self-protective systems as a reaction to trauma, which also means, he says, that the self remains locked up in the inner dissociated world of trauma. Hiding becomes part of the shame pattern that keeps individuals from feeling free. Approaches like Hooge's do not seem to include any benefit for the individual in processing shame, but points at the social benefits of shame. There is no real protection of the self and certainly no restoration without a conscious effort to make it.

There has been some discussion regarding ways of measuring shame. Considering the fact that most shame scenes are connected to right hemisphere and the implicit memory system, it will be difficult for individuals to communicate their experience of shame because they do not remember them. Using a phenomenological approach based on self-evaluation and bodily reactions to shame is therefore a vulnerable procedure, because shame is most of all an unconscious self-related condition with many different faces. We will need research methodology that also includes the patterns that operate in the unconscious related to cognitive, emotional and instinctive processes. Using the arts and the projected images of the unconscious is one way of getting information about the different images we have of ourselves and recalling forgotten stories connected to early development.

Freud's concept of the unconscious is unlike Jung's in the sense that Freud understood the 'id' as a sexual instinct searching towards satisfaction more than towards meaning. Freud did not have a psychic and archetypal component in his understanding of the unconscious, and therefore the unconscious could not be trusted as a guiding principle in the psyche. I think it makes a big difference how the unconscious is defined before we actually dip into it. What can we expect to happen when we let go of control? Are we confronting the unbearable shame again or is there something else for us in the unconscious? Something we don't know of? Something good?

Lee and Wheeler (1996) think that an individualistic approach can communicate shame to the client, because the client will become the subject to objectification by the therapist. They are referring to Freud's reductive method and to the therapist as a shaming other to the client, as if there are no other options than to use a Freudian paradigm.

The focus on the object-relational approach to the healing of shame is relevant during the phase of integrating personal traumatic scenes from life, when someone else was part of the shame experience. Continuing a development beyond shame is for me the whole purpose of processing shame. I think it is important to address the interaction with the greatness of the self, as well as integrating personal shame scenes. Jung's archetypal psychology and his approach to the *inner* object-relational connection between ego and self gives us a possibility to discover new original shame-free parts of the self that were never made conscious before. This process of individuation is deeply connected to original creativity as something new to the world as well as to the individual.

Few clinicians include Jung's concept of the collective unconscious layer in the psyche, indicating that the unconscious is 'no more' than personal rejected memories. Using a Freudian understanding of the unconscious may support an integration of shame memories, but cannot initiate a development of new and original aspects of the self.

This book attempts to fill this gap by showing a connection between the personal and the archetypal dimension in the psyche related to shame and to creativity. I think shame puts us in a box with no access to the unknown. The unknown outside that box is then feared as the enemy, and we are stuck in dynamic patterns that repeat themselves endlessly. This is what we call a normal life. The increase of control makes the walls thicker and thicker. As the tension increases inside the box, the more experiences we collect from life. Now and then we see boxes explode. They become the opposite of normal, because the tolerance to shame has reached its limit and the fragmented pieces are put in bigger boxes labelled 'anti-social behaviour'. As a society we do not tolerate anti-social behaviour. It becomes part of the enemy outside the box instead of a learning experience that could change the box and society with it. The creative process that would initiate social changes based on reactions from the individuals does not take place because the link between social control and individual responses remains separated and gets personal instead of relational.

Ego, self and shame

We need to think out of the box in order to free the creative process and to become the individuals we really are. Jung was a good example of a creative thinker. He moved out of the Freudian box and became isolated from the scientific milieu of his time. He was considered a mystic more than a scientist because of his interest in the spiritual, which at the time was considered dangerous to rational thinking.

His concept of self as a guiding principle in the psyche was therefore also difficult to accept, because who was in control if not the conscious ego?

The challenge in working with the archetypal self and the greatness attached to experiencing the self is that when this meeting takes place before the ego is prepared to remain in a modest position, there is a risk of developing an inflated ego as a compensation to an unconscious shame. We need to have some shame available in consciousness that will help us stay grounded when we meet the greater reality of the self in the image.

Jung was well aware of this risk of becoming inflated and he often suggested his patients should use creative methods and dialogues with the projected image in order to avoid identification with the self.

Jung's differentiation between the ego and the self is based on two paradigms. One is that the ego is constructed as a result of a hermeneutic interaction with the world, while the self is an unchangeable core in the psyche that instinctively searches for wholeness and manifestation. Most clinicians use a self-concept that is based on an understanding of the self as a construction, defined through the interactions with others, corresponding to the ego concept in Jungian psychology. This approach in therapy can in best cases lead to a stronger sense of ego consciousness, because that is all there is, but it does not create an inner connection between ego and self as a condition for original creativity and wholeness.

In the process of healing shame we can understand and experience the self as 'the greatness of the soul' through the image. According to Jung, the self has two basic functions in the psyche. Firstly, it instinctively tries to correct one-sidedness in the ego through compensation. This can be found in dreams, images or behavioural patterns in life.

Secondly the self searches for wholeness, which Jung refers to as the individuation process. These two qualities connected to the function of the self are important when working with shame, and I think this is the main difference between a Jungian approach and other psychodynamic approaches. The clinical implication of including the collective unconscious is that the individual can discover a new voice within, which has not been known before because it is not part of prior experiences.

One client said she could paint only when she was together with someone she trusted who would not criticize her artwork. So when she participated in courses, she would do whatever task was expected by the trusting other/teacher, but when she was at home, she would end up in a depressed state, where nothing would work and she felt bad. When we were discussing her background for this, she remembered a scene from age two and a half, when she came to her mother's bedroom with an enthusiastic expectation of praise and a drawing of her vagina, as she had just discovered that mysterious hole in her body. She remembered the disgust on her mother's face and the shame that followed of having shown her discovery. She became dependent on someone outside of herself who would permit and take responsibility for her expression as a way to avoid further rejections.

When she was at home, the inner judge became too strong, because the good, accepting mother was projected to someone outside, who was not present when she was alone. The challenge was to find her good mother inside her own psyche, so she could be able to paint when she was alone. This 'good mother' image could not be found in her personal life experiences. All she could find was the judging eyes of her mother. When using her imagination she was able to create a clay sculpture of a good mother sitting with her daughter, and this good mother image came from within her archetypal self. The clay mother was given a voice she could repeat inside, whenever the shaming mother appeared.

According to Tomkins (2008), shame is a rejection of the two positive affects, joy and interest, which makes the child withdraw from the relationship in order not to be rejected again. Miller (1996) disagrees with Tomkins and does not think it is possible to reduce the number of affects to nine (Stewart reduced those to seven), because it 'is too simplistic a brain model to account for the full range of human emotional experience' (p. 16). This was in a sense similar to Jung's view, because he saw the affect as the instinctive side of an archetype, where the other side was the image. Jung did not discuss instincts as a limited group of specific qualities because they followed the nuance of the psychic image. We must remember that the affect of shame is part of our evolutionary survival strategy, as it helps us to socialize and stay connected to others, while shameless behavior can lead to exclusion from the collective, and to death (Dissanayake, 2000).

Akhtar (2016) addresses shamelessness as a condition that is not always pathological but "also exists in the setting of a child's innocence and a great man's self-assurance" (p. 112). In expressive processes we need to be shameless so that we can allow new parts of the self to be expressed. Therefore, we need to be innocent as a child or feel great as the self in the moment of expression. We cannot care about what others think of us during this process, because then we allow 'them' to decide what to express and no new discovery can be made. Using the creative process as a safe place to explore parts of the self that were rejected earlier in life is not always easy, because most individuals have experienced shame, even when they were 'shameless' as children. Being shameless in the creative process means to take a step back to the time when life was still like paradise and before we were able to see ourselves through the judgemental eyes of another.

Shame and empathy

Another quality of the self, according to Jung, is that human ethical behavior is a result of being connected to the self, while Freud's concept of the id was more related to the principle of pleasure based on negotiation with a moral super ego. I think the cultural potential in working with shame is that we can begin to use our shame vulnerability as an attunement to each other based on empathy and human ethics, not because we are expected to do so under threat of exclusion from society, but because it follows a coherent self-structure.

Today, when interest in shame is emerging, I find it important to emphasize the spiritual attitude to shame in order to avoid a too-narrow clinical approach related only to the psychology of the ego and the personal unconscious. I think we need to ask what a consciousness of shame can lead to in a person's life. Why would we voluntarily want to get closer to a self we might find is defective unless we trust that there is a better life hiding on the other side? A differentiation between what we see and the attitude of seeing might be appropriate here, so we can come to understand that it is our way of seeing that is defective and not the self as such.

Dearing and Tangney (2011) discuss ways to regulate shame and suggest self-compassion as an effective method. They refer to Gilbert's compassion-focused therapy, where clients learn to become more accepting of their feelings and needs. Their main point is that empathy makes shame disappear. This may be the argument for using a relational approach to the healing of shame, where the therapist comes to represent an empathic other, as opposed to the shaming other from the client's past.

Brené Brown has developed a 12-step psychoeducational approach to the healing of shame as a tool for clinicians as well as for the lay community (Dearing and Tangney, 2011). She found more interest in shame as a topic from the lay audiences than from the clinicians, and she calls it "a silent epidemic" due to the fact that most clinicians do not study shame (2011, p. 356). Part of her approach to shame is to practice empathy in a relationship. She says, "Being able to practice empathy is predicated on a person's ability to relate to the shame experiences of another" (p. 363). She emphasizes the sharing of shame stories and says that sharing "allows individuals to practice sharing vulnerability, empathic listening, and compassion" (p. 370). I find her psycho educational approach important, because it combines teaching with individual shame processing. This also means that shame is normalized to include us all and not just those who need professional help. Shame vulnerability is an openness of sharing as well as of listening to each other, which is an opposite of shame communication.

The limitation of her work is that she does not include discoveries of new self-parts in her program, because working with symbols is not included.

When true original creative patterns are discovered at the bottom of shame, what then? How are we as individuals able to use this spiritual potential that has never been shown to the world before? I don't think there is any narcissistic failure in recognizing the greatness of the self. I think it can lead to more creativity, joy and love in a world so controlled by shameless corruption, terror and narcissistic needs. Therefore shame is *more* than humiliating experiences of self-disgust. It is also a key to a more caring way of seeing life and the meaning of being here.

In most literature about shame the relationship between the client and the therapist is the place of transformation, and creative methods are hardly ever mentioned. I think the therapeutic relationship alone is a vulnerable focus when it comes to processing shame. It is in relationships that shame is first experienced, and when therapists are unaware of their own shame they may unintentionally transfer shame to their clients through objectification, reductive methods and countertransference reactions. If we also recall the unconscious need we have to repeat shame scenes, the odds are in favour for using creative media in order to avoid shame experiences in therapeutic relationships.

Shame is still a personal and cultural taboo in our patriarchal culture, though more books are being published on the subject. Shame is something we do not speak about, and in most cases we no longer remember the shame we have experienced. As therapists we are also part of a shame culture, and the study of shame processes is included in few therapy curricula.

Also I think we need the physical aspect of creativity together with imaginative language to match the location of shame in both brain and rational mind. We cannot process shame using just our rational mind alone, because shame scenes from our lives are located in the right hemisphere and not in the left.

Experiencing shame

Knowing shame when it hits us is a first step towards changing a shame pattern. As we catch these sudden moments, when shame replaces our positive expectations to others and to what life has to us, we can feel it in the body, in our self-esteem, in our social relations to others and as a spiritual disconnection to something greater than our personal ego.

In general, emotional conditions are considered to be symptoms that we should try to get rid of rather than get to know better. We see the destructive effects of those who lose emotional control and blame the affects more than our relation to them. They have become signs of weakness in cultures where having control is more important than losing it, which further activates a shame of not living up to social ideals when we fail. The more we attempt to control emotional states, the more they seem to control us, and the result is found in depression, psychoses, terror, anxiety and addictions to the point of a collective breakdown.

Approaching emotional regulation from a Jungian and affect theoretical understanding, we need to allow affects to be released without the humiliating voice of shame and as a protection of the individual as well as our culture. But how can we do that with emotions that we don't want to know about? Or with emotions we consider dangerous and uncontrollable by ego consciousness? The affects *are* dangerous when they are activated and then left unattended as complexes in the psyche. The rational mind has a good argument in what we see from outside, but seems to miss the psychological fact that it is the *rejection* of the affect that creates the compulsion to live them out in distorted ways.

Expression through making art is an opportunity to 'let the steam out' without abusing others and to explore the deeper meaning behind emotions. It is a way to compensate for years of control that we have learned is a necessary condition for living together. Freud claimed that our normality was built on the rock of repression of the instincts, and that a failure to do so represented a failure of the individual. For many years the individual became the scapegoat for shame, without including a shaming other as a responsible factor in the reactions to shame. Something was considered wrong with the control function in the individual, and parents remained off the hook for shaming others. This is not the time to blame individuals for being wrong, especially because most shame is transferred in the name of love or according to the moral laws of socialization. This is a time when we have to face the ugly shadow of socialization and make our own choices.

Summary

A general consensus is that before change can happen, we must come to know more about shame and what shame does to our motivation to live. Avoiding shame is no longer a solution to the negative influence that shame has on our lives. Our free will to act is restricted by the power coming from the complexes in the unconscious, and we need to know what goes on in the unconscious in order to regain control of our emotional life.

Jung's psychology and self-concept introduces a different potential in processing shame beyond personal exploration. Getting to know the function of shame, we might prepare ourselves to re-connect with the greatness of the self as a soul aspect of original creativity.

Another general agreement in present literature on shame is that compassion cannot exist together with shame. Again, from a Jungian perspective it is the ego-self connection that facilitates compassion, and therefore we cannot just replace shame with an attitude of compassion without also allowing the process where ego and self can re-connect.

Shame and inner relationships

The shadow and the inner judge

According to Nathanson (1992), shame is experienced as inner voices that devalue the dignity of an individual to the extent of self-disgust. From an object-relational point of view these voices once came from someone outside who convinced us that we were no good. When shame becomes part of who we are, we no longer want to be visible and fully present in life. We want to hide and pretend to be someone else, because we do not expect that others will like who we are.

Getting to know the shameful part of us means being able to see and tolerate whom we are inside. DeYoung defines shame in its relational aspect as "an experience of one's felt sense of self disintegrating in relation to a dysregulating other" (2015, p. xiii). Her relational approach to shame takes the focus away from the inner life of the individual as she maintains 'the other' as an outer person. I think the relational approach is needed in order to understand and process shame scenes in therapy, but I also find that awareness of inner relationships is equally important when the focus is to repair the ego-self axis and develop new patterns to live by.

While clinicians have focused on the cognitive approach to life's experiences, especially since the beginning of the past century, individuals have lost connection with all the not-so-visible aspects that also operate in an object-relation. We learned not to trust our own feelings if they could not be verified by the rational mind. Objectivity became superior to subjectivity, and still we do not trust the individual unless we can understand the signs rationally. Shame is such an irrational experience. It comes all of a sudden, claiming that the individual is a failure. A positive reaching out towards the other is rejected without warning and the individual feels isolated from the other or from the group.

When we want to transform our shame patterns and reconnect to that inner place of dignity and self-esteem, I find the Jungian approach useful as a practical tool as well as a paradigm for understanding the journey. This is because the transformative process itself is considered to be an inner process, while the developmental process can be seen as a result of relational interaction. Through the development of personality the child uses the outside world to create inner relationships, which then take control of behavioural patterns. I think an understanding of the early relationships is not enough for transformative work. We also need to know how far we can go. What is a self's potential? What is possible? How do we change?

Getting to know the shamed part of our inner self becomes relational as we open up to different 'others' inside our own psyche. In general, when we talk about 'our self' we refer to a *consciousness* we have of our self and we do not include all the unconscious inner parts that are operating within us, because we usually do not know them. The battle between inner shaming voices and the voice of the self is therefore a beginning conflict when we first begin to listen to the inside.

An example may illustrate this.

A 31-year-old student from an eastern country, who had lived in Denmark for six months, dreamt that she was going to visit 'home' but missed the plane. When she woke up she felt a great relief, because she did not want to return to the strong influence of her parents, who wanted her to come home and to live a life like they did. She wanted to become an artist free from their influence. The next night she dreamt that her mother came to her bedroom (in Denmark) and said that they were going shopping, and that I (the leader of the course she was participating in) had been informed about her not coming for the day's teaching. She could not resist and followed her mother, and then she woke up with a fear of being late for the class. These two dreams illustrate the struggle we can experience in making a conscious decision about which voice to follow. When the self is activated through images, dialogues and group processing, the shaming voice will also be activated, trying to pull the ego away from the self and back to the protected family expectations, based on the belief that this will be the best thing to do. The ego of this student was stronger when she was awake than when she was dreaming. Her fear in real life was to let her parents know what she really wanted from her life, so she travelled to the other side of the Earth to avoid the confrontation. But her dreams were pushing her to take a stand in relation to them, because the struggle created a conflict in her consciousness as well as in her artwork.

Most of us have learned to keep a focus on the outside, avoiding that magical dialogue with someone inside who can inspire us to make decisions that are good for us. We come to trust the voices that we internalize from someone else and lose connection to our own original voice, which Jung would refer to as the voice of the self.

One student said after a group drumming session that she heard the voice of her mother as soon as she began to play in a different way than the others. She played louder, speeded up her rhythm and felt that she stepped out of invisibility in the group. Her internalized mother told her to go back to being invisible – that she was in danger of being excluded if she stayed visible. She decided not to listen to her mother and enjoyed the experience of freedom in the process. Later the other group members said that she had been such an inspiration to them that they wanted to follow her rhythm. They all became part of the new inner voice that would help her manifest more of herself in the future.

Jung has described this journey towards the self as the individuation process, and the first relationship, closest to consciousness, is what he termed the ego-shadow relationship. The shadow represents a personality opposite to what we have identified with during our upbringing. If an individual identifies with shame, the shadow will come forward in the most shameless manner as a way to balance a one-sided self-image in consciousness. Opposite to this, a shameless individual, who seems to have no self-consciousness, will keep the inner shamed shadow part locked up in the personal unconscious as an invisible and rejected part of self.

In a group there was a participant who came with a history of having been shamed in her family all her life. She was rather withdrawn in the group and seemed controlled and stiff in her body in her interaction with the other group members. After two weeks of working with shame and her inner shadow parts, she became the omnipotent child in all creative group processes. In a group painting, she would practically swim in the painting, so no one else could find a space there. In drumming, she would play so loudly and chaotically that the rest of the group would withdraw and just play in their own world. She had so much power that the other members of the group felt unable to make contact with her and with each other. She was finally accepting her shameless shadow and did not care about anyone else. The group shared in her pleasure of having discovered her inner shameless child, but in the end it became too much for them, and they had different ways of reacting to her. One escaped into the mother role, trying to support this wild child. Another turned her focus inside to find her own centre of balance in the middle of chaotic sounds, as a test of returning home. Another gave up and stopped drumming and said that she 'would come back later', like tomorrow! Another waited for the right timing but never found it. The lesson was that when finally the shameless child unfolds, it needs protection from a good inner mother, who can let the child know when it is a good time to express and when to hold back in order not to be rejected by potential playmates. As adults we have that possibility by creating the *inner* mother and child relationship, while a child depends on the outer mother's ability to regulate the child without using shame as a communicative tool. As adults in a group setting, we can discuss these things after the creative processes and all learn something about our own reactions. The participant who reacted with a motherly attitude towards the shameless other in the group felt that she had to abandon her own inner child and discovered that she had done the same throughout her childhood. Her mother was mentally ill and unable to mirror her needs, and so she gave them up and began to support her mother instead, without a father to protect her. I find these recognitions between present and past behavioural patterns very important, because we can make group interactions conscious and meaningful without projecting the shadow onto other members in the group. It also gives each individual a possibility to imagine new behavioural patterns for future relationships.

Working with rejected images of who we think we are opens up the shame we experienced when these ways of behaviour were rejected because someone did not approve of them. In artwork there is a tendency to recognize such fragmented parts of the self as inner personalities that have a voice of their own, which is different from the voice of the ego. Because the shadow is projected and held in the artwork it is no longer fused with many other rejected parts of the unconscious and therefore we have a chance to create a conscious relation to the shadow as well as to many other inner personalities.

Creative nakedness

When individuals try to live out their shamelessness in an expressive process, the inner shaming judge often appears, attempting to cover up the naked expression. While shame is holding the individual in the dark, the creative process is doing the opposite; it enlightens individuality by making it visible for others to see. Consciousness of self therefore also creates a vulnerability to shame as we transfer inner parts to the outside. We may shame our own expression by judging the artwork as ugly, primitive, bad, stupid or no good and start all over. From time to time I have observed how shame operates in creative processes without the individual being aware of it until we discuss the process afterwards. Sometimes important and vulnerable parts in the image are painted over as a way to protect consciousness from being shamed again. Instinctively there is a sense of vulnerability and risk of being excluded from the group when we stand out naked as individuals. As one student said, "It was as if my father's voice came into my head and made me confused".

Without knowing that this is happening, the autonomous forces of the complex take control of the creative process and of life, preventing true originality from unfolding (Skov, 2015). Therefore we do need to discuss artwork. Without paying attention to the artwork and to the expressive process itself, we may not discover this self-shaming function, which covers or hides authentic parts of the self in the image-making process. These are the self-blaming patterns that we have not chosen, but that were given to us before we were able to make our own decisions.

The majority opinion regarding shame in the literature is either developmental or pathological. Few, among them Kalsched (2013) and Stewart (1996), have attached the spiritual dimension to shame/trauma as a loss of soul connectedness, which in Jungian psychology would be similar to a broken ego-self axis. Also there seems to be some consensus related to the treatment of shame with a (traditional) focus on the transference relationship, but with an increased awareness on the therapist's own unconscious shame and its effect on the client. The connection between shame and narcissism has gained most attention in the pathological approach, basically due to early rejections of the greatness of the self. Morrison (1989) says, "Thus, shame and narcissism inform each other, as the self is experienced, first, alone, separate, and small, and, again grandiosely, striving to be perfect and reunited with its ideal" (p. 66). Morrison describes the relationship between shame and narcissism as a dialectic relationship where the ego strives to become perfect through merging with an idealized other and at the same time wants to be separate and independent. The motivational drive towards perfection is seen as a reaction to the experience of the self as flawed and defective. Narcissism is therefore a reaction to shame experiences during the time when a child lives in the early symbioses with the mother before the phase of separation. When the mother is experienced as a shaming other during the symbiotic phase, the child will internalize the self/mother as an inner shaming other and stay wounded in its own uniqueness when the next phase of independence follows. Using a Jungian concept of the self means that the self will later strive towards balance by attempting to merge with an idealized mother because the 'first' mother was a disappointment to the self. A Jungian approach to narcissism could therefore be considered as the self's creative urge towards repair of an internalized bad mother image. In narcissistic behavior the need to be the center of attention, to be seen and mirrored by someone else, will relate to the inner child's drive towards fusion with the idealized mother. But at the same time there may be an older part of the ego that has matured in life, becoming more independent from the mother realm, and these two parts can create an inner tension, where one wishes for merging and the other for individuation. When Morrison refers narcissism to a dialectic relationship we might understand this as an inner relationship between a young shamed self and a more adult and conscious drive towards individuality. Again, from a Jungian perspective, we can see narcissistic behavior as an attempt to repair the ego-self axis by getting a good mother's attention and admiration, so that the process of individuation can continue.

In art therapy, narcissistic behavior is manifested through images of the archetypal self. The inner greatness is explored through the symbolic image, and for a narcissistic personality it is important to mirror and accept these images without reducing them to the ego. The process of repairing the shamed self through compensative images is an important use of art in therapy, because the images are experienced as coming from the inner self and not, for example, from an idealized other.

Another shame activator in the use of a client's artwork is when the client expects that the therapist can 'read' the image and thus get access to hidden shame parts without the client's permission. Using a reductive method can therefore lead to re-experiencing shame, because the client may feel exposed and objectified.

The nakedness that we can experience when we express images from the invisible reality in the artwork have a parallel in the biblical story of Adam and Eve eating an apple from the tree of knowledge and discovering that they were naked in front of God. Jacoby (1991) describes this as the ego's first experience of a self in the image of God and sees it as the beginning of the individuation process. The shame that follows makes sure that the ego does not identify with the greatness of the self, but "stands in relationship with that which is greater in us, the Self, drawing a certain confidence from it" (Jacoby, 1991, p. 19). Knowing shame therefore also means knowing self, and the step in psychological maturity can be described as a transition from oneness with the self towards being separated from self, as a pre-condition for dialogue.

In relation to shame, the physical activity of externalization is in itself a release. The advantage of including creative media is that you can share inner shamed and fragmented parts in a symbolic way before you even know what they mean on a personal level. You can talk about the image and stay protected from the shamed self until you feel ready to share shame scenes with another.

Not all personalities in artwork are representatives of the personal shadow. Some are too archetypal and should not be integrated into consciousness until the ego can tolerate such images of self without being overwhelmed.

I remember a client who started by drawing the devil and ended up drawing a man on a motorbike months later, with which he could identify without the danger of becoming psychotic (Skov, 2015). The art therapist can support the development of ego strength by the way questions are asked and by maintaining the ego position in relation to the image. Methods of identification with images might be useful during the last part of shadow integration, but not at the initial meeting with the unconscious, because the affect might have a more compensative nature that can be overwhelming for the ego. In such cases of compensation, the ego is often not represented in the image at all. The gap between the content in the unconscious and ego consciousness is still too big to be imagined and expressed in the artwork.

I think it is important to understand the role of shame during this process of getting familiar with the unconscious. If the image one has of one self is contaminated with shame, the ego may not want to look at the shamed self even through the image. The motivation to start working with images in therapy may therefore have to go through the therapist as a trusting other. By keeping the focus on the artwork as an external image, the individual can get the time needed to become familiar with the 'strange' language of the inner reality as a preparation to a more psychological and personal sharing. Jung explains the ego "as the complex factor to which all conscious contents are related" (1959, p. 3). Being a small part of a whole, he also refers the ego to the "subjective feeling of freedom" (p. 5). Our so-called free will is limited to ego consciousness, while the will of the self remains outside conscious cognition and control. Therefore, when unconscious parts are made conscious we gain more control of the forces within, simply because we know more of ourselves. Edinger (1996) brings to mind the experience that Jung had when he was 11 years old, of walking out of a cloud, only to discover that instead of everything happening *to* him, he suddenly felt that he had a will of his own. Consciousness of having an ego was not the same as having one! Most people do not have a differentiated experience of an ego, but are merely follow-ing collective expectations without having reflections of their own. Their inner authority and will to make decisions are merged with collective demands of who they are supposed to be. A first step in knowing shame is to find the bravery to reflect on the self-image that has happened to us.

One student made the image shown in Plate 1 (see plates between pages 112 and 113). She said that it illustrated her shame at not having reacted to the shame she experienced in her childhood. How could she have just put up with it for so long? She was shaming her own self for not knowing and for not having done any-thing to change it. This is one of the initial self-blaming reactions to not-knowing what we are living as life happens.

Jung emphasizes that "integration of the shadow, or the realization of the per-sonal unconscious, marks the first stage in the analytic process, and that without it a recognition of anima and animus is impossible" (1959, p. 22). Getting to know the shadow parts of the personal unconscious related to self-images is a preparation to create a dialogue with the inner masculine and feminine parts in deeper layers of the psyche. We need more imagination to work with the inner masculine and feminine parts as they are operating further away from our ratio-nal awareness.

The inner masculine and feminine

According to Jung, the feminine part, anima, is related to a man's unconscious soul aspect, to Eros and to the principle of relationship. A woman has an inner masculine part, animus, as her unconscious spirit related to logos and to the prin-ciple of differentiation. This layer in the unconscious is seldom made conscious without an effort, and is experienced in its projected form on partners of the oppo-site sex.

In art therapy we activate both the feminine and the masculine principle as part of the method. As therapists we try to initiate clients to create new relationships with inner personalities through therapeutic dialogues with the artwork. We use the artwork as representations of the self, as we search for some rational meaning of symbols and colours.

Jung points out that lasting change can come about only when the ego keeps its separateness from the different inner personalities, the shadow, the animus/anima and the self, and when these figures are granted "relative autonomy and reality (of a psychic nature). To psychologize this reality out of existence either is ineffectual, or else merely increases the inflation of the ego" (Jung, 1959, pp. 23–24). Exploring images is far from psychological. The image often convinces us of a psychic reality as it becomes alive and connected to feeling. This aspect of the dialogue becomes a vitalizing part of the process as meaning and value come together.

I would like to approach the masculine and feminine from two angles in this book: firstly, as a relationship between the conscious ego and the unconscious inner man *or* woman and secondly, as an inner relationship between the conscious ego and the masculine *and* feminine. In the first relationship the ego of a woman is expected to be feminine and therefore the animus would be more unknown and closer to the self, and the opposite applies to the man. This was Jung's approach to the animus/anima discussion, so the masculine and feminine relationship was in reality a relationship between the ego and the inner partner.

As a post-Jungian approach to the masculine and feminine polarity, we can also use the conscious ego as an observer or 'therapist' in relation to the inner couple. I like to think of them as people living inside us, defining our life quality by the way they relate to each other. Because they usually function as an *unconscious* relationship, this behavioural pattern may not change, because they are disconnected from consciousness. Using a creative medium, like clay, we can create them as two representations of the feminine and the masculine and discover how they are doing with each other. Working with this couple is more imaginative than working with the shadow, and therefore needs some preparation.

As I see it, the ego is not always to be trusted because it is coloured by parental expectations to have a certain preference for either the woman/mother or the man/father. One student had made the inner couple as two clay figures, and there was a sword illustrating the masculine and a snake lying on top of the sword illustrating the feminine. When I asked her about the snake, she said it was evil and unpredictable and no good for the man. This was how she had experienced her own mother and her own father, and so it became her opinion of women in general. She had no personal experience of the positive aspect of the snake, referring to the instinctive nature of feminine freedom and sensuality. Her ego consciousness was coloured by her childhood experience with a mother who became overwhelming and frightening in her unpredictable and rejecting attitude. In order to make any changes in the masculine and feminine relationship, the ego must find a more balanced position in relation to the snake in order not to be biased when she begins to have dialogues with the couple. We can compare it with a couple coming to therapy. If the therapist is more accepting of the man than she is of the woman, the woman will not feel she is understood in the same way as the man, and there may be no progress in the therapy at all. The therapist's personal expectations of women will block the transformative process between the couple. This is also an example of the importance of working with the shadow before working with the inner couple, as the integration of shadow qualities makes the ego less rigid and able to work on this deeper level.

If the relation between the mother and father was experienced as un-loving, the little girl will not want to be like mother, because she will not get her father's love, as she can see that her mother did not. She might identify with the father because he has more value or power and she will end up rejecting the feminine part of herself that her mother represented, simply because her father did. Qualities that her mother represented will then become shadow aspects in her personal unconscious. This is when the development of identity becomes entangled with shame. The shame of being like mother becomes associated to the shame of being a woman.

The same goes for the man. If the mother was living out the masculine part in the relationship and the father was experienced as weak and unable to protect the child from a shaming mother, the son may not want to be weak like father, and will take the mother's strong masculine side as his role model. Qualities related to his father will then become shadow aspects in the man. The shame of being like father becomes the shame of being a man.

These 'inherited' parts of inner dynamic patterns define the way we approach life creatively in everyday functioning and transfer shame from one generation to the next. When un-reflected, our creativity is far from original; it is merely a reaction to our childhood experiences of shaming others close to us. It may be easy to understand with our rational mind that shame is connected to the rejected shadow in the personal unconscious, but it is more difficult to connect shame with the feminine and masculine, because they are also rooted in the cultural unconscious. Clinically this means that we need to process shame on two levels, a personal and a developmental level, as well as a more cultural and archetypal level.

During the last 30 years I have invited clients, students and couples to express their experiences of their masculine and feminine sides as two figures in clay. When they do so for the first time, they usually associate the couple with their parents, without having thought about it during the expressive process. This tells me that the inner couple do not easily change and that they stay similar to the role models we internalized in childhood. I have also experienced how fast they can change their relationship when first they are created and explored through active imaginative dialogues. The ego will ask them questions (as a therapist would in a therapeutic session with a couple) in order to awaken their relationship so they can put into words their dreams and feelings of being together. Active imagination is not an easy method to use alone, because it does not follow the rational logic of the ego.

We need some preparation to accept the psychic reality as a reality populated with inner personalities having their own voices and will. When we have no awareness of the rejected self-images opposite ego consciousness, we are merely fulfilling others' expectations without questioning the 'truth' for us in these expectations. Confronting the shadow creates a separation and stronger independence in relation to outer collective morality, and this is needed as a firm ego foundation in active imaginative work. The ego must stay separate when the imaginative dialogue between the masculine and the feminine begins. The ego also needs to have a certain self-reflective awareness in order to avoid childhood biases controlling the dialogue.

In the beginning of working with the inner couple, the actual therapist can be the one asking questions like, "How does he feel about the woman when she turns her head away from him?" Or "How will she respond when he says . . . " When these inner voices are experienced as surprisingly true in their affective component, it becomes easier to do active imaginative work alone.

The process of separating from these early identifications that 'happened to us' leads to a strengthening of the ego position, as new decisions are made during the therapeutic process.

The mother–child relationship

In most literature about clinical methodology the focus is on a good relationship between the client and the therapist as the healing agent in therapy. Following Jung's understanding of therapeutic change, the transcendent function in the psyche needs to be activated before any transformation can take place. In order to activate the transcendent function an inner opposition must be present in the client, as for example hate-love, good-bad, strong-weak self parts. The tension caused by the opposition will create a third image, which will be the new transformed aspect of the self (Skov, 2015). The challenge is to hold the opposition long enough for the transcendent function to do the job instead of projecting one of the parts onto the therapist.

The client-therapist relationship is therefore only a pre-condition for change and not responsible for change itself. I think we need to separate these different processes in therapy in order to understand the true nature of psychological creativity and transformation. Of course the therapist is important as an-other who is capable of emphatic understanding and who has some kind of toolbox available to use together with the client, but it is the client who does the actual inner transformation through the creation of a third position coming out of the tension from the inner polarity. It is not the therapist. When the good relationship is created and the client trusts the therapist's good intentions, the relationship fades out to be only secondary to the transformative work. It becomes a conditional space that both parties can relax into as a creative matrix for change. From that time and forward, the focus must be on relational connections inside the client where the methodology for this work becomes the bridge.

The inner good mother who wants the best for the child must be found and activated within the client. Some of the transference on the therapist must flow back to the client and become a resource within the client's psyche. This is the *time* aspect to every integrative process in psychotherapy, namely the time it takes for the client to discover and 'own' the qualities of good mothering in order to create something new within the psyche. If the good mother is experienced solely as qualities that the therapist can get access to, this inner tension in the client does not develop. The therapist needs to be able to let go of the identification with the good mother image while waiting for the good mother to appear as an inner voice and attitude within the client. I think this is a difficult task for many therapists. To let go of the identification with the positive helpful and supportive mother is not easy, because it also gives the therapist a bright personality of goodness. It belongs to the traditional therapeutic identity and seems to be one of the motivational reasons for wanting to become a therapist. In my opinion this is one of the traps in the therapeutic profession. It is a classical countertransference vulnerability that goes with the job. The client needs a good listening mother in order to create the therapeutic matrix to start the healing process of integration, and the therapist often *becomes* the positive mother without clearly realizing that it is a *function* that the client needs to become familiar with in relation to the inner child. It is not the full identity of the therapist but a human empathic quality that the therapist is trained to use together with the client (and hopefully also with others). From being more or less dependent on the therapist, the client will eventually seek to develop more independence and inner freedom to think in different ways and to make decisions without the therapist being present.

The creativity of the therapist is shown in the ability to take different roles following the development of the client. When the client experiences overwhelming affects like sadness, the therapist may relate to the client as a good mother would to his son or daughter in order to create the therapeutic matrix needed for transformation. If the therapist remains in the good mother position by being overly helpful for longer than the client needs, the client may feel that the therapist expects him or her to stay dependent, which can lead to shame experiences of having independent thoughts or impulses. Eventually the client must leave the therapist in order to avoid shame and belittlement. It all depends on the therapist's creative listening to the client's growing need for independence.

Another aspect is the use of creative *modalities* in the therapy to facilitate a creative process within the client, based on the creativity of the therapist. This will be the art therapy toolbox. Directives, expressive processes, imagination and dialogues are based on both left and right hemispheres. When a Jungian orientation to art therapy is suggested as a therapeutic method to heal shame, it is first and foremost because Jung's approach to creativity as a transformative process rests on the transcendent function.

One client came to her therapy session saying that she felt that she was 'going to pieces'. She had been angry with her teenage daughter and had shouted at her in a way that her good mother image could not tolerate. She definitely did not want to be like her own mother, who always shouted at her when she was a teenager. She felt an inner opposition between being a good and bad mother, and her identification with the good mother image was breaking apart. The inner opposition was present and if she could hold it long enough to allow the transcendent function to operate, she would have a chance to transform her self-image into a more whole position.

Creativity and inner relationships

Table 1.1 illustrates the most important inner relationships that I have found in relation to shame.

Working with the relationships to inner personalities has for me always been a practical way to relate to unconscious patterns in the psyche. The unconscious is often experienced as a big mixture of undifferentiated affects, emotions and personal memories that comes and goes in consciousness, depending on outer stimulation. For someone who has never listened to the inside, or who feels too much shame trying to do so, I find it helpful to approach the artwork as if it were a person. Therefore I often invite clients to imagine that their painting represents someone else, and ask how they would describe that person. If the person could speak, what would they say, and how would the client respond back?

As Table 1.1 shows, I find the relationship to the shadow, the inner masculine and feminine and the self to be a helpful structure in practical work as a reference to these personalities coming out of images. By recognizing the personality in the image as one of the archetypes (shadow, anima/animus and self), we can use a therapeutic method with more precision. For example, when a shadow is found in the image as a rejected self-representation from childhood, we can play with that personality as if it were an extension of the ego, attempting to accept and integrate this rejected part of ourselves. When working with the personal shadow, there is usually a story of shame connected to the rejection of the shadow, which leads to a sharing of personal shame scenes.

Table 1.1 Inner relationships and shame

Inner relationship	Shame relatedness	Potential
Ego–shadow	Shame related to rejected self-images	Self-esteem
Ego–anima or animus	Shame related to gender identity	Inner authority
Ego–anima and animus	Shame related to psychodynamics	Synchronicity between inner and outer reality
Ego-self	Shame related to self	Individuation

In working with the ego–anima/animus we are dealing with the way we relate and express ourselves to the outside world.

I remember one woman who could only be supportive of others in a group painting and who showed no expression of her own self, and it turned out that her inner man had been sleeping for a very long time. He was just not available in the psyche as a self-manifesting force of interest to become visible. Therefore she could not give birth to her own self in the group painting, because that would also need to include the dynamic of the masculine. The problem in that relationship was that the woman lost her freedom when the man was awake, because he wanted to dominate her and take away her wings.

There is an association to the story of Lilith and Adam, where Lilith, who was Adam's first wife, flies away to the desert and the Red Sea, because Adam would not respect her as his equal. This power struggle is here solved by putting the man to sleep so she does not have to fly away. I think it shows a pattern where a woman can stay in a relationship with a dominating man by manipulating him into a passive role in bed as well as in daily life. She can rule the house and he the outer world, and she can have a shelter and some order in her life. By de-activating the inner masculine, women survive the threat of loneliness but lose the connection to the inner self. This was especially the case in past generations of women who became identified with the mother archetype who had no inner personal life. She was there to support her husband and children and found her identity in the role of Eve. This tradition of identifying the feminine principle with the mother archetype is changing. More women today are following their own need to live an independent life guided by the inner self, even when it means to live alone.

When women turn their attention to the inside, the earliest inner relationships that often appear are not only a sleeping man but also an inner neglected child.

This connection can bring back a consciousness about inner needs that we forgot existed and which calls for attention. I think the most important part of inner relatedness is the feeling of compassion that we can experience in relation to these rejected parts. Getting to know the child/shadow we create new attachments to the self, replacing the shaming attitude with a voice of acceptance and empathy.

Shame and the loss of original creativity

One of the archetypal images of a 'shaming other' is the Greek gorgon Medusa, whose hair was made of snakes. She was raped by Poseidon on the altar of Athena and was further punished by Athena, who made her one of the three horrifying gorgon sisters. Anyone who looked at her would freeze to stone. When the hero Perseus finally cut off Medusa's head, he held a polished shield, like a mirror, so he avoided being paralyzed from looking directly at her.

The mirror shield represents the artwork. It gives us an opportunity to confront shame scenes without being re-traumatized by the direct confrontation with a 'shaming other'. This is one important purpose of using creative methods in working with shame. Another purpose is to free the creative energy that has been held in the body in fear of being shamed again. As one student said; "I have been a listener all my life, because nobody ever listened to me when I was a child, so now it is difficult to know which questions to ask about the image". She had abandoned her curious mind and voice when she became a listener to others.

When Medusa was killed, the white winged horse Pegasus was released from Medusa's bleeding body, representing the spiritual creativity behind shame. This story offers an important key in confronting shame in its paralyzing effect but also as a release of original creativity.

This is not a gender-related issue. Men as well as women experience shame and the dreadful consequences that shame can have on our lives. Using a Jungian perspective throughout this book means that the feminine side is also part of men's psychological structure referring to the body, to imagination and to the unconscious.

Using Medusa as an image of the traumatized young maid who became abusive to everyone around her, original creativity was held in the body until head and body was divided and original creativity released directly from the body. When the creative psyche goes through the complex of shame, it does not want to become visible. It will try to pull consciousness back to the fusion in the maternal unconscious womb of safety, preventing the soul from true original creativity. The inner struggle that takes place in this polarity where one part wants to be set free, while another (shamed) part wants to stay invisible, creates many different resistances to the use of creative modalities. One client kept saying to herself that she 'could not', 'did not know how', 'it was properly wrong', all the time she was painting her family portrait. Other clients long to be creative at home, but always something 'comes in the way', and time goes by.

The wounded feeling function

According to Jung's typology we have four psychological functions; sensation, feeling, thinking and intuition. Thinking and feeling are rational functions, while sensation and intuition are irrational functions. Jung found that we usually identify with one function, while the other three functions are more or less unconscious. When thinking is the main function, then feeling will be the most unconscious function, because they are placed opposite each other, and the same goes for sensation and intuition.

He described the individuation process as a process where we could become conscious to all functions as a way to perceive reality from all corners of the soul. When shame experiences are rejected and stored in the unconscious memory system, then the feeling function is not trusted in its potential to evaluate a relationship. The feeling function is then operating from the unconscious and no longer available as a rational psychological function that helps us understand what goes on in a relationship.

The feeling function is our ability to evaluate emotions in order to see the objective pattern in a relationship. With a wounded feeling function we tend to isolate our experiences with both the external and internal other, thus making experiences personal instead of relational. This is especially the case in shame experiences, where one of the reactive instincts is to move away from the shaming other and withdraw to the inside. When this happens we can no longer evaluate the experience on an objective level and the operational function of feeling is wounded.

In Jung's understanding a feeling is therefore not the same as an emotion, even if we tend to link the two words. A feeling is like an inner knowledge about the emotional connection to another person without judgement. It is those moments of enlightenment when we just 'know' what is going on between ourselves and someone else. One moment later, our thinking may take charge again and ridicule what we were just feeling, because it did not make rational sense. When for example a therapist is giving the client good advice, the rational explanation is what it looks like, that she wants to help the client to mature and develop. The therapist believes in her own motivation to be helpful and may not question her intentions or her actions, because giving advice is what is generally expected from a therapist. The understanding is based on our interpretation of what we see, related to thinking.

In the feeling relationship something very different may also take place that is often not put into words. The client may feel belittled, followed by the shame of being rejected as a responsible adult who can make mature decisions. The expectation in helping someone else is that the person who is helped is not as mature as the helper, so the balance of knowledge is unequal as one is now superior to the other. Even when this is part of the deal in therapy, it still may activate an old pattern of shame whereby this child–adult relationship was once connected to experiences of being dominated. When such emotional reactions are activated, it can be almost impossible to make a decision to act, especially because the feeling of inner knowing stays inside and is not shared with anyone. The psychological understanding is that there is no such thing as being wrong. There can be different experiences, but they both belong to someone and therefore exist. The problem is that when we only use thinking as a psychological function, only one of the explanations can be true and therefore the other experience, like shame, cannot also be true at the same time. According to thinking, one of the experiences must be rejected, and here the individual stands, less strong than the collective accepted reality. The real potential for growth happens when these two realities meet without one being truer than the other. If the client expressed her honest reaction when someone gave advice, the therapist might learn something new that would give her more sensitivity to shame in her work.

Nothing is more damaging to the feeling function than shame, because shame isolates the individual in relational terms. The feeling function is based on Eros and the feminine principle of relationships and stands opposite to the thinking function, which is based on Logos and the masculine principle of separation. As rational functions, they are both 'explainable' and contain a certain order of logic, but each comes from a different paradigm and approach to reality.

Many women come to therapy with a wounded feeling function and a problem of not trusting their own emotional experiences. Should they leave their husband or not? They blame themselves for being weak and often stay too long in unhealthy relationships.

When we lose our trust in what we experience, we do not know which actions to take. We would like someone else to just give us the right answer, and maybe we seek therapy with an expectation of finding someone who is willing to tell us so we can get on with our lives. As therapists we want to make our clients happier, and unconsciously we may live up to this expectation as a countertransference reaction and the feeling function then stay un-functional in the client.

When a man identifies with the traditional masculine principle he will see reality through the glasses of thinking and often ridicule arguments based on emotions. On the other hand, when a woman becomes opinionated by identification with the masculine principle of reason, she loses connection to her feminine roots through her identification with Logos. Nothing is more irritating to a man, Jung says, than a woman with strong opinions (1959). If the *woman* identifies with the masculine principle, the man is in danger of losing his masculine power to her animus and the feeling function will create a bad atmosphere between them as a result of an unconscious battle on the feeling level.

In a group of students, there was one very opinionated and problematic student. A casual remark would activate her ego-animus and she would argue that something else was truer. What she did on a feeling level was to reject the other student's experience as if it was wrong and she was right. At the end of the course other members from the group began to reject her as well by not listening to her, not wanting her to comment on their images. She did not understand what was going on, and felt rejected, 'as always'. In the psycho-logical reality she was rejecting her own feeling function and became 'blind' to what was going on in her communication with others. She had so much shame that she could not look at her own self without dissociating into her rational reality that once made her survive early family rejections. So she was living with one conscious reality of thinking and one unconscious reality of feeling and they were not connected.

When a man has identified with the feminine principle, his behaviour is controlled by his moods more than by reason and his self-esteem becomes vulnerable. A wounded feeling function is bad for both sexes and is the cause of many problems in relationships. When it comes to processing shame, the challenge is to look at shame in its relational aspect so that responsibility is shared between the shaming other and the one being exposed to shame. Healing shame will therefore also restore a wounded feeling function.

Psychological creativity

The general understanding of creativity is related to the making of something new and valuable – something related to a product more than to the psyche. Newer brain research has been more interested in the process that takes place in the brain *during* a creative activity than in the product itself. In this book creativity is understood as a transformative psychological process. Psychological creativity includes an expressive process as well as an impressive dialogue with the artwork, where the creative product, the image, is felt as an inner reality.

The interaction between the conscious ego and the *collective* unconscious is considered to be the birthplace of original creativity, while the interaction between the conscious ego and the *personal* unconscious is considered to be an integrative process, which lays the ground for original creativity. The concept of being creative is therefore also related to our *ability* to change as well as to the methodology used to facilitate this process.

Ehrenzweig (1967) has described the creative process in three steps. The first phase is schizoid, where we put fragmented parts of the self onto the canvas as an opening of the process. We try to loosen the control that we may have had during the day in this moment of release. In this phase we may be torn between the two realities, the physical and the psychic. Which reality should we trust and follow? Can the process facilitate a new wholeness, or is it just another waste of time? The feeling function is not yet active as an evaluative function in the psyche, so no decisions can be trusted. When we finally let go of the rational doubt and discover something in the expression that we recognize as part of the fragmented self, we move into the second phase, the manic condition, where we work to integrate all the split-up parts into one whole. In the manic phase we are reorganizing the self as a projected image. We are in an inflated condition, dancing with the gods, moving around with colours, forms and rhythms in a flow of synchronicity. This phase leads to the third and last part of the creative process, where consciousness is back in the physical reality of the ego and the image is recognized as an inner state of mind. Ehrenzweig refers to this phase as the depressive position. According to Ehrenzweig we switch from one condition to another in order to complete a creative process. He suggests that different conscious states are involved in the creative process. First we are extroverted, then we are in the space between extroverted and introverted, in the doorway, so to speak, and finally we withdraw from the outside, going back to the introverted position. Looking at creativity as a process in constant movement between the inner and the outer reality is an interesting perspective, because then we can actively change the inside by working with the projected outside image.

In shame-related behaviour there is no flow between the inside and the outside. Expectations of being shamed will prevent individuals from becoming visible and the manic phase of expression therefore cannot take place. Here shame functions like a stick in the wheel, destroying the pattern of creative circulation. On the other hand, the art-making process can re-stimulate the manic phase for a person who feels trapped in the inner reality because of the outgoing activity in the expressive process. In art therapy, the image is explored after the expressive phase using imaginative language, which is a schizoid way of approaching the world, because we are confronting the psychic reality and yet we are in the physical world doing so. The uncertainty about which reality we shall trust is a beginning issue in therapy, because we think we must choose only one of them. When imagination is connected to personal associations at the end of an imaginative exploration of the image, the last phase of depression is activated. We are back on Earth and back in the personal reality where there may not be any flow. It is the moving back to the inner space that is associated with the depressed position. The value in having a personal dialogue with someone else related to the artwork makes the depressive phase in creativity a felt experience of discovering something new in the image that can be integrated into life.

Dacey and Lennon (1998) describe the most important personality factor in creative individuals as a tolerance of ambiguity: the ability to hold an inner opposition emotionally and mentally until the creative process has been completed. This has a parallel to the description of creativity in the old alchemical procedures, where the alchemist had to stay focused on the vessel. If the cork was not properly put on, the transformed content would burn away, and there would be no creative outcome. What Dacey and Lennon are pointing at is the necessity to 'hold' the attention in the creative process until the process has finished, otherwise we will have missed the news in consciousness, because our mind went somewhere else.

There is a parallel here to Jung's concept of the transcendent function. When we can contain an opposition in the psyche without projecting one of the parts to the outside, the inner tension leads to a solution indicating a third and new position in consciousness. Like Jung, Dacey and Lennon (1998) also claim, "There is no longer any doubt that creative ability can be purposely enhanced" (p. 226). Using an academic approach to creativity they also found that "fostering creativity . . . can help people with psychopathologies more effectively" (p. 226). The point here is that creativity is approached as an activity of psychological change and not restricted to making a product.

I suggest that the experience of shame in the creative process is related to each of the three phases in creative processing, as described by Ehrenzweig. In the first (schizoid) part, we have to decide if we want to change the pattern of hiding and to tolerate the fear of becoming visible in the artwork. One student said that she had to paint in a naturalistic style before she could use more imagination and free expression in her work. She said she needed to feel 'safe', and this was her way of preparing herself for more spontaneous expressions. At the end of the week, she managed to make one spontaneous painting in a more imaginative and free style, and that became her favourite!

Many individuals who long for more creativity in their lives start painting nature scenes or other nice objects from the outer reality. What else should they express?, they say. Is creativity not identical with the mere expression and the use of a medium? In the schizoid phase, we just allow fragmented pieces to come out in a more uncontrolled manner in order to start the imaginative dialogue with psychic reality.

During the manic phase we are shameless in the way we express. The inner judge stays in the physical reality, while we fly away to another, more magic world. This is because of the lack of self-consciousness in the manic condition. We move outwards following the flow of projection. In order to do so we need to let go of the shame that keeps an eye on us, judging every move we make. And how can we do that? How can we forget about our shame for this short moment in time? I think many individuals dream of letting go in an art-making process as a way to finally let go of shame, but inner judging voices keep pushing them back into hiding when they try.

The step in moving from the schizoid towards the manic phase is also a trust in the psychic reality. It is like an ecstatic letting go of the familiar as the interest in the unknown becomes more important. When there is no trust in the process you can do nothing, because fear of the unknown is in control. This is when a therapist, teacher or someone else who trusts the psychic reality can come to play an important role. In the transference that person can become the 'trusting other', allowing the individual to let go of shame in order for the self to do the work.

When the creative process and flow experience reaches its natural ending, as we get hungry or tired, self-consciousness returns and shame may take over again, when we look at it through the eyes of a shaming other. The judge may doom it wrong, ugly, disgusting and a complete waste of time, and the shame pattern does not change but is rather reinforced, being just another experience of having done something that revealed the ugly side of the self.

When looking at images, we can always find something in the image that is not affected by a shaming other, some part that is free from shame. It may be hidden behind a colour or in the corner or held within a figure, but it is there.

The difference between a therapeutic process and individuation is that in a therapeutic process the goal is to integrate personal unconscious content into our conscious mind in order to connect ego and self. The inner connection between our conscious mind (head) and the unconscious self (body) is called the ego-self axis and is the foundation for the process of individuation (Skov, 2015). The creation of something new is therefore related to the process of individuation and not to the therapeutic process, because content from the personal unconscious has already been created once before and was then, in the past, repressed because of the overwhelming affects. Therefore they are not *new* memories, when they are brought back to consciousness during therapy. They are re-created memories. The integration of personal unconscious content into consciousness leads to a stronger mind-body coherence, while the individuation process leads to the creation of new original parts of the self that have never been conscious before.

Making personal forgotten memories conscious through psychotherapy can therefore not be considered creative in the sense of original. Where is the original aspect to a forgotten memory? Levine (2015) talks about implicit (unconscious) and explicit (conscious) memory and says that often our conscious states are activated through an unconscious implicit memory. Early experiences of shame that are stored in the implicit memory may foster present experiences of shame when something in the presence has something in common with the early shame experience.

It can be a tone of voice, a smell, a word, an attitude and so on. When the relation between the implicit and explicit memory system is disconnected, we also lose the possibility to understand our own behaviour and response to a present situation. We might say such behaviour is inappropriate, because the reaction in a given situation does not seem to match the present situation and the vulnerability to shame has therefore increased.

Psychological integration means to make such implicit, personal unconscious memories conscious in order to create a link between the past and the present and between the unconscious activator and the pattern of behaviour that follows.

Many individuals have described how they seem to work with the same themes again and again in therapy, and wonder why they do not change. From a Jungian perspective change comes about when new parts of the self are developed and lived out. But often this aspect is not considered as important in most therapies as working with negative life experiences.

One student was working with her inner imaginative man and woman and discovered the unspoken shame between them. Through movement it became clear that the woman was trying to seduce the man in spite of her inner disgust for him and as a reaction to his attempt to dominate her. When she was invited to express her disgust instead of hiding it and pretending it was not there, he stopped his domination and sat down. After a short separation, the woman took initiative to contact him again, but this time she seemed more mature, and with eye contact and within a few minutes they were dancing a tango as two lovers would do. No words were spoken and this union was original. It had never happened before, and the key learning process for the woman was to be more honest in her emotional expression, instead of hiding behind a seductive behaviour, castrating the man with her unspoken disgust. When the student was asked later what she felt was most important from this experience, she said that the woman's shame made the greatest impact on her. She had completely forgotten about the joyful union between the two as the original aspect of the therapy. The tendency to hold on to shameful experiences even when a new potential is felt as a living reality shows the way our brain holds on to the past and the challenge we have when it comes to lasting change.

How do we change?

When self-reflection becomes a self-shaming activity, individuals may prefer to use medical treatment in order to avoid re-experiencing shame. We all know that being in therapy means reflecting on ourselves, depending on the method, and some individuals may not feel that there is any potential behind shame. They may only experience shame and disgust when looking at their self, and therapy is therefore considered to be just another shameful experience unless there is some understanding of a positive outcome beyond shame.

Grawe (2007) argues that the therapeutic dialogue alone does not make long-term changes in the brain, even when the dialogue is experienced to "flow well and seem important and interesting to both parties" (p. 40). He says that new neurological activation patterns must be established in the brain, and that the client must hold a positive expectation to the outcome of therapy as a drive to accomplish therapeutic change. Part of the therapist's role in this process of change is to support the client in repeating new patterns of behaviour after the therapy hour, because the risk of going back to old patterns in 'real' life is there until new pathways have settled in the brain.

Many processes in the brain are involved with therapeutic change, and one of them is imagination connected to right-brain activity. Research on placebo effects shows that change is dependent on our ability to imagine a change before it actually takes place (Kirsch, 2009). When we imagine that we get better because of a pill or therapeutic technique, the outcome is significantly higher than when we do not have any expectations of reaching a goal. This finding confirms Grawes's research on positive expectations related to therapeutic change mentioned above. Cozolino (2016) refers the "miraculous" imagination to our ability "to escape the present moment, create alternative realities, and then begin our journey to find our new narratives" (p. 26). Imagination is a biological function in the brain that we use in order to escape from shame, and therefore imagination can refer to dissociated conditions as well as to therapeutic change. I think the difference lies in whether imagination is used as a dissociative tool for survival of a shame experience, or later as a tool to facilitate change. The point is that imaginative activity reduces the pain of shame experience, as it relates to a reality where all dreams can come true. In dissociated states there is usually no connection between the two realities because the imaginative activity is compensating for a humiliation of the conscious ego. We know this from children's play, where they play the roles of the abuser in order to recover from trauma. They use their imagination and reverse the actual situation as a way to re-gain the power and loss of control from the traumatic experience.

In art therapy we use imagination for different purposes. First of all, we create novel thoughts and new pathways in the brain that can replace old patterns of mental processing. Secondly we use imagination to activate personal memories that are stored in the right brain as unconscious scenes from life. In the dialogue with a client we may start with imaginative exploration of the artwork, with no focus on the personal story. My experience is that during that exploration, an associative memory often pops up in consciousness from the client's personal life. The image of a dragon becomes identified with mother, when she was shouting for no good reason, or the house is recognized as the ex-husband with no windows, and so forth. The image becomes personal as a surprise in the dialogue and has created a bridge between the world of imagination and personal repressed memories.

What we need to do as therapists is to wait for those moments when the client makes the connection between the two realities as organic associative links between implicit and explicit memory systems. In this way we use the artwork as a centre of reflection during the integrative process.

Stewart (1996) refers imagination to the activity of play and suggests sand play as an active imaginative media for playful activity. I am left wondering why he never introduces painting or other creative media with his clients.

The connection between imagination, creativity and therapeutic change is an argument for moving beyond verbal and cognitive methods in the attempt to activate new and lasting pathways in the brain.

According to Cozolino (2006), "prolonged shame reduce levels of endorphins, . . . and dopamine and increase stress hormones and noradrenalin . . . inhibits plasticity and creates a vulnerability to psychopathology" (p. 86). Considering the amount of individuals living with stress, I think that shame processing could become one of the solutions to many physical and psychological unbalances of our time.

Shame of the feminine

The patriarchal paradigm began its development when Adam's first wife, Lilith, insisted on maintaining her individual freedom in sexuality as well as in life. Adam would lie on top of Lilith, and she refused to surrender. (Some call her the first true feminist. Others feel that she should have understood Adam in a more symbolic way.) But Lilith thought that since they were both created from the same dust, they should be equal. God stepped in and shamed Lilith for her lack of obedience, and she flew to the Red Sea and the desert to hide. We all know that Eve was later born from one of Adam's ribs, indicating that she had lost her independence and freedom and belonged to him. She adapted to his needs and became known as someone who longed for knowledge more than freedom and sensuality.

The strength in Lilith to consciously choose freedom instead of surrender to an outer law is a quality I see many women fighting for today. The longing for a partnership where the woman is true to her own inner spirit as well as loving to her husband often makes the woman stay in a not-supportive relationship for too long. If only he would change and appreciate her for her Lilith characteristics, then all would be good and she would not have to take the risk of being shamed by God for leaving him or fear being alone. Much too often she projects her fear of following Lilith onto her partner and expects him to set her free before she can actually find her own trust in the feminine. The collective rejection of Lilith, as an aspect of the feminine archetype representing freedom and sexuality, becomes part of a dependency pattern in which individuals are held in relationships that are not supportive of the individuation process. The fear of being shamed by the collective (and by God) for the need to separate and to 'stand out' is a challenge that often appears in groups, where individuals 'surrender' to their experience of what is expected from them in order to be accepted. Instinctively they do not want to run away, like Lilith, but wish to change the patterns in their lives that cause them to feel inhibited in their self-development.

When original creativity is understood as an interaction between the inner feminine and masculine as equal partners in the creation of self, this mythological foundation in the psyche becomes a barrier for the individuation process. How can the creative process lead to any original outcome without this feminine part of the soul being present? Creativity will be biased from the very core of creation, and masculine values will dominate in both men and women, such as logic, rationality and usefulness of the product. The basic attitude to creativity will be oriented towards what is already known to us, in fear of what the unknown can bring. This may explain why shame has been so absent in both literature and clinical practice, because when we return to the feminine realm inside, we also meet the dark goddess of shame: the irrational, emotional and revengeful aspects of the soul that were once rejected and known as Lilith.

Lilith has been called many names, among them witch, baby-killer, hag, demon, whore and destroyer. She is reacting to her experience of being rejected and shamed by God. The many women that were burnt as witches during the 'age of enlightenment' are good examples of the fear of feminine qualities that evolved together with the attempt to separate science from religion. Everything that was mystical, irrational, sensual and related to nature was dangerous to society and judged as demonic in an attempt to separate religion from science.

This is not a question of gender. This is a question of valuing feminine qualities as equal to masculine qualities in both men and women, creating a new paradigm for creativity.

The rejection of Lilith limits the creative process as an everyday creativity in life. The arts become compensative instead of original, and psychological transformation is restricted to follow outer laws instead of inner needs.

Some months ago I was invited to give a radio interview about colouring books. How did I understand the therapeutic process for individuals who would put colour into structured lines, illustrating an outlined flower, bird or house? Individuals described the relaxing benefit of colouring and the publisher claimed it was therapeutic. Was it? I think we need to differentiate between therapeutic and compensative ways of using creative processes. Colouring books seem to reduce stress due to the focus of attention and the relaxing benefit of the activity, but since the flower, bird or house is dictated by the book and does not represent an image of the inner self, the transcendent function cannot facilitate change, because one part of the polarity is still projected to the outside. The transcendent function, as described by Jung, refers to our ability to transform an inner opposition into something new and original. When one part is projected to the outside, this transformation cannot take place (Skov, 2015).

Abramovitch (2014) has studied the relationship between brothers and sisters and found that siblings tend to divide the world into polarities: "Everything you are, I am not" (p. 22). He further argues, "To live within the framework of polarized identities is to live within a fragmented world" (ibid. p. 22). This pattern of polarization refers to Jung's shadow psychology and to the difficulties we can have when we attempt to integrate polarized content.

According to Levine (2015) we can only change negative patterns of behaviour by developing a capacity for "self-exploration and reflective awareness" (p. 31). Turning awareness towards the self instead of towards the other can initially re-activate shame, depending on how we have learned to see ourselves through the eyes of an-other. Hopefully the therapist represents the 'good mother' for a while, the mother who can see us behind our shame, but we also need an inner mother voice who can love us for who we are. In art therapy the good mother image can be created as a sculpture or painting, and through imaginative dialogues, she is given a voice that eventually replaces the voice of the rejecting mother.

In a training group where the students knew each other well, I asked them to do a little meditation. They were to close their eyes and imagine seeing themselves from outside for 15 minutes. They would then write down what they saw in words that would be like a presentation of themselves to the group. We compared their subjective experiences with statements from the other ten group members related to how they saw them. One student could not see herself from the outside at all. No images; no special qualities; just an empty body sitting on a chair. The group members gave her statements that she could reflect on as images of how they perceived her. Others described themselves in a more negative way than the group in general did. One person saw herself as more lovable than some of the group members did. Only few had a close match between their own experience and the reflection from the group. The uncertainty of not knowing how other people see us makes us vulnerable to shame and more dependent on other people's categorization. As one student said: "I hate it when someone else defines me and puts me in a box". She soon realized that this was what she did to herself by limiting her creative and free expression through the eyes of the 'other'. Her ability to reflect on herself was contaminated by shame.

Shame as an opening to the self

While repression of shame scenes is caused by unbearable emotions in relation to another, the process of individuation brings forward new original parts of the self, often symbolized as a gifted child. This special child represents a new beginning as a *result* of the integrative process. When shame is transformed to be a special sensitivity in relation to others, we react to it in a different way. Instead of moving away from the shame scene either psychologically or physically, we move outward towards the other, protecting our dignity and self-esteem. This behavioural change is in symbolic language the birth of a child, and the child symbolism can often be found in images created during the last part of a shame process.

In the beginning of getting to know shame, other children can appear in artwork and dreams. They are often wounded children who have been traumatized, neglected, are hungry, ill or close to death.

One student, in her first week of training, dreamt that she was holding her friend's twin babies. She was going to breastfeed them, because their real mother was not there. In the dream she thought that the milk from their own mother was healthier for the babies. The image of the mother–child relationship is connected to the theme of being able to take care of the needs that we have, and the dream may show that my student was feeding her friend's needs instead of her own.

I think the spiritual aspect of the self, as a source of creative originality, is one of Jung's most important contributions and a strong motivational drive in processing shame. Understanding the self as a guiding principle in the psyche can facilitate a trust in the process as a replacement for fear of the unknown.

The connection between shame and creativity therefore has a personal connotation as well as an archetypal one. The personal part is connected to trauma and life experiences that have been repressed to the implicit memory system, from where they influence the present life's behavioural patterns. Because these memories are disconnected from consciousness, we cannot use our conscious will to control the impact, they have on our lives. To gain more self-regulative control, we therefore seek therapy.

The archetypal approach creates a possibility to release more original parts of ourselves that are not traumatized, split-off parts. They are new and vulnerable because we do not know them well, and they still need to be protected and mirrored in order to become part of our life.

This double nature of the child archetype illustrates the two layers in working with shame. One is psychological, personal and integrative, while the other is developmental, archetypal and transformative. Most of the clinical methods used in psychotherapy are related to personal integration and do not include the spiritual creation of new parts of the self, because the definition of self in most psychotherapeutic paradigms is only related to the personal.

When patterns of shame control our life, the inner spiritual child lives in an isolated world, protected from the danger of the shaming other. One example will illustrate this. A student made a free painting after teaching hours, as shown in Plate 2 (see plates between pages 112 and 113). The following day she used the painting in a training process, where another student represented her therapist and the rest of the group observers. She described the painting as follows: the woman is reaching out towards freedom, illustrated as birds. The circular form down left in the painting illustrates the inner (blue) child, who is held captive by the red circular form.

The student was then invited to use a drum together with her voice to explore the image. Her therapist held her hands on the woman's back to support her expression. The woman's voice was angry and tense, and she stopped and said, "It does not feel right".

She then began to push away the therapist's hands, and when the therapist respected her need for aloneness, she continued to create sounds and discovered a much softer, slower and more sensitive voice that made her feel deeply connected to her self.

She realized that the therapist was representing her mother, who did not trust her ability to support her self. Her mother communicated to her that the world was a dangerous place and that she should stay in her mother's care. In the therapy she used her aggression to push her mother away before she was able to discover her more feminine side.

When Koltuv (1990) describes the challenge for women of today to choose between freedom and love, women are confronted with the same choice as Lilith. Will she sacrifice her own inner creative child in order to fulfil outer expectations of giving her full attention to an-other, be it mother, husband, child or work? The many women who experience stress in our culture are women who run faster than wolves in order to live up to such outer expectations. This is a dependency pattern. They depend on others to give them an understanding of who they are and permission to say 'enough'. When women choose freedom like Lilith (and my student), they must be able to stand on their own two feet, avoiding the pressure from outer expectations. My student's anger towards her mother did not make her free, but it did help her to make a space where she could create a new self experience through the use of her voice. Her anger was a reaction towards her mother for having limited her need to explore the inner and outer father world.

Timing and the story of Demeter and Persephone

Another and more mythological aspect of the mother–child relationship can best be explained through the story of the grain goddess Demeter and her daughter Persephone.

One day when they are walking in a meadow enjoying the flowers, Demeter strays from her daughter. Persephone reaches out to pick a beautiful narcissus flower in a moment of ecstasy. The earth opens and Hades abducts Persephone to the underworld, where she is to become the queen. The abduction is described as a rape of the innocent girl. Her grieving mother, Demeter, searches for her everywhere and finally finds out that Zeus has given Hades permission to take her daughter. She warns Zeus that if she does not get her daughter back, she will let all cereal on Earth die, creating a famine, and when humans die there will be no one to honour the gods, so they will die too. Zeus agrees to arrange for Persephone to return to her mother, but because Persephone eats a pomegranate while in the underworld, she is connected to the underworld forever and must stay part of the year with Hades. When spring comes she appears on Earth with her mother, and when autumn comes, she returns to the underworld as the queen of Hades.

This myth refers to the initiation of the feminine moving from the maternal domain of being protected by the mother to the inner realm connected to the masculine. It is a movement from dependency towards independence.

One of the important themes in this transition is the aspect of timing. When the girl is taken away from the mother too soon because of the mother's absence, the influence from the masculine can become abusive because the girl has not yet matured to this meeting and she still lacks the motherly protection. The shame that follows experiences of abuse can keep the daughter held captive in the underworld, as she cannot come back by her own power. She needs someone to fight for her and to make sure that she returns to the upper reality alive.

When the mother is overly protective of her daughter for too long, the daughter will be captured in the dependency to the mother, always fearing the unknown father world. The mother must, as Demeter did, leave the daughter unattended in the moment, where the daughter can follow her own interest as an initiation that leads her to the inner relationship with the underworld king. The guilt of leaving mother can lead to a shame of having a need for independence.

The creative process is always to some degree an independent process from the mother, and to some degree an exploration of the unknown. Using the arts as a bridge to the self can activate strong bonds to family expectations and the pain of sacrifice and choices that must be made.

When fear is overwhelming it indicates that the attachment to the mother world is stronger than trust in the father's world. Working with the affect of fear as a preparation to process shame is therefore based on personal experiences of the transition between the mother and father realm. Was the mother a safe enough model for the girl to internalize? Did the mother trust the father enough to let her child become more independent? Will the mother be able to process the 'loss' of her child without involving the child in her own grief? And will she accept the inner empty void when the child is no longer with her? Does the father have a feeling for the child's personality and need for independence, and can he trust and guide her into the social world? Looking at the father world of today, many things can go wrong in this transitional process of developing independence. Part of the preparation to process shame is therefore to process fear.

In the story of Amor and Psyche, Psyche confronted the affect of fear every time she had a new task to solve. Fear made her surrender to her instinctive side, the ants, the voice of the rush, the eagle, the tower, and she succeeded in fulfilling each task without her conscious ego in control. Gradually she gained more confidence and was able to trust her instincts as a guiding voice towards wholeness and joy. She was ready. This was the right time for her to move towards the unpredictable masculine world and succeed.

The man has a different journey. It is a major challenge for him to stay in touch with his feminine side and with his own feelings without losing his power and self-esteem. He may lose his male identity in going back to the time when this connection was broken, and when he was still dependent on his mother.

From Freud we learned that the guilt of killing father and marrying mother would lead to blindness, as Oedipus blinded himself when he found out what had happened. I don't think it was guilt as much as shame of who he had become. He completely forgot that it was his father, King Laios, who had rejected him as a baby and left him in the mountains to die, based on his own fear of change. This is the time when the relational approach becomes relevant to use as a way to understand what was really going on in the shame experience. As Ayers (2011) points out, "One of the most important things about being a man is not being a woman" (p. 110). This paradigm in culture, she says, leads to a devaluation of the feminine wherein both mothers and fathers use humiliation as a tool to make boys repress emotions, indicating that "being a sexually adequate male means not being loving" (ibid, p. 110). The rejection of the feminine 'weakness' in a man means that he must use power in order to separate from the feminine and from the body. According to Ayers, this leads to a heroic development of the ego searching for "achievements, glory, and domination, dissociating his real feelings by identifying with symbols of power and control" (ibid, p. 109).

The separation between ego and self or between head and body is therefore different for men and women from a developmental perspective, and therefore the re-connecting process, as an opening to the self, will also be different. A woman is already to some extent identified with shame because she is a woman, while shame is a much more repressed side of a man, if he succeeds in following the social requirement of a true hero.

Summary

In this first chapter I identified shame as an experience connected to inner rejected personalities and to creativity. I think it is important to know the potential of the unconscious in order to avoid the mistaken expectation that the unconscious consists only of rejected and unwanted personal experiences. Knowing about the greatness of the self is an influential motivator to confront shame before actually doing it. To me it is not sufficient to know about shame without also addressing the meaning of this confrontation, which I see as the process of individuation.

The paradox is that shame prevents the self from unfolding, even as it is the very key to further development. The pattern of living is based on internalized role models from our early lives, and these patterns do not change by themselves as they are more or less identified with whom we believe ourselves to be. Using the art-making process, imaginative dialogue and a handful of trust in the psychic reality, a more archetypal world can become known to us as we turn our attention towards the inside. Images of the greatness of self are revealed along with personal scenes where shame made us feel less powerful, and this dynamic between ego and self must be kept alive throughout the journey. Getting stuck in one pole while avoiding the other only leads to a fragmentation of the world where creativity becomes restricted to function in one of them as a compensation for the other.

I think there are important shifts in present paradigms in psychotherapy that need reflection in order to use shame as an entrance to the individuation process and I would like to name a few.

1   We need to define the self in its archetypal potential in order to trust the possibility of change. Otherwise the healing process of shame will lose its meaning and purpose.

2   We need to approach the unconscious with curiosity and openness instead of judging the self to be the enemy of well-being.
3   We need to understand psychological creativity as a projective tool that is useful as a bridge between the inner and the outer reality.
4   As therapists we need to pay more attention to the self-regulatory and guiding function of the client's self, leading to the therapeutic relationship being supportive to therapeutic change more than the agent of change itself.

Literature

Abramovitch, H. (2014). *Brothers and Sisters*. College Station: Texas A&M University Press.
Akhtar, S. (2016). *Shame: Developmental, Cultural and Clinical Realms*. London: Karnac Books.
Ayers, M. Y. (2011). *Masculine Shame*. London: Routledge.
Cozolino, L. (2006). *The Neuroscience of Human Relationships*. New York: Norton & Company
Cozolino, L. (2010). *The Neuroscience of Psychotherapy*. New York: W.W. Norton & Company Ltd.
Cozolino, L. (2016). *Why Therapy Works*. New York: W.W. Norton & Company.
Dacey, J. S. and Lennon, K. H. (1998). *Understanding Creativity*. San Francisco: Jossey-Bass Publishers.
Dearing, R. L. & Tangney, J. P. (2011). *Shame in the Therapy Hour*. Washington, DC: APA
DeYoung, P. A. (2015). *Understanding and Treating Chronic Shame*. London: Routledge.
Dissanayake, E. (2000). *Art and Intimacy*. Seattle: University of Washington Press.
Edinger, E. F. (1996). *The Aion Lectures*. Toronto: Inner City Books.
Ehrenzweig, A. (1967). *The Hidden Order of Art*. Berkeley: University of California Press.
Garfield, D.A.S. (2009). *Unbearable Affect*. London: Karnac.
Grawe, K. (2007). *Neuropsychotherapy*. East Sussex: Taylor & Francis Group.
Hooge, I. E. (2014). The General Sociometer. In: Lockhart, K. G. (editor). *Psychology of Shame: New Research*. New York: Nova Science Publishers.
Jacoby, M. (1991). *Shame and the Origins of Self-esteem*. London: Routledge.
Jung, C. G. (1959). *Aion*. London: Routledge & Kegan Paul Ltd.
Kalsched, D. (2013). *Trauma and the Soul*. London: Routledge.
Kirsch, I. (2009). *The Emperor's New Drugs*. London: The Bodley Head.
Koltuv, B. B. (1990). *Weaving Woman*. York Beach: Nicolas Hays.
Lee, R. G. and Wheeler, G. (1996). *The Voice of Shame*. Santa Cruz: Gestalt Press.
Levine, P. A. (2015). *Trauma and Memory*. Berkeley: North Atlantic Books.
Miller, S. B. (1996). *Shame in Context*. London: The Analytic Press.
Morrison, A. P. (1989). *Shame: The Underside of Narcissism*. Abingdon: Routledge.
Nathanson, D. L. (1992). *Shame and Pride*. New York: W.W. Norton & Company.
Nathanson, D. L. (1996). About Emotions. In: Nathanson, D. L. (editor). *Knowing Feeling*. New York: W.W. Norton & Company.
Sanderson, C. (2015). *Working With Shame*. London: Jessica Kingsley.

Schore, A. (1994). *Affect Regulation and the Origin of the Self.* New York: Psychology Press.

Shepherd, L. J. (1993). *Lifting the Veil.* Lincoln: iUniverse, Inc.

Skov, V. (2015). *Integrative Art Therapy and Depression.* London: Jessica Kingsley.

Stewart, C. T. (2008). *Dire Emotions and Lethal Behaviors.* London: Routledge.

Stewart, L. H. (1996). The Archetypal Affects. In: Nathanson, D. L. (editor). *Knowing Feeling.* New York: W.W. Norton & Company Inc.

Tomkins, S. S. (2008). *Affect Imagery Consciousness.* New York: Springer Company.

Part 2

Living shame

About affects

When I first read about the affect theory, where shame is suggested as one of nine innate affects, I had just finished my work on depression without even considering the affect of shame in my analysis. As I became more interested in shame as an affect behind not only depression but also life quality in general, I began to realize the depth of shame as the invisible cause behind many of the problems in our time. I therefore thought that processing shame might become a key to solve some of these challenges, and I began to look for ways to use creativity as a tool for this transformation. As a therapist, I also liked the idea of a limited number of affects, which I thought would bring an archetypal frame to the many aspects of human experience. I believe this in spite of the critiques from other sources arguing that human emotions cannot possibly be reduced to only nine affects, because it would mean ignoring the variety and individuality of emotional experience (Miller, 1996). I have found the affect theory useful in my work alongside a Jungian orientation. When Tomkins first published his work about the affects in 1962 and 1963, the affects were not considered as powerful to human consciousness and behaviour as they are today. They were merely confined to biological action–reaction patterns that were controlled by forces of evolution, and they were further ignored by the professions of clinical psychology and psychiatry. When Jung suggested that complexes have us more than we have them, he was referring to the affective/instinctive side of the complex that we cannot control. Affects may be repressed up to a certain point, depending on ego tolerance. They may create bodily unbalance like stress as well as behavioural patterns that destroy both individual and society. They may be sublimated into something that is socially acceptable, like art, work or science. They may break through to consciousness, creating madness and lack of direction. In their positive aspects they contribute relationships, vitality and passion to our lives.

Getting to know the psychology of affects has also added a new dimension to my understanding of psychological creativity and to the way shame interferes with transformative processes. When an affect is activated through some life experience, it becomes emotional in the sense that we now have a personal setup related to one or more affects. These activations of affects in our personal lives make it possible to express and verbalize aspects of this otherwise uncontrollable power in the psyche. It gives us a possibility to change our attitude to this part of human energy and to learn different ways of using it in life.

We can work with these emotional scenes in therapy as we try to integrate memories that were either repressed or forgotten in order to create more wholeness in our lives. By connecting affects, emotions and language, we are creating a transformative cycle as described by Schore (2012) and the challenge in therapeutic work is to develop methods that include all steps.

The Jungian orientation is focused on the transformative function of active imagination and the use of symbols as the bridge for changes. The symbol is, in itself, more connected to the psyche than it is to the body, which is why the theory of the affects offers a relevant supplement to Jung's psychology. Although Jung did describe the instinct/affect as the physical aspect of the symbol, he was always more interested in the soul than he was in the body.

In practical creativity there is a physical activity involved, which means that the affects are stimulated in ways that are not possible when we only use language. As a basic paradigm to creativity I think we as therapists need to know about the life of the body as well as of the psyche, since they are both involved in art therapy methodology. Otherwise we may lose the connection to the body when focusing on the symbol.

In working creatively with shame we bring the psyche out from hiding while we build up visual representations of the inner life. I have come to understand that the act of creation is just as important as the image, and that the body has a life of its own, as it moves through different emotional conditions during the art-making process. Usually we are more focused on the image after the creative process has finished and we don't think much about the change that has occurred in the body during the process. I sometimes wonder whether the change we find in the artwork has already taken place in the body, only the client did not notice it because s(he) was busy making the artwork meaningful. When we tend to focus on the symbolism more than the process of art-making, the dialogue often has a more psychic character. In order to involve the body in the therapeutic dialogue, I find it useful to use a second medium to explore the artwork before verbalization. It can be movement representing figures or colours in the painting in order to explore the symbol through the body, allowing it to activate the affect that is connected to that specific image. It can be drumming together, as in role-play, where one is red and the other is blue. It can be body sculptures, or that members from a group are given a specific role, and they all improvise together as if the painting is moving and changing form. When the affects may be too overwhelming, I suggest that the creator of the image observes, while other group members bring the painting into movement. The point is that there are many different ways of stimulating the affects by using the image as an activator.

Affect theory

Tomkins categorized nine innate affects: joy and interest are the two positive affects, surprise is neutral, and shame, anger, sadness and fear are negative, while the last two, dismell (warning response via the nose) and disgust (warning response via the mouth), are related to our hunger drive (2008). Louis Stewart (1987), who is a Jungian psychologist, excluded dismell and disgust as independent categories, because he saw these two affects as a biological side of shame/ humiliation caused by rejection of another or of the self. Stewart also named the four negative affects to be crisis affects related to the fourfold structure of the self, while the two positive affects were considered to be our life instinct and motivational drive to play. Finally, he saw the affect of surprise as a reorienting affect of the self, connected to the function of ego consciousness.

For me, the limited number of affects became an interesting and useful description of those uncontrollable forces in the unconscious. I came to recognize the affects behind other emotional signs, such as depression, and found that art therapy was a method that could create the matrix for the interaction between the crisis affects and the life instinct. Connecting the positive affects of joy and interest with the crisis affects of sadness, anger, fear and shame was in itself a transformative process and facilitator of change. This was what I had experienced so many times in art therapy processes, where clients would begin a painting based on one of the crisis affects and end up joyful and surprised by the sudden transformation of an emotional state. In my attempt to understand more deeply the key to processing shame, I became aware that all the affects were important players in this process and it gave me a somewhat different perspective to processing shame. A certain connectedness between all the affects became like pearls on a string, indicating an overall procedure to the healing of shame, which I came to name the 'Blue Diamante model' (shown in Figure 2.1).

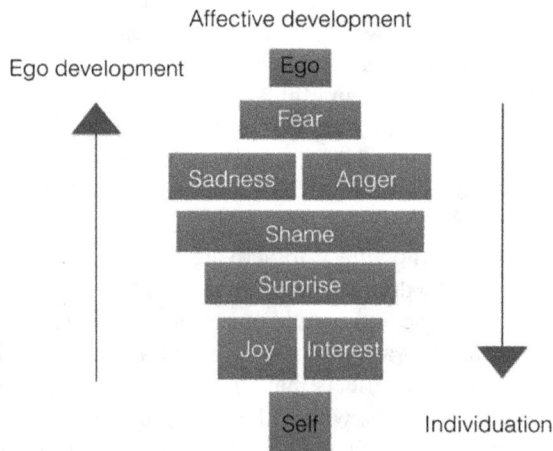

Figure 2.1 The Blue Diamante model (shown here in grayscale)

The negative influence of the affects is caused by the inability to transform a crisis affect into a more mature consciousness where joy and interest again can play their role in life. When a crisis affect is left un-connected to the life instinct, our transformative ability to grow and change are limited, as is our access to original creativity. These are the patterns that we grow into during our first development in life. We do not choose these patterns as much as they choose us, and they become part of how we see our selves.

All affects have a scale of intensity ranging from little to more intensive stimulation, like surprise–startle, joy–ecstasy, interest–excitement, anger–rage, sadness–anguish, fear–terror and shame–humiliation. The affects can connect with each other and create a more powerful force to make individuals behave in an uncontrolled manner. The affects can also bind to different needs, as for example when an eating disorder is the result of the fusion between shame and the hunger drive.

It is important to remember that we need the affects to feel alive, and that we cannot avoid the crisis affects as part of our life's journey. When the affects become a problem for the individual and for society, they are experienced as meaningless and as having a will of their own against conscious influence. When we do not mature through the crises we meet in life, we lose that feeling of meaning, which motivates us to get out of bed each morning. Trusting that something new can come out of a crisis can make us continue to search for meaning as part of the process of change.

One client, who had cancer and had recovered, got cancer again one year later. She also recovered from the second cancer trusting in good faith that she would beat the cancer as she had last time. But when she was diagnosed for the third time, she lost her trust in the body and in the self. Until that point she thought that when she kept a dialogue with the unconscious through dream work, the self would not punish her with cancer. So she became angry with her body and with the self and just ignored both, and this was when she entered art therapy.

Table 2.1 Stimulus, image and affect (part of model by Stewart, 1996)

Stimulus	Image	Affect
Loss	The void	Sadness
Rejection	Alienation	Shame
Restriction	Chaos	Anger
The unknown	The abyss	Fear
Unexpected	Disorientation	Surprise
The familiar	Illumination	Joy
The novel	Insight	Interest

In one artwork she made a dead, 'isolated' tree in the middle, green nature on the left side, and the ocean on the right side. When she finished the painting, she felt that the tree needed roots, and she made a boat at the bottom in which the tree could stand and be supported. At the end of the session, she was invited to imagine how her painting would look in the future, if the film kept rolling. Then she placed the boat into the ocean with the tree in it and said: "I would just surrender to the ocean and lie in the boat (as the tree) and suck in the nature".

She was challenged by shame of being rejected by her body and by her self when she got the cancer, as if it was a sign of failure. When she tried to imagine a state of letting go, she experienced sadness, which replaced the anger that had kept her separated from her body/self. In the painting she was represented by the tree and was surely alienated from both nature and ocean, standing in the middle with no connection to either. This was not about fear but about anger–sadness as reactions to shame. Stewart (1996) has made a connection between stimulus, image and affect as interconnectivity, which can be useful in processing shame.

As Table 2.1 shows, the shame stimulus is rejection, and my client's reaction to being rejected (by the self) was anger and behind the anger was sadness. To discover shame underneath, as the activator for these other two affects, could very well have remained in the unconscious, because my client had no awareness of an underlying shame before she was asked.

The images Stewart refers to can be found in artwork as archetypal themes, and the connection to the matching affects can become a useful tool in processing affects through the image.

In the therapy room, we often see that activation of one affect can lead to other affects and that this connection also creates the possibility to explore the positive affects through the stimulation of negative affects. In a creative process we may start with joy and end up in tears, or we begin a painting process in anger and end up laughing. The affects can trick each other during the creative process when we 'hold on' to the affect instead of leaving it for some other activity. We need to finish the painting in order to complete the self-regulative process.

This example shows how consciousness more easily allows anger and sadness to be experienced than shame. Shame hurts more and is therefore left behind in the unconscious as an affect too painful to know of. The challenge as a therapist is to approach sadness and anger as a protection of an underlying shame too vulnerable to expose, because it is directly related to the core of our being. Developing the Blue Diamante model helped me to keep an overview of the transformative process and to find ways to acknowledge shame when it is hiding underneath sadness and anger. In general, I think there is a tendency for therapists to get caught in the countertransference activity of wanting to help clients when they feel trapped in the spiral of sadness or anger. We want our clients to feel better and not worse, which may be one of the reasons why shame has been left behind also in therapy sessions. When traumatic shame experiences can become a doorway to the spiritual self, by adding a Jungian understanding of the self, more therapists may find a motivation to address their clients' shame when it appears in disguise.

The Blue Diamante model

When we consider shame to be experiences that take us away from connecting with our inner self, a therapeutic challenge in working with shame is to reconnect ego with self. The space between these two layers in the psyche was described in the first chapter as different inner relationships. Getting familiar with these relationships was considered a pathway to the self. Combining Jung's concept of the ego-self axis with the theory of affects, the Blue Diamante model illustrates ego development moving from the self towards the ego. The model also gives an overview of the individuation process, moving from the ego back towards the self. I now use this model as a reference in therapy, teaching and supervision and it helps me to remember shame as an underlying and self-related affect to sadness, anger and fear, as well as a bridge to the positive affects of joy and interest. It also makes clear that the affect of shame is operating on a deeper level than fear, sadness and anger, farther away from ego consciousness and closer to the self.

According to Tomkins (2008) life begins with the positive affects of joy and interest, as they make sure that we start life with an inborn motivation to become part of it. As we grow and develop, our positive expectations of the world are replaced by surprises of not being allowed to control our own actions. These surprises can in worst cases be traumatic experiences of being attacked and humiliated by someone, replacing the experiences of the first greatness of self with the shame of being a failure. Reactions to shame are sadness and/or anger, depending on family values and emotional priorities from those around. Based on these experiences the developing ego may internalize an attitude of fear of being exposed to rejection again, leading to a split between ego and self.

When we later decide to make therapeutic changes in our lives, we enter therapy and the journey back to the self begins. The first affect we meet is fear. Fear of the unknown and fear of the repressed past, where scenes from life were forgotten in order to keep the self from going to pieces. When trust has been restored in a holding environment, the confrontation with sadness and anger can take place as a release of withheld emotions from the past. Continuing the process, we meet shame as an underlying identity behind the sadness–anger polarity, and the process of healing shame is now directly related to the self and to the imaginative work of creating a new inner good mother. This new relationship between the inner good mother and the shamed ego can lead to different surprises, as the ego is invited to bring new parts of the self into play. Of course we must add the subjective reality to this more archetypal frame of developmental processes, but as an overall view of processing shame it gives an indication of the roles all the affects play in processing shame.

The affects in art therapy

Stewart (1996) suggests that joy and interest are representations of the archetypal feminine and masculine principles in the psyche.

In creativity I see joy being activated when the client or group feels safe to express themselves freely and without expectations of surprises that can communicate shame of wrong behaviour. Therefore it can take some time to build up an environment for joy and interest to unfold in art-making. First of all the environment must be a safe enough space to allow for unpredicted impulses, like throwing paint, working with hands or feet and sometimes other parts of the body. The relationship among participants is also important – there must be trust among the group in showing new parts of the self without being ridiculed or shamed.

Sometimes there is no interaction between the affect of joy and the affect of interest during the art-making process. The inner relationship between the masculine and the feminine is disconnected and the creative process becomes either joyful *or* interesting. When there is only joy in the process and no interest in the projected image as such, it does not matter what is projected from the unconscious and attention is on the joyful release of the affect and not on the content or the search for meaning. At times the inner woman needs the freedom to just *be* without looking for meaning, especially when life is full of stress and always occupied with something to *do*. The creative process then becomes compensative, attempting to regulate the body from holding on to the demands from a rational society.

At other times, the inner man takes control and there seems to be less joy in the process and more interest in some specific symbol or scene that may already have been created in the mind before starting the expressive process. Then it can be difficult to follow new impulses from the body during the art-making process, allowing the inner woman to influence the outcome. Basically this is a fight between control and letting go of control instead of an interaction between the two forces, where trusting chaos would lead to a surprise and novelty related to the outcome.

When I watch creative processes, there seems to be more passion in the art-making process when joy is activated than when the affect of interest dominates. In this way joy seems to be more related to the body, while interest stimulates the head.

When individuals begin to express themselves creatively after many years of doing other things, they often have some ideals related to their creative skills, which they cannot live up to because they may not have painted since they were 12 years old. They get disappointed, shameful, irritated or angry with themselves for not being able to control their body well enough to express what they want, and they may give up further creative expressions. When this happens I suggest they express their emotional reaction in the painting, instead of thinking that such 'ugly' emotions do not belong to the creative process. They want to paint an idea and leave out the affects connected to the body and to chaos, as if they are not as important as the idea. This is a true repetition of the priorities we learn to make for the masculine principle of reason neglecting the feminine and the body. When there is a split or opposition between the inner man and woman, the creative process becomes either compensative or rigid. This inner relationship is therefore the key to develop a creative expression that is original and meaningful in the arts as well as in life, because they are mirroring each other.

What usually takes place when the affects are involved, is that the painting becomes alive, the art-making more joyful and more interesting to look at. In moving forth and back between the paper and the body allowing some dialogue to take place during the activity, we can sometimes experience how they can interact and bring more wholeness to the process.

When head and body play together, the two positive affects of joy and interest are both activated. The woman might lead the process at the beginning and some colour and movement from the body are freely expressed on the paper. Then the man may take over by following something of interest in that first expression made by *her*. Having worked like that for a while, the woman may interfere again, expressing her felt reaction to the direction he has taken. She may add a new rhythm or colour that he had not thought of, and their differences will be visible in the final artwork in the relation between meaning/form and passion/rhythm.

When individuals have become more familiar with creative expression, they often find it easier to let go in the art-making process by following the inner woman enjoying the body in the process. Then the affect of interest may not be stimulated before the therapeutic dialogue, where the search for meaning continues the expressive process. In some way the art therapy process makes sure that joy as well as interest is stimulated, but maybe not as a dialogue *between* them as much as one after the other. I wonder whether this is one reason why so few men seek art therapy, because they run the risk of being overwhelmed by the feminine, when she is finally set free from her cage and allowed to express years of built-up emotions. A more masculine approach would be to introduce a technique or a task to hold on to, so the interest in solving the task is not being overruled by impulsive reactions. A new trend is to colour pre-defined figures in colouring books. The shape and form are already given, and the job is to add colours to the figures. This activity reduces stress on a biological level, and joy in not being responsible for the content. The affect of interest is in my opinion not included in this process, because someone else defined the content, and so the split between man and woman is maintained. It becomes a meaningless process, because no new insight is gained from it.

The inner couple both have important roles to play. She is able to let go of the already known when she feels safe enough; he is able to focus on something new that happens in the moment and together they can create something original.

Stewart (1996) calls the inner couple "the twin affects of libido" as they make sure that we have a motivation to interact with the outside world as an instinct of survival.

When positive expectations are not met, it can lead to shame for being wrong, depending on the intensity of rejection. A surprise in the middle of playing can also stimulate play in a positive way, when the surprise is not experienced as judgemental.

Stewart (1996) sees the affect of surprise as a reorienting affect attached to the ego, while I find it much closer to the self and to the two positive affects. I think the ability to be surprised is connected to the disappointments of joy and interest, and therefore some individuals avoid situations where they might risk being surprised in a negative way and then the two positive affects are also restricted and held back. The scale of surprise can move from traumatic humiliation to creative stimulation. When shame begins to replace joy and interest in life, we see sadness and anger as reactions to the humiliation of the self.

My experience is that when the affect of joy is made wrong (by others or by one's self) the negative affect of sadness is stimulated by the loss of something that felt good. Likewise when the affect of interest is made wrong, the affect of aggression is activated. This creates a connection between sadness and joy as two levels in the feminine archetype, and a connection between anger and interest in the masculine archetype, as illustrated in Figure 2.2.

Connecting the personal experience of sadness–anger with the archetypal experience of joy–interest then becomes the reconnecting activity of original creativity and wholeness. Tomkins also thought that if we had enough experiences of joy–interest during the first, important years of our lives, we would have the resources to deal with the crises that come later in life. But if we did not have that opportunity, we might be able to create that foundation later in life through play.

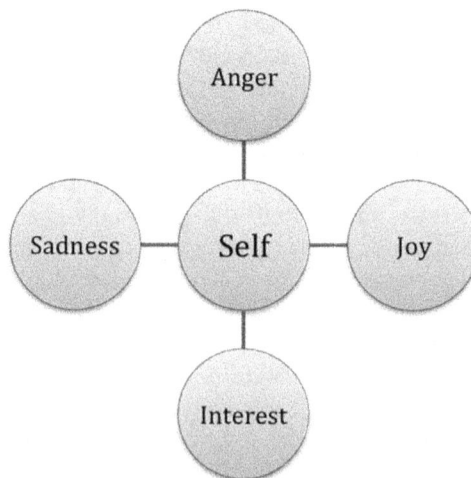

Figure 2.2 Feminine and masculine relations

Moving from the sadness–anger opposition towards the ego, fear is activated as a protection from re-experiencing the trauma of being shamed, and the intensity of fear then decides the openness to further interaction with the unconscious.

In the movement from the self towards the ego, the child's personality and behavioural patterns are formed, as something that happens to the child during relational interactions.

When we later start a therapeutic development, usually with a conscious awareness of sadness *or* anger based on what others have done to us, the regulative process will be about getting access to both of those emotions before confronting shame.

Some individuals think that this is the purpose of therapy. When the ego is no longer victimized the balance seems to be restored. We feel better. That is true, but the pattern of creating the unbalance may continue to operate as the complex of shame is still undiscovered. In order to process shame we need to move *beyond* sadness and aggression as a compensative reactive pattern to shame. We need to include the experiences of how we have come to think about ourselves as a deeper level of reflection beneath the emotional states of sadness–anger.

Usually clients have access to sadness or anger and all the *signs* of shame, like low self-worth, victimization or bad relationships. The client seldom verbalizes shame as a topic directly. Therefore the therapist can support verbalization of shame and shame relationships, attempting to bring awareness to a deeper connection with the self, beyond the sadness–anger polarity. Working therapeutically with the release of sadness and anger can therefore function as a bridge to the self and to the restoration of self-worth. When we discover the relational scenes where sadness–anger was experienced, we are able to address experiences where someone else in these situations rejects us.

The process of individuation goes through different affective states, moving from fear of the unknown to the sadness–anger polarity. When this polarity is processed and when sadness and anger are 'equal' as available affects, the deeper affect of shame can be confronted without destroying the individual's integrity. I think this therapeutic process of becoming familiar with both sadness and aggression is an important preparation to working with shame.

Most individuals tend to hold on to either sadness or anger as the most familiar affect, while the rejected affect is operating from the unconscious. The bipolar condition of moving forth and back between the two affects, sometimes depressed and sometimes manic, illustrates the movement between these two affects beyond conscious will.

These emotions can be expressed and explored through creative activities as a safe way of becoming familiar with otherwise overwhelming affects. Using the sadness–anger polarity in life means that we no longer have to be victims of abusive behaviour. My point is that there is more to life than emotional balance. We also have the opportunity to become conscious about our original creative potential and spiritual purpose of living.

Fear is such a powerful voice because it is based on what has happened to us and we may not feel that our ego is strong enough to confront all the rejected parts inside. This is a motivation to seek therapy in order to strengthen the ego and to regain trust in the self. The following example may illustrate this.

A client felt deeply sad whenever she thought of losing her grandmother, because her grandmother was the only trustworthy person in her childhood. Her narcissistic mother kept up a social façade but she was unpredictable and sadistic to her daughter while her father was distant, passive and unable to support her. She felt a deep shame because nobody believed her when she tried to share her experience. She said it was as if reality was 'hidden behind a sky', and therefore she kept her knowledge a secret. She said that she always felt hungry, as if there was a hole in her stomach.

We can follow the connections between the different negative affects in her story as sadness, shame, fear and anger directed at her self. It all leads back to the trauma of losing her grandmother and with her, the access to the positive affects of joy and interest.

She was searching to re-gain more joy in life as was the Greek goddess Demeter in her search for her daughter Persephone, who had been taken to the underworld by Hades. My client had become her mother's helper in order to survive. The Demeter part of her was now working as a therapist in a psychiatric hospital, while another part (the inner child) was held captured in the underworld, as were her patients. By projecting the inner wounded child onto her patients, she was caught in the childhood pattern of self-rejection until she had to leave her job because of stress. Her fear was related to the unpredictable and shaming mother inside herself and she feared the power of craziness in the unconscious.

In creative processes she was able to explore the Persephone/child aspect by following her intuitive ideas in painting, drama and clay. She preferred to be guided from the inside, and in her own way she transformed through the expressive process every directive she was given. The regulation of her emotional condition based on trusting her own intuition was fun, surprising, imaginative and joyful.

This connection between madness and creativity has been well described in literature. Rosen (2002) describes creativity as a process of ego-cide, initiation and return, where the phase of initiation is a meeting with the deepest strangeness of the soul. The return phase in Rosen's model is based on trusting the psyche's ability to find a way back guided by the self. My client did not have a good role model in her mother, because she never returned to sanity but eventually was hospitalized. Ulanov (2013) has described Jung's personal journey after his break with Freud as an example of the connection between Jung's experience of madness and his coming back with new, original ideas that he spent his life fulfilling. There is a cultural aspect to the condition we name 'madness'. It is seen as a symptom of not being able to socialize. We medicate individuals who surrender to the unconscious because we have no trust in a creative return. The unpredictability of chaos is a threat to our attempt to control life, and we think our social system depends on it. The process of initiation is trapped by this dissociation between the two worlds, and we learn to fear the unconscious as a place of danger and social isolation. This was the experience of my client just mentioned. She was too young to be responsible for her mother's madness. At the age of 54, she was introduced to 'mad' experiences in her artwork and to the original creativity that came out of it. I think she learned to trust the creative aspect to madness, as she felt joy and interest unfold in her artwork. The feminine reaction to shame is sadness (in both men and women) as a circular movement towards the big inner empty space of being nobody, while the masculine reaction is anger (in both men and women) as a direct and linear movement towards somebody, either an outer somebody or the inner self.

When these negative affects are not allowed to be expressed but are held inside, due to social standards, they can be re-activated later in life when a situation provokes the unconscious memory.

One participant from my research study was brought up in a very religious home, where anger was the most forbidden affect to show. When her husband suddenly left her for a younger woman after 32 years of marriage, her first reactions were sadness, despair and confusion. How could he do that to her after she had sacrificed her own career in order to stay home with the children, while he was successful in his work life? First of all she felt dependent on him and feared a life on her own. When she became stronger and gained more trust in her ability to develop her own interests, she could also feel her aggression slowly replacing her sadness. She began to do more things on her own, like travelling, taking courses, seeking jobs and the like.

We cannot be active in life without the dynamic energy that goes with aggression, and when aggression is connected to the archetypal affect of interest, we can use our aggression with a different purpose than as a reaction to shame.

The sadness response to shame is also a fear of being aggressive towards the shaming other. When sadness is active for too long and subverts the affect of aggression, depression may develop as a consequence. So from an affect-theoretical point of view, my experience is that the solution to depression is to activate the affect of aggression, and the other way around, so the two affects can both become tolerable to the individual. This also means a transition from being dependent on others towards a more independent pattern of behaviour, as we must be prepared to lose the relationship when we use aggression.

When working practically with creativity, there is always a certain degree of independence involved. Small or big decisions are made during the expressive process: which colour to choose, which form, which style, which size and so on. In chronic depression, creative processes can be difficult to initiate because of psychological dependency patterns and limited imaginative ability (Skov, 2015).

Summary

When shame is repressed to the unconscious we have only the reactions to work with in therapy, which seem to be either sadness (moving inward) or anger (moving outward). Usually we first meet the affect of sadness in therapeutic processes where individuals have lost a vital part of them selves. They often blame themselves for the patterns they live by, and the task is to activate aggression related to earlier object relations, when somebody else took their power away from them. Using the expressive process to stimulate aggressive energy to balance this polarity is part of this work, along with an object-relational approach. We define ourselves according to the relationships that matter to us, and we need to include these relationships in order to re-define ourselves and make a different choice independent from their judgements. When shame becomes part of who we think we are, the shadow personality will have a more aggressive character in order to compensate for the shamed ego. We must have access to both emotions before we can work through shame, as they both have a quality needed for that work. If we shall defend ourselves against a shaming other, we need aggression to do that as a resource to say *stop*. Likewise we must have access to sadness in order to explore the deep feeling of aloneness when we break the dependency bond with a shaming other.

Stewart suggests the potential in sadness to be a connection to sensation and to the body, while the affect of anger is related to thinking and to the head (Stewart, 1987).

Working with the sadness-anger polarity therefore refers to a potential integration between head and body or between the conscious and the unconscious. This may explain why it is important to pay attention to both emotions in therapy instead of focusing on the one most conscious in the client.

From a Jungian perspective, this is first of all an integration of shadow qualities. We need to pass those inner judges who demand us to be perfect before we can endure to see ourselves as whole.

When clients have worked through scenes from life, where they reach a more object-related understanding of themselves, their relationships in life are also changing. They may want to take new initiatives based on a better head-body integration and new connections with inner needs. This part of individuation is a consequence of shadow integration. It mirrors a dynamic between the masculine and feminine parts of the psyche. We need to listen to the inside (following the potential in sadness as an inward movement) in order to become aware enough of those needs to take action. Becoming conscious does not in itself create a change in life, and this is where the dynamics from the masculine principle are necessary as a movement towards the outer reality (following the potential in aggression). Both introverted and extroverted, we circulate between the inside and the outside as a complete creative cycle and result of inner listening. When the sadness–anger polarity is unbalanced, the inner masculine and feminine is wounded, separated and shamed. They do not speak with each other in a friendly manner based on the role models we have had in life, and therefore inhibits the two positive affects of joy and interest. Sadness is therefore the *emotional* aspect of the feminine archetype of joy, while anger is the emotional aspect of the masculine archetype of interest. We have no joy when we are sad and we cannot concentrate on what we are interested in when we are angry. When sadness and anger have become equally accessible in the psyche and self-image, without making one condition more valuable than the other, the possibility to explore joy and interest also becomes possible, because the inner judges are no longer in control.

I consider joy and interest to be 'older' archetypal affects in the psyche, because they were present in the psyche *before* sadness and anger. In their origin they are not attached to relational experiences like all the other affects and they are therefore vulnerable to outer influence from beginning of life. They are experienced as positive until they are rejected or not met by someone in the environment. Then sadness or anger replaces the positive experience of playfulness, which is referred to as a 'flow experience' in creative processes. Flow is often characterized as a condition where the ego 'forgets' about the outer world, allowing the body-mind relation to unfold freely and playfully in an expressive process. DeYoung (2015) also mentions the importance of play in processing shame, because she understands the importance of using a right-brain approach to shame, but she does not suggest play as an actual activity for adults. Instead she suggests that the therapist should include humour as an attitude in therapy sessions and that "our stance of playfulness is our standing invitation that our clients join us in open-ended exploration and discovery" (p. 83). This way of introducing the positive affects – as a tool to avoid the negative affects – is of course a behaviour that both client and therapist may use in therapy, but often this behaviour remains compensatory more than transformative, because the affect of shame remains protected from being revealed. I think DeYoung's relational approach to the healing of shame has the limitation that the transformative process is held within the transference relationship between client and therapist, instead of held in the client's ego-self relationship.

Returning to the Blue Diamante model, we find shame underneath the sadness–anger polarity, and therefore I see the therapeutic work with sadness–anger as *preparation* to work with the affect of shame. Most individuals do not experience shame behind sadness or anger, until the therapist asks them to reflect on the self-image behind these emotions. Working through shame scenes and getting back the power from the shaming other can activate the two positive affects of joy and interest as a different way of using the energy that was attached to shame. The transition between shame and the positive affects is led through the affect of surprise, and this is where I find the use of art media important. When the power returns to the individual who has been living with shame, it is usually turned towards the shaming other as aggression that compensates for the experience of being shamed. I think this is part of the release of the power that was held in the body, but I find it important that the process does not end in compensative expressive processes, because that does not change the cycle of shame.

In creative processes the joy of using this power often becomes more valuable than the need for revenge. The pain of having been victimized is replaced with the joy of original creativity as the affect and the image come together in the creative process. Working with these images has the potential of making a *psychic* connection to the greatness of the self as the dialogue with the image reveals the story of new parts of self. The coming together of a physical expressive process and a more psychic- and spiritual-oriented dialogue is quite unique with art therapy and is often experienced as more convincing for ego consciousness than words alone.

Affects and creativity

The positive affects of joy and interest

The inner foundation of the libido energy of the psyche rests on the archetypes of the feminine and the masculine. The interesting part is that it seems as if the inner couple is left in the unconscious as an internalized pattern that does not change unless consciously re-activated. Most individuals do not think of connecting their life energy with inner feminine and masculine personalities. They may have no knowledge of how the inner couple are relating to each other. Do they fight or avoid each other? Do they even know about each other? How do they speak together? Do they speak at all? Do they listen to each other? Do they want the same kind of life, or are they focused on different things? How do they connect emotionally? In my research study the participants created the inner couple as clay figures, and in most cases the woman was shamed or dominated by the man (Skov, 2015). One woman made a standing turtle as her inner man and a lying dishcloth as the woman. Another woman made an ugly duckling representing the woman while the man was standing above her with his arms crossed looking down on her. Another participant made a woman who looked like a small girl with no arms, and a much bigger man with an erect penis who "had been sleeping for 40 years"; she described him as "primitive, controlling and stubborn". She said, "[It's] difficult to do something with him because he wants to lie on the couch and sleep all the time". No wonder she found it difficult to use her talents in life! The general consensus is that the traumas we get during our upbringing when joy and interest are seen as wrong or just ignored must be made conscious so new choices can become possible. One important finding from neuroscience is that we can create new pathways in the brain and through repetition make them more useful than the old patterns. However, the new pathways are located outside our memory system and therefore we need to use imaginative ways to create them.

In depression there is little imagination. Imagination has been replaced with hopelessness and negative expectations. Life is on 'stand-by'. The inner man and woman are not interacting to create joy and interest in life. The question we should ask regarding depression is how we can re-activate the relationship between the inner man and woman so the positive affects can influence our lives again. They are the ones who need therapy, because they control the ego. One male client came to therapy and said that he would like to work with his relation to his mother. She had taught him that he should always be a nice boy and not make his mother feel sad by becoming too independent and wild. And now his girlfriend complained that he was always the nice one, leaving the bad role to her. What did she mean and was she right?, he wondered. I invited him to choose an object in my room that he could identify as the boy his mother wanted him to be, and he chose a box of oil crayons neatly organized. Then I invited him to select another object in the room that represented the part of him that his mother did not allow him to be, and he chose a drum. Next I invited him to express on the drum what the crayons would say to his girlfriend when she accused him of being too nice. He played a soft, 'well-behaved', repeated sound, as if he was inside himself while playing. After that I invited him to allow the part that his mother did not accept to respond to his girlfriend, using the drum as his voice. He became aggressive, direct, playful and unpredictable in his sounds and movements. He was able to explore the affects of joy and interest through the personality that was not allowed to develop in his childhood.

At some point in our development we need to make a decision regarding our attachment to mother and father. My client's father had not been able to take his son away from a narcissistic mother and had left his son in a dependency relationship with her. How could he survive the shame and guilt of hurting his mother if he left her? These are some of the issues for all of us when we move from childhood dependency patterns towards individuation.

Some individuals have problems with controlling their affects and are overwhelmed by the intensity of energy that can lead to a lack of emotional control in situations where they end up hurting themselves as well as somebody else. Other individuals are able to repress their affects and to live primarily in their heads in fear of losing control. In both cases the body-mind relationship is disturbed and creativity is either compensatory or rationalized.

Using Schore's (1994) research on the importance of the early relationship between mother and child in their right-brain to right-brain interaction, the communication of shame as an overwhelming affect is more subtle and non-verbal than was earlier believed. The child's perception of the mother's face, movement, mirroring and timing is now understood as a foundation for the child's later functioning and well-being. Since the left hemisphere (language and explicit memory) is developed later than the right hemisphere (emotion and implicit memory), it is difficult to use a rational and verbal therapeutic approach as a method to heal early trauma. The child experiences the world through images and sounds before language sets in, and these implicit early memories can therefore best be activated through images and not through rational language. The implicit memory system related to the right hemisphere is not only visual and emotional but also symbolic and imaginative.

The neutral affect of surprise

In a shame experience the neutral affect of surprise is more or less a shock experience due to the degree of humiliation. The surprise can be so overwhelming to the ego that it becomes impossible to escape from the situation because the body freezes and then the psyche dissociates to survive the moment. Individuals describe it as feeling like they are un-real, dizzy and not really present in the situation. We know from neuroscience that the ability to be present in the moment is connected to right-brain functioning, which leads to an understanding of shame as an inhibitor of present awareness (Schore, 2012). Considering the number of individuals in our culture suffering from stress, which often leads to depression, we might think of stress as a reaction to shame. Stress is a condition where part of consciousness is living in the future thinking about all the things we must do in order to be perfect according to outer standards. Being present in the moment is difficult when we live with stress, so part of our conscious mind dissociates from the moment and lives in the thoughts of future accomplishments. We also know that individuals living with stress have difficulties in taking care of emotional needs because awareness is not present enough to register with them. This explains why cognitive methods such as mindfulness have become so popular in relation to stress as a method supportive of bringing consciousness back to the here and now. Personally I think these methods ignore the possible re-activation of shame scenes that are kept in the right hemisphere. When consciousness becomes mindful of the present moment, shame-related self-images also move closer to consciousness because they are part of who is present.

Our ability to be mindful in the moment depends on the intensity of shame experiences. The more we feel ashamed of who we are, the less we want to look at our selves. This means that we are living in more than one reality at a time: one that we can tolerate enough to make sure that we do what we need to do in life, and one where we compensate for the life we are not living.

Kalsched (2013) has described how we come to live in at least two realities based on dissociation. We develop a 'pretend' personality that does not feel real because it is based on outside expectations more than on whom we feel we are inside. The other inner reality we mostly keep to our selves as a personal hiding place to avoid shame. That inner reality is not identical with the unconscious, which by definition is unknown to us. The inner reality is a reality of a more compensative nature wherein shame cannot reach us and hurt our sense of dignity and self-worth. It stands in opposition to the physical reality we live in and has a more psychic nature wherein magical things can happen that make us feel better. We can transform our experience and our self into whatever we need to be, and no one can tell us that we are wrong, as long as we keep it to our selves.

By not sharing how we *also* feel and think, the split between mind and body is maintained.

One client, who had a traumatic childhood with repeated violence from an unpredictable father, had developed a spiritual personality of kindness and compassion and her imagination included daily conversations with angels. She could talk about her past experiences without any emotional reaction to her memories because part of her consciousness had left the room.

Or, like another client once said, she wanted to be happier but she did not want to let go of the other reality that had been available to her for so many years. The fear of being paralyzed again without her usual place in nature to hide was un-imaginable.

The negative affects of fear, sadness, anger and shame

The affect of shame can bind to other affects like anger, sadness and fear and therefore all the negative affects can become part of processing shame. Shame is a more quiet and self-conscious affect that hides behind other emotional expressions, and we may only discover shame when we know the physical signs of hiding the body – head bent down, eyes avoiding contact, red face and a lack of connectedness in the relationship. Some clients do not have access to the affects because fear is keeping them locked up in the unconscious, and they complain about a head-body split and not knowing their direction in life because nothing feels 'right'.

I remember a client who had painted the image of her father sitting at her bed and she was paralyzed by his sexual behaviour. When talking about the painting she felt no affects towards the father. No need to push him away. No anger, no fear, no sadness. In making the painting she had already dissociated from the abuse and the affects were gone. Then I asked her to imagine a good mother standing in the room knowing what was happening to the child, and what did *she* feel? That imagination gave her access to aggression in her body towards the father and some connection between head and body was made.

Other individuals explore the affects *while* they are painting and the affect becomes meaningful during the resulting dialogue.

The negative affects are reactions to experiences we have had in our lives and therefore the intensity of the affect is connected to those relationships. We experience fear when we are confronted with the unknown before we feel ready and strong enough in our selves. We experience sadness when we lose someone who was important to us. We get angry when we are prevented from expressing ourselves freely and we experience shame when we are rejected as individuals (see Table 2.1).

My suggestion in the Blue Diamante model is that the intensity of the affect of fear is a result of the overwhelming character of our sadness and anger experiences, where fear functions as an *attitude* we develop in relation to the unconscious part of the psyche. Experiences of sadness (stimulated by loss) and anger (stimulated by restrictions) are in reality learning experiences that determine the intensity of fear. Underneath we find shame as an image related to consciousness of self.

The family as matrix for shame

The patriarchal society is based on the father archetype being more valuable than the mother archetype. And what does that actually mean for the developing child? How is this transition made from the maternal containing archetype of intimacy and relationships towards the rational and much more independent life held by the father archetype?

The mother in a family is living in a patriarchal society and is brought up according to rules and values based on the rational principle. Her consciousness is coloured by the values of right and wrong that go with the ruling father of society.

A client explained how her father and mother always argued when she was a child and she was forced to take sides. She would try to negotiate between them, but often they would end up blaming *her* for their problems. Eventually she became a social counsellor, because that was what she was trained to do her whole life. Finally she had to leave her job because of stress and depression. No matter how hard she tried, her inner parents never paid *her* inner child the attention she needed in order to stay connected to her own needs. The little girl or boy sees how father and mother relate to each other, and this becomes the way their own inner polarity learns to communicate.

When Jung describes the inner man in a woman (her animus) and the inner woman in a man (his anima), he does not consider the inner masculine and feminine *relationship*, as Stewart brings forward in his affect theory related to play (1987). He is more concerned with the interaction between the ego and the anima/animus as a self-relational dynamic in the psyche. In relation to creativity I think the interaction between the two life-forces plays a significant role as to how we transform a crisis into an opportunity for new learning. The process of balance and mutual respect between the two life principles then becomes a precondition for the interaction between ego and self and for the process of individuation. One female student, aged 74, had the following experience. When she started on her first psychotherapy education 30 years ago, she thought she knew more than her teachers and all the other students and she liked to confront them with their lack of knowledge. Then she began to remember her childhood life of abuse. How her parents had 'lent her out' to friends and other men, and the shame that she had survived by repressing it to the unconscious. She began to understand that her superior self-image had been her protection against the shame and self-disgust. She had to some degree identified with the self as a compensative activity in order to tolerate her shame. Her long journey back to herself and to her body also became her dis-identification with the greatness of the self and a new relationship based on dialogue. She now works as a psychotherapist helping others to process shame. In order to maintain some psychic integrity, she allowed her inner masculine side to dominate her consciousness and self-image, rejecting the humiliation she felt from early abuse. The dis-connection between her head and body was also a dis-connection between the inner woman and man, and without their interaction there cannot be a dialogue between ego and self.

The self-caring system

When we protect ourselves from shame by moving into another reality, we experience this as a self-caring system (Kalsched, 2013). We do this in order to avoid being destroyed by someone else. It is a creative solution to a dangerous situation, and illustrates the instinctive reaction to the affect of shame. As time goes by and we become adults, we forget to evaluate our defences. Without reflection we continue using the self-caring system that we learned as children. Many individuals experience a sense of isolation from vital parts of themselves and they seek therapy. This vital part is often experienced as an inner child/innocent psyche held in the other reality.

A client was asked to express her inner child by choosing an object from my therapy room. She chose two drums and put them on top of each other. This was a representation of her inner child. Then she put a number of black chairs around the child. She said that the child was captured within an iron box. She did have the key to get out, she said, but the door was too heavy, and she was not strong enough to open it herself. I invited her to sit opposite the child pretending to be the child's mother and asked what she would do. She said that she would not help the child to become free, because she knew that the child would be hurt again if she got out, and she wanted to protect the child. The self-caring system is operating with help from an inner mother who cannot support the child in living a more independent and free life. The mother's voice in this example could be something like: "Because I love you so much, I can never let you free. I don't trust that you can ever become strong enough to take care of your own self when you are in danger". Referring to Neumann (1954), this child is captured in the matriarchal realm and there is no one to support the transition to the patriarchal reality. The child is basically left alone.

When the inner mother in the psyche does not support a transformative process of freeing a potential in the psyche, represented by the child, who else can support the inner child in further development? Every time the child experiences an affect like fear, sadness, anger, joy or interest, the mother will try to prevent the child from showing this affect to the outer world, because of the danger of being rejected. The child will remain dependent on motherly 'protection', because the father and mother do not co-operate in their parental responsibility. Another example of how the two realities are used in a self-protective pattern is shown in the following instance.

A woman aged 50, whom we can call K, participated in an art therapy group and was invited to have her painting dramatized in the group. She appeared to be a strong woman with a grounded sense of herself, and she also seemed caring and helpful towards other members in the group. After having described her painting, she chose five participants in the group who would each act as one of the colours in the painting. One would be red: she was asked to play the role of being structured and function as a holding frame for the other colours. Another participant would be the empty space and function as the background for the others. Another would be blue, which was defined as rigid and linear (which K associated with her husband). One would be green and play the role of mediator between yellow and blue, defined as love. K herself would play the role of yellow, which appeared in the painting like a flash moving down through the blue. They were instructed to act out the roles that they were given in a non-verbal group painting. They did not know one another's roles, and the relationship between them would be based on their improvisation together.

In the painting process K remained almost invisible. She put small yellow marks all around the painting, but they were quickly painted over by someone else. Nobody seemed to relate to one another, and it seemed as if they all just had a job to do. I wanted to see what would happen if she and the blue (her husband) would find some connection in the painting process, so I stopped the process and took the blue outside the door and gave him the role of trying to create a contact to the yellow (wife) in the painting process. When they continued painting together the yellow (K) ran away every time he, the blue, tried to contact her by letting his brush touch hers and just following her around. She was clearly trying to escape intimacy and contact. Again I stopped the process and took K outside and changed her role. I invited her to become more visible in the painting and to leave her marks so others could see her more clearly. Continuing the group painting, she had found a box with golden powder that she began to give to the others from a standing position. Everyone else was moving around on the floor, busy with their own doings. Again she was available to others, but did not leave any personal marks in the group painting, though she was invited to do so.

In the following discussion, she came to think of a period in her life 20 years earlier, when she had been shamed in the press for having used shamanistic rituals in her work with unemployed individuals to help them feel better. Her parents had both turned their backs on her, and she had felt humiliated in the eyes of others. Since then she had held back her own creativity, afraid of being misunderstood, and instead she had become more helpful towards others from an invisible position.

In spite of her very powerful physical and verbal presence in the group, she was in her psychological life living in a spiritual and 'golden' dimension where she thought that no one would notice her.

Dissociation and the journey back to the self

The individuation process is described as an inner friendship between ego and self or between the two realities where one is conscious and the other is unconscious. The shamed individual has lost the meaning of this interaction and survives partly by escaping into another reality with secret thoughts and dreams. Before the individuation process can really begin, the challenge is to find the way back to the self in order that this lifelong friendship can be re-established.

Sometimes we seek someone else, whom we see as a person who has gone through that process, and we transfer our inner self on to that person, hoping for a safe journey. This is the basic mechanism in therapeutic relationships as well as in any student–teacher relationship. It does not change the fact, however, that the individual must make the journey back to the self alone. This is the journey that I have found described in the story of Amor and Psyche. It is a story that in many ways illustrates the challenges we meet during the search for *inner* connectedness.

The experience of living in two realities is for most people a lonely experience, because the full presence of being together in a moment with someone else feels fake and unreal. We leave our affects in the other reality and pretend to be here, hiding the shame of being who we are. Fear of being discovered and negatively judged may be more important than to enjoy being together. The absence of wholeness creates an inner void of loneliness and isolation, and from a Jungian perspective this is an experience of a broken ego-self axis.

Dissociation and loneliness

The beginning of Psyche's development starts with the same lonely position, as we experience in shame. Psyche is living isolated from the masculine and therefore also from her own self. Following Psyche's development as a psychological movement from loneliness towards her marriage with Amor shows a process of developing the feminine in both men and women. Apuleius originally wrote the story in his novel, *The Golden Ass*, as a small part of his initiation into the Isis mysteries (2008). As such, the myth refers to his anima development as part of his journey towards the self. Neumann also used the story to illustrate the development of the feminine, while Hillman calls this myth the myth of our time (Skov, 2000). Our time is the time of a dissociated psyche growing up in shame cultures where doing is more important than being. Moving attention back to the inner life is a first step towards the self, which in the story is located on Olympus, where Amor and Psyche finally unify. For a while I wondered why they were unified at Olympus and not on Earth, until I realized that the myth illustrates the journey from ego to self, with no instruction of using the self in practical life on Earth. Therefore I see it as a story that shows the steps in healing a dissociated psyche caused by shame. In my understanding, we cannot use this story as steps in healing shame, because that would include some kind of return phase as we find, for example, in the (much older) story of Inanna's descent and return. We can use the story of Amor and Psyche as an archetypal image of repairing the ego-self axis before working with shame.

I have divided the story into five parts according to the different experiences that Psyche goes through on her journey, and I will add these as headings to the story (Skov, 2000).

The story of Amor and Psyche

I LONELINESS

Psyche is a princess, living with her mother and father in a castle, and no man will marry her, because she is so beautiful. Instead they bring her gifts in admiration of her beauty. Her father is worried and asks the oracle for advice. He is told that he must leave his daughter to her destiny on the highest mountaintop.

2 FALLING IN LOVE

Psyche is left alone, trembling with fear of the unknown, when the west wind Zephyr comes and carries her down into a valley where she lives with the invisible Amor surrounded by invisible servants. Because he is divine she must not see him. Her two sisters are jealous when they discover that it must be Amor himself whom she lives with, and they convince Psyche that he is a monster that will swallow her and the child she is now expecting. Psyche is lonely and confused about reality and decides to trust her sisters. They tell her to cut his head off when he is asleep, and one night she holds the oil lamp in one hand and the sword in the other and by the light she sees his divine beauty and falls in love. A drop of oil from the lamp falls on one of Amor's wings, and the pain wakes him up. As a punishment for having seen him, he leaves her.

3 SEPARATION

Psyche persuades her sisters that Amor is waiting for them, and they are both killed when they throw themselves from the top of the mountain expecting the west wind to bring them to Amor.

Psyche now searches for Amor and is finally told by Pan to develop her own feminine nature in order to win him back. She confronts Amor's mother, Aphrodite, the 'real' goddess of beauty, who is furious with Psyche for having received the admiration that only she should experience. She keeps her son, Amor, locked up in a room in her house.

4 INNER COMMUNICATION

Aphrodite gives Psyche four trials that she must solve. First she must sort a stack of corn before midnight, and she almost gives up solving the impossible task, when the ants come to help her make it in time. In the second task she must fetch some golden hair from aggressive sheep, and again she is about to give up, when the green plants tell her to wait until darkness when she can pick their wool from the bushes where they spend their day. In the third task she must bring a bowl of water from the deep Styx waterfall, but two dangerous dragons are protecting the water, so she cannot get close to it without being killed. Again she is about to give up, when suddenly the eagle comes to her rescue and collects the water for her. In her final task she is sent to the underworld to get a box of beauty cream from Persephone. She goes up in a tower to jump out in despair of the impossibility of the task, but the tower speaks to her, telling her how to get down through a hole, remembering cookies for the dogs and money for the ferryman. She is not allowed to help the many dead souls who call her in the underworld river, and when she returns she must not open the box but deliver it to Aphrodite immediately.

5 BEING

She succeeds in everything, but when she comes back from the underworld, she does the forbidden thing and opens the box. She falls into a death sleep. Amor, who has been held in his mother's house, wounded by the drop of oil, is now healed and comes to her rescue. He wakes her and gets permission from the other gods to marry her on Olympus, where she drinks ambrosia and becomes immortal. She later gives birth to a girl whom they name Joy.

Psychology of Amor and Psyche

Loneliness

Loneliness becomes a condition that starts the process. It is to be associated with the lack of connection with the affects and with the body. Psyche is just a pretty face with no inner passion in life, which means that she is disconnected to her animus. The text says that Psyche is well aware that it is Aphrodite who is seeking revenge, because humans have mistaken Psyche for the real goddess of beauty. Psyche voluntarily accepts her destiny.

She understands the meaning of the coming process before she experiences it, but is full of fear of the unexpected when her family leaves her on top of the mountain. There is no outer teacher, guru or therapist available from this point, and this is when the relationships to different parts of the unconscious take over, indicating that the self is activated within Psyche.

As a parallel it corresponds to Rosen's concept of the ego-cide stage of development being the initial sacrifice of an immature personality (2002). The oracle is a calling from the archetypal self for the ego to follow a new orientation, and so Psyche leaves her childhood protection and her family, starting her inward journey towards the invisible reality of the self.

In a creative process this can be compared to the preparatory warm-up to start the expressive process. The canvas is hanging there in front of us, paint is ready, and we try to make contact with a bodily impulse to move us into the process of painting. We are longing to unify with an-other (affect/animus) and we wait for the self/oracle to call us into movement. The doors to the house are locked, the telephone down and there are no dishes to wash. The inner journey has begun.

Falling in love

Then we let go. We fall into the empty void and the west wind carries us as a reward to the invisible reality where we move around in our new home, surrounded by invisible servants. Amor comes in the night and we make love. There is no understanding, no rational explanation to what is going on, but we accept the condition. The enjoyment of creation is a uniting process of making love to the principle of love itself for no rational reason. This is not an easy task due to the stress of living in a society that constantly demands results and explanations for every action. Therefore it does not happen by itself. We need to choose it and prepare ourselves to let go of other, more familiar things to do. We hear the calling from the self and follow it. It is the instinct of the individuation process that has no rational meaning other than a need to listen and to express what we hear through the creative process.

This phase in the creative cycle is often referred to as mystic or mad, but in reality it is merely invisible to the human eye. We are not allowed to see Amor because he belongs to the spiritual upper world and we are earthbound as humans. This is one of the positive aspects of shame, because we will need some modesty at this beginning part of the journey. Otherwise we might be inflated by being so close to the greatness of the self/Amor, as we see in manic states and in narcissistic self-love. The balance is delicate: not too much shame, because that will close our curiosity to move on, and not too little shame, because then we will lose our earthbound and more humble identity as humans.

As time goes by, Psyche begins to long for other humans, and her sisters are allowed to visit her, though Amor warns her against them. I think we can understand Amor's warning throughout the text as an inner self-protective voice that wants to avoid further separation from the mother world of oneness. He himself is wounded by the new consciousness in Psyche when she sees him and seeks rescue in his mother's house. We do not hear anything about his pain while Psyche is challenged by his mother, because the story is not about him but about the psyche's maturity to meet the greatness of the divine reality and the instinct of love itself. So his warning to Psyche helps her avoid the danger of being inflated too quickly by the closeness to the divine and at the same time serves as a self-protective behaviour towards his mother's rage of leaving *her* for another woman. The story is that Aphrodite sends Amor to punish Psyche because Psyche takes attention away from her. Instead he falls in love, which is the first sign of separation in going against his mother's will. The initial activation of Psyche's development comes from Amor as an aspect of the self, and not from ego consciousness. *He* is the true mover of the soul, indicating that we cannot decide to fall in love using our conscious will.

In creative processes the shadow sisters are that manipulative voice in us that makes us feel shame about not knowing who we are making love to during the art-making process. They are jealous because they know that it must be Amor and they both want to have him themselves. The sisters represent an unhappy union with the masculine, because, we are told, they are married to some old and rigid kings, where there is no love. In daily life they represent the jealousy from others, when *we* can surrender to the affect of joy and inner togetherness and they cannot. They want to have what we have, and because they have not been called themselves, they forget about ethics and good manners. They are the direct opposite to the innocent Psyche and represent the Lilith voice tempting Psyche to become more independent from her invisible lover. Psyche follows that instinct by following the sisters' advice to kill 'the monster', and she ignores Amor's warning. While holding the lamp during the night, she sees Amor for the first time and she falls in love.

In the creative process we discover new and original parts of our own selves that we never knew existed and which have not been exposed to shame. They are images of the soul's beauty that are revealed through the union with the positive affects of joy and interest. They are the true original aspects of the soul that we discover because we left the outer world for a little while. But the price for this taste of heaven is that we must separate again in order to keep our sanity. When Amor wakes up, hurt by a drop of oil from the lamp, he must leave her because she is not yet ready to stay with him.

Separation

When we have finished the creative activity where we felt protected from the outer world, we wake up to face reality the next morning. First we must deal with the jealous sisters, who are far from innocent. Psyche does that by manipulating them to think that Amor wants them more than he wants her, and when they surrender to the empty void from that same mountaintop, there is no west wind to carry them into a valley and they die. Psyche integrates the sisters' manipulative side by being able to act like them, and she is no longer just an innocent girl.

Amor has now left her and the experience of joy and interest has changed into a psychological longing to get back to that creative flow. Psyche seeks help from other gods and finally, when she is about to give up, she hears the voice of Pan, the natural feminine instinct, telling her to win back Amor by developing her feminine depth.

This is the moment of changing our direction from being regressive, wanting to hold onto the past, to a more progressive attitude to the future. Going back to the unconscious unity we felt in the painting process means that we can start a new painting process and cross our fingers for the west wind to carry us to that divine place once more. Pan is telling Psyche instead to develop her own divine being in order to become conscious of her feminine soul and equal to Amor. In the story of Lilith and Adam, Lilith never came back to Adam. She did not develop her Eve shadow side in order to win back Adam but remained in opposition to him. She got stuck in the affect of anger, while Psyche used the affect of sadness to go deeper and deeper inside. Therefore we cannot use Lilith as a guide towards the very freedom that she represents, but must remember her for the *instinct* of freedom that she is. And maybe she could not hear the voice of Pan because she was too ashamed of being rejected by both Adam and God. Lilith and Psyche therefore represent two different feminine archetypes. Psyche's development starts with an innocent and lonely position, which shows her detachment from the affects and the body, while Lilith is rejected from the beginning with all the negative affects activated. Psyche therefore is a more mature aspect of the feminine, because she has an interest in developing her own self, while Lilith is more primitive and affective in her response to being rejected.

Psyche is rejected in her curiosity to become conscious, motivated by her loneliness in the valley, but instead of flying away like Lilith did, she follows her longing without listening to Amor's warning. This is what she does again and again when confronted with an impossible task on her journey. She listens to her inner animus instincts more than the warnings from Amor or Aphrodite, just as Pan suggested.

In creativity this means that the compensative process of creation is over, and the journey back to the body and the affects begins. The Pan archetype is challenging the immature ego to 'stay on track', and to resist the draw of regression back to the unconscious union from whence she came.

Inner communication

Now comes the time when the creative expressive process is replaced with a creative dialogue. Aphrodite is both a compensator and a guide. She seems to be full of rage towards Psyche and at the same time she is guiding Psyche towards her deeper feminine self. This contradiction in the figure of Aphrodite represents an interesting polarity in the feminine archetype, because how do we know whether she is just another jealous, narcissistic woman, as Psyche's two sisters represented, or a guide to wisdom and union with the self? Should we run away, as we always did before when someone shamed us with their rage and unpredictable affects, or should we trust the shame to be developmental and part of the individuation process? Psyche does not run back to her parents to hide in the castle; rather, she surrenders to the voice of Aphrodite when she sends Psyche out on the four tasks. There is no rational logic in Psyche's decision, and we must assume that she has an instinctive trust in the process to come. After all, Aphrodite is a goddess and mother to her lover, so she is merely following a voice of the self.

Psyche's initial test shows the first step of integration of the masculine instinct: the ants. She is overwhelmed by the task and cannot use her rational side to sort out the corn, so she gives up.

One client was stuck in this first phase of development. Even when tears were running down her face, she did not know what she was feeling, because she was trying to figure it out, instead of allowing the ants to do their job.

In the dialogue with the artwork, we need to use a bodily sensation to differentiate one aspect of the painting from another, in order to create some beginning order of the projected image. Many decisions are made in this process, with no rational purpose other than to describe the image. The ants represent this working mentality wherein we take one step at a time and thereby avoid being overwhelmed by the hidden emotional content in the unconscious. The ability to differentiate one aspect in the painting from another is a first approach to the artwork. For a shamed ego this is not easy, because all the emotions are piled up in the implicit memory system, just waiting to break through to ego consciousness when the chance is there. The projected content makes this process possible without the risk of being overwhelmed from the inside because the focus is on the artwork and not on the body. It is a first animus principle of separation that we need for further exploration of the image.

In the second task Psyche needs to learn to withhold her impulses and to be patient. She must wait until darkness in order to avoid being killed by the aggressive sheep. This is a self-regulative task and it is about timing. She learns to control her affects in order to survive, and again she is advised by an inner voice represented by the image of the plants. Self-regulation is more difficult than differentiating one emotion from the other, and we are using a deeper animus aspect than in the first test. I remember one participant from the research group who described the figures in her painting as a woman, a black circle of anger and some dancing angels. She said that the woman had to become stronger in herself before confronting her anger, and then finally she could dance with the angels. Somehow she understood the depth of this task and knew she had to be patient before confronting her rage towards her unfaithful husband.

In the third task Psyche is asked to get a bowl of water from the waterfall connected to the river Styx. Because Amor so often has helped Zeus with his many affairs, Zeus sends his eagle to help Amor in return, and Psyche is then able to bring Aphrodite the bowl of water as requested. This is guidance to use when shaming voices – the dragons – try to get us away from the deep connection to the underworld inspiration. To pass the dragons, we need to take an eagle's perspective and distance ourselves from these shameful voices that we know so well. We must see the story of our lives from a more objective point and separate from our identifications with childhood emotions. A new animus is introduced here who has the ability to see things from above. He can teach us to separate from the affect of shame by approaching the potential of original inspiration represented by the water from the underworld. Using artwork makes it easier to solve this task because we have already separated from the emotions during the creative activity, and what was inside the body is now projected to the image. In the therapeutic dialogue we can focus on the potential and the original aspect of the artwork instead of doing regressive work as we might have done so often before. It is an important shift in therapeutic orientation that helps to keep an overview avoiding the trap of shame when receiving great ideas and intuitive understanding that we normally don't think we are capable of. This inner greatness is explored through the symbol being a product of our own imagination.

In the fourth task Psyche must go to the underworld to get a box of beauty cream from the underworld queen Persephone. She follows every instruction that she gets from the tower except that she opens the box when she returns to Earth. It seems as if her feminine vanity makes her act irrational as she imagines winning Amor by using the beauty cream herself. This is not the case. She knows exactly what she is doing, and this we know because Amor suddenly recovers and comes to her rescue. The consequence is clear, and is this not what true love is all about? A 'loving' gesture that leads to disaster is hardly love in the spiritual sense of the word. We might think so when we shame our children because we love them so much and it is in the name of socialization, but when we look at the consequences we can see that such communication often leads to self-destructive patterns in the child's further development. When defining love or true empathy, maybe we should look more at the consequences than merely trust our own moral judgement. This can in many cases lead to shame for having been a 'bad' parent, but it is also a necessary first recognition in healing shame and stopping it continuing through generations. Psyche's 'vanity' in opening the beauty box is also a healing of Amor's mother-wound, because, we hear, he is now cured.

In the creative process this is where guidance comes directly from the image. One client said that she could enter the green triangle in the image and get access to 'all knowledge'. Most of us have forgotten to use imagination as a language of the self and to trust the information that comes from images in the artwork. Language is a left-brain activity and imagination is a right-brain reality, and together they create an equal pair of opposites that make original creativity possible. I remember a lecture I once gave on this subject when a man asked, "But how do you get people to paint all these strange symbols?" He could not imagine the leap from left-brain rationality into right-brain imagination. I told him that when individuals are hungry for personal development, they are motivated to try new methods, and if they have a little trust in me, they will use art-making as a possibility. When the imaginative dialogue with the artwork gets emotional, they are moved by the experience in a way that left-brain thinking cannot predict. These are short moments of ego-self connections when shame does not disturb the relationship. The development through the four tests corresponds to an integration of four different aspects of the inner masculine: 1) sorting based on body sensation, 2) self-regulation based on patience to withhold the instinct till timing is right, 3) overview to avoid the affect of shame and 4) surrender to the 'forbidden' instinct of love.

Being

When Psyche is awoken from her death-sleep by the kiss of Amor, they are both healed – she, in trusting the instinct of love, no matter what others may believe and tell her, and he, in separating from his mother and creating a more healthy relationship to the feminine and to the body. When Psyche drinks ambrosia and becomes immortal, she also becomes equal to Amor and, the story says, their daughter was named Joy.

Referring to the positive affect of joy as the archetypal feminine, the child symbolizes a new conscious attitude to life based on joy more than shame.

Summary

Using the myth of Amor and Psyche as an image of re-creating the lost connection with the archetypal self is also a guide to re-orient the shamed ego from a diffuse and lost position in life. In order to gain more access to the positive affects, ego consciousness must first of all change the focus of interest, moving from an extroverted position towards an introverted position. This myth guides us through different creative processes. It gives an understanding of a psycho-logical creativity and shows us how we can reach the self again.

Many artists are motivated by loneliness to start a creative process, hoping that the flow experience will help them create a masterpiece. When they enter the phase of separation next morning, they may start from the beginning again, hoping that next time will be more successful. So they go through the first three phases of the Amor and Psyche myth – loneliness, falling in love and separation – but they avoid the last two phases of inner communication and being, because that would mean that awareness would leave the outer artwork for a while and focus on the *psychological* experience of the creative product.

This is how the story of Amor and Psyche also illustrates the archetype of art therapy: the movement out and the movement back to the body as a creative cycle of projection and introjection.

Neuropsychological understanding of shame

One of the main discussions related to the affects is the issue of emotional control. How does the brain process innate affects like shame, and how can we work with individuals and adjust the ability to control the affects when they become 'too much'? What is the key activator that makes the brain cross this line between a healthy surrender to the affects, as we see in play, and a letting go of responsibility and ethic in behavioural activity? Getting to know shame as an experience behind many affective conditions is now also coming forward in brain research.

According to Cozolino (2016), core shame develops within the first months of childhood and leads to decreased immunological functioning and increased levels of cortisol and adrenaline, together with decreased neuroplasticity. Also, the child's experiences of shame scenes are stored in the implicit (unconscious) memory system. Bodily reactions to shame are therefore without conscious connection to the experience of shame, which makes it more difficult to process. Cozolino (2016) also found the key symptoms of core shame to be a) longing to be perfect, b) lack of self care and c) abusive or non-supportive partners. Taking into account the tendency (especially amongst teenagers) to desire perfection, the use of drugs and other self-destructive tendencies of our time, together with the rate of divorce and domestic violence, makes the need to process shame in our culture seem more than relevant.

Hill (2015) mentions deficient affect-regulation to be the course of dissociative conditions at low levels of stress, which prevents individuals to be able to process the present moment. The ability to listen to others as well as to listen to the inner self is disturbed by shaming internal voices, leading to a disorganized right-brain functioning. Without a right brain to process the present moment in which we act and live, we step into that other reality created in the dissociation as described by Kalsched (2013). The importance of the right brain related to the experience of the present is interesting considering that the function of the left brain has been emphasized much more in Western culture. The way we learn to value categorization and labelling of experiences before the body actually feels the present moment has created not only a split between head and body but also between the left and right side of the brain.

Hill (2015) suggests that repair of the self-regulative ability is "brought about by emotional experiences co-created in the implicit therapeutic relationship" (p. 205). The therapist's ability to listen to the client's unconscious communication, and to respond to the non-verbal subtleties that lie behind verbal and bodily interaction, is the repairing strategy to process shame, according to Hill. The client will use the therapist as a new role model and will eventually internalize the therapist's more positive attitude to the self. This process can, of course, lead to a better quality of life for the client living with self-shaming patterns, but from a Jungian perspective, the client is merely re-doing the early process of socialization, only with a different role model. Instead of having an inner negative mother as an internalized voice making life miserable, the therapist will appear as a more caring 'mother' and hopefully be able to minimize the bad influence from the early role model.

Referring to the early life of a child when the attunement of the mother was the foundation to a healthy ego-self relationship, this process could take place only because the child projected the self onto the mother during the first phase of development. It was the *mother*, as a (small) representation of the self, who regulated the child's affective needs, and only later did it become the ego-self relationship within the child (Neumann, 1973). As a parallel process in therapy this projection of the self also happens in the transference on the therapist as a condition for change. The therapist must become a safe other in order for the client to develop those parts of the self that were once rejected or not met by the mother.

During the following independence phase the child must redraw the projection of the self from the mother, thus establishing the ego-self relationship inside as a pre-condition for the process of individuation. From this time on, the client's *artwork* becomes the mirror of the original self and replaces to some extent the focus on the therapist. The client's self is so much more than the positive mother image that is transferred onto the therapist, and the individuation of the client's self becomes the novelty of the further development. The individuation process is vulnerable especially because of the lack of collective support, and the experience of self must be repeated many times in order to replace the old patterns. The challenge for the therapist is to let go of the past and to work more progressively with the new self-parts that are revealed in the artwork. In neuropsychology this process stimulates new neurological pathways in the brain by making them familiar through repetition.

The developmental transition from dependency towards independence patterns in the client's behavioural system also leads to an important change in the therapeutic relationship, because the client's ability to make decisions and to follow the inner self is thus being established. From a neuropsychological approach this transition indicates a stronger interaction between the right and left hemispheres in the brain. The child's dependency upon the mother's regulation of affective states in the first years of life is due to the slow development of the left hemisphere and the subsequent ability to control body and mind. The child depends on someone else to make sure that needs are fulfilled so life can be felt as good.

If the therapist becomes insecure without the good mother role to identify with, s(he) may want to keep the client in the dependency phase communicating shame, when the client attempts to individualize. This all happens in the right-brain to right-brain communication between therapist and client, and the good transition to the independence phase depends on the therapist's own inner ego-self relationship. If the ego-self axis in the therapist is not well enough established, the creative interaction with the client cannot take place either, because the therapist can only feel whole or meaningful when projecting her/his own inner wounded child onto the client. This is a main argument for the vulnerability in therapy, when the therapist has not been working with her/his own personal integration before working with others.

There is always to some extent a loss of control in creativity, because nothing new can come out of the creative process if we stay within the knowledge we already have. The opposite position, when the affects are disconnected from consciousness, is just as vulnerable when emotions dominate, because no creative activity can start without some connection to the body. It becomes an activity without soul or feeling and again, nothing new comes out of it. The 'Jungian' answer is to re-connect ego with self. We have discussed the role that shame plays in the developmental process, where the ego is formed according to outer demands, but what do the brain researchers say about this? And why is Jung so poorly mentioned in the literature with his practical solution to this major problem in our time?

Using symbols and imaginative ways of working is stimulating right-brain activity. One of the therapeutic values in using symbolic dialogues with clients when discussing their artwork is that at some point there is a personal association to the symbol, which leads the dialogue into more personal scenes from life. Starting with describing the symbolism of the artwork, with no personal memory activated, it seems like the focus on the symbol activates a personal memory track in the brain. This might be a result of the symbolic stimulation of right brain, where both the symbolic and the repressed scenes from life are located. This is also part of the surprises in art therapy dialogues, because neither the client nor the therapist knows which memory will be activated by the symbol.

Jung's concept of the self as an inner self-regulative centre in the psyche leads to a very different approach in psychotherapy. Trusting the self as a healing agent based on instincts more than on consciousness and willpower includes working with the affects in therapy using a symbolic language. When we no longer trust the instincts to be on 'our side' but see them, as Freud has explained it, as irrational impulses that aim only at satisfaction and not wholeness, we begin to fear losing control. In practical creativity we can lose control without killing anyone. We can find out what the affects are compensating for through working with the images that mirror the affects and thus we can gradually develop more trust in the affects as meaningful conditions.

One example

During a seven-day workshop one student was working with her shame of expressing her self, having grown up with a patriarchal father who 'always knew best' whenever she expressed her own thoughts. He would beat her if she dared to go against him, and the shame made her hide her true feelings inside. She had been a good 'mother' for everyone else in her life and now, at the age of 62, she expressed a longing to 'take care of her own self'.

In her first image (Plate 3; see plates between pages 112 and 113) she saw a womb as the white circle between the two red parts and associated this with a birth process. It calls to mind Grof (1986), who describes four phases, from conception to birth, as a) endless space in the womb, b) beginning pressure, felt as an outer aggression, as the child grows bigger, 3) beginning pressure/aggression from inside as the child's reaction to the limited space, and 4) the birth process, where both mother and child are active.

Using Grof's model with this painting, we can see that all the red power is outside the womb and that the child is neither pushed from outside or has the power to push from inside. What does that mean? My student associated to her lack of connection to emotions. She was painting her *idea* of a birth process, but without the affects being alive in her body. Or we can say that the affects are in the picture but extroverted from the womb, leaving the child unable to help in the birth process because the aggression that the child needs inside is absent. When she felt the connection between her need to help others, her father's abusive behavior and her lack of emotional connection, she felt sad about having lost so many years to no inner connection and made the following painting (Plate 4; see plates between pages 112 and 113).

She named the painting *Sadness and Anger.*

The two birds in the painting are equals, she said, and they meet here for the first time. Remember the Blue Diamante model, in which we discussed the importance of having access to sadness *and* anger as a precondition for working with shame. I see these two affects coming together in this image, creating a balance in the feminine and masculine polarity.

After this painting she made a painting of a blue snake and went to bed. During the night she woke up and felt such rage in her body that she had to go to the studio to 'attack' the snake. She used the birds as the attackers and in the image they bit the snake. As we looked at the painting the next day, she associated the snake with her father and realized that the snake did not seem to be affected by her anger as he was still just smiling in the painting. My feeling was again that the anger was captured in the archetypal image more than it was felt in the body. The true passion of rage, as she had felt the energy in her body during the night, was still held back and not visible in the artwork. I invited her to free that energy in a new painting by using the experience she had felt during the night, without looking for symbols and meaning. She painted over the blue snake and the result of this process is shown in Plate 5 (see plates between pages 112 and 113).

Interestingly she felt that her bad hip felt so much better after this painting!

The next night she dreamt the following: "A five-year-old girl comes out of a black tunnel with a lamp in her hand. She is dressed in white and looks very determined as she walks towards me. I wake up screaming as I see her standing beside my bed".

For so many years she had lost connection to her inner child, and here she comes walking out of a dark tunnel to meet her as a bringer of light. Also, she exists in both the psychic dream reality and the physical reality, and the two realities are no longer separated. When this fusion between the two realities takes place, the ego must of course be prepared to see the dream image become alive without being afraid of the strangeness in this fusion. This woman had known about her ability to 'see' the other reality since she was a child, and it turned out to be a secret that she had kept to herself and almost forgotten.

When the psychic image and the affect to that image come together, there is a sense of wholeness in the head-body connection, which is a new beginning/birth of a different attitude to life.

This example illustrates the limitation of using *only* symbolism in transformative processes. The language of the soul may be symbolic, but the language of the body is more primitive, raw and direct. The creative process is less psychic and more connected to body *movement* and to the physical *sensation* of painting during the release of affects. The true purpose of this kind of expression is to cleanse the body from such withheld affects as rage, sorrow and fear.

Self-regulation is a big topic in almost all psychotherapeutic approaches, due to the unbalance in our time to regulate emotions. We have seen the terror of letting the affects go free, as destructive and un-empathic activity directed against others or oneself. The general reaction to this is that we have become more suspicious of the unconscious and fearful of the consequences of letting go of control. When we learn new ways to protect ourselves from being influenced by the unconscious, these projective ways are created as oppositions to the affects. They are compensating for the un-controlled affects through the increase of control in almost every aspect of society.

From a Jungian and affect-theoretical approach, we do not gain anything by reinforcing the outer attempt to control affects, since this is where development went wrong in the first place. It would be more sensible to trust the affects as attempts to regulate the ego from having a one-sided attitude. The attention would then focus on ego development and not only on shameful affective behaviour.

Following Jung's suggestions in the debate on human change based on his understanding of the self, the relationship between the client and the therapist should be considered only supportive to therapeutic change. Strengthening the inner relationship between the ego and the self in the client (and the therapist) is more important because of the restoration of the self-regulative function itself. The unfolding of the original self, the individuation process, may be the deepest function of psychological creativity. The images of a self in transformation, which Jung discovered through mythology and alchemy, give us a depth of information about the process of individuation.

The role of a therapist in a Jungian-based art therapy process is therefore different in many ways from the role in a verbal therapy without a projected image of the self. As Schaverien (1999) points out, the transference onto the therapist might be explored through the image, but in my experience, this is only the case when the relationship to the therapist is unsafe and the client is afraid to verbalize this directly. If images are reduced to represent only transferences involving the therapist, the self within the client is ignored as if the therapist is more important. This can easily facilitate a shame reaction in the client, who again needs to stay invisible according to the therapeutic code.

The therapist's interest in the image and positive expectations to engage in the image invites the client to do the same, and the togetherness that characterizes the vitalizing relationship, as described by Hill (2015), is now activated in the relationship between the client and therapist, as a precondition for establishing the ego-self axis in the client.

In an art therapy process there is an implicit attunement to the image from both client and therapist. The client's vulnerability to the way the therapist relates to the image is an important right-brain attitude to the projection of the client's self. If the therapist reduces the image to mean something specific before the client has had a possibility to express in his/her own words what is revealed in the image, this act can take away the client's experience of being listened to in the therapy session and also the possibility of being able to connect to the inner self. The attempt to restore right-brain processing will then fail. Wilkinson says, "The right hemisphere, the seat of the bodily based self system with its store of early relational patterning, is the source of originality, creativity, and emotional growth and development" (2010, p. 9). What seems to be a general new emphasis on the function of right hemisphere in therapeutic relationships will hopefully lead to new attitudes in treatment, where the client's self is more directly involved.

The three brains and creativity

Creativity is not only related to the right-left brain interaction in the prefrontal brain. Looking at the brain from an evolutionary point, the neuroscientist Paul D. MacLean developed his theory on the triple brain in the 1960s. The oldest part of the brain (the reptilian brain) is located in the brain stem, which is the homeland of the affects and the autonomous self-regulative system (Stevens and Price, 2000). The archetypes would also seem to originate in this oldest part of the brain, which means that symbolization would be an activator of the instincts, as Jung suggests. The second and younger brain (the paleo-mammalian brain) is connected to the limbic system and the process of emotions. When affects are stimulated in the reptilian brain, it results in some emotional reactions in the limbic system, which controls "basic psychophysical responses and attitudes to the environment" (ibid, p. 17). The third and youngest brain is the neocortex (the neo-mammalian brain), which is connected to cognitive processes and rational thinking. This is the most conscious part of the brain; the reptilian brain is the most unconscious.

Stevens and Price also include the division of the neocortex into the right and left hemisphere, where the left hemisphere is controlling the right hemisphere. The bottom line is that the younger the brain is, the more consciousness has become part of the complicated neurological processes. When Jung talks about the ego-self relationship, this could in neuropsychological terms be associated to the relationship between the neocortex (ego consciousness) and the reptilian brain (archetypal unconscious).

Our survival depends not only on our instinctive reactions but also on the way our consciousness is formed according to the response we get from others. Because of the preference of left-brain processes, we tend to reject what we cannot control and what seems irrational to consciousness, which blocks the natural flow from affective activation towards conscious integration. This means that the attitude in consciousness becomes very important when we want to understand the key to creative stagnation, and how to re-open the flow between the unconscious and consciousness. The change of attitude towards the unconscious is maybe the biggest challenge in our time, because there are so many unhappy examples of affects that have gone wild. The rational left-brain thinking can easily assume that affects must be dangerous, without considering the attitude in consciousness to be the controlling agent. I think this could become Jung's contribution to neuropsychological research, because his main concern was always man himself.

Shame as a guide to inner wholeness

I have come to understand creativity according to the four domains that we know as the biological, psychological, social and spiritual (Skov, 2015). The way we process our experiences in the different life domains connects to different orientations as we try to solve the problems we meet in each domain of life. If we look at the domains from a developmental perspective, the new-born child is first of all interested in physical well-being. All the biological needs are regulated by the mother/caregiver while the other domains are less important for the child. Gradually the regulative process of biological needs is replaced by psychological ego development and the forming of a personal identity. The focus is on the self-image as it develops through the relationships in the family, while the other domains are more in the background. Moving forward in life, the young individual prepares for social integration and to find a role to play in relation to society. The focus here on the social domain is to develop a mask/persona, which will connect the individual to social groups. The development through the first three domains will in best cases lead to some sense of life being meaningful. Jung found that the spiritual domain was activated through midlife crises, when the outer life became meaningless and the inner life called for attention.

The four domains seem to represent the flow of life from birth towards death. When individuals experience crises in one domain, it would be most supportive if the therapeutic method addressed the same domain. The goal is to develop art therapy directives that fit the individual need for transformation.

If an individual has problems with the body and emotional self-regulation, it would be appropriate to re-gain connection to the body through free expression, without directives from a controlling ego. If the psychological domain and the topic of self-image were more important, individual therapy and the integration of personal scenes from life would seem to match the problem best. If an individual feels lonely, group processing would be most relevant as a frame for working with relational issues. When inner meaninglessness is activated, the creation and dialogues related to symbols would be the language where the spiritual self would gain most support for development.

If we add the topic of shame to the four domains (Table 2.2), we see how shame experiences can block the transformation of moving from one domain to another and the individual gets stuck in a type of problem that relates to the specific domain. This is why I think that a therapist must be familiar with all domains in order to follow the transformative process together with the client. When shame shows its face in therapeutic moments, we can relate the shame experience to one or more domains in life leading to different creative methods.

Table 2.2 Integrative model of shame

Shame domains	Signs of shame	Shame potentials	Purpose of creative activity
Biological	Bodily neglect	Health	Balance
Psychological	Low self-esteem	Dignity	Self-reflection
Social	Isolation	Belonging	Socialization
Spiritual	Meaninglessness	Meaning	Individuation

One client experienced shame on a biological level. Her body reacted strongly in relationships, showing signs of pain and loss of energy according to the dialogues she had with different people. She would blame herself for not being able to tolerate as much as she wanted from other people and did not experience the loss of energy as an *emotional* experience involving someone else.

Another woman who was also stuck on the biological domain saw herself as having a 'noise-vulnerability'. She felt more sensitive to sounds than 'normal' people are, and often had to leave the group she was in when she could not tolerate more sounds. In our group discussion it turned out that it had become part of the group culture not to be sensitive to others in how they made noise in the social room. Instead of lifting a chair in order to make as little disturbance to others as possible, they would carelessly drag it along the floor, and so forth. Instead of pointing that out to the group, she blamed her self for having a sensitivity disorder.

Creativity in the biological domain will always be compensative according to the special sensitivity we have in relationships when affects are activated. These kind of creative processes are controlled by the affects and the unconscious patterns that we have created in our life. The compensative expression of affects helps us to keep a balance in the body, but may create psychological and social difficulties and rejections, which we cannot control.

Another woman was stuck in the psychological domain. She did not sense many of her body signals, but felt controlled by the inner judge in all aspects of her life. She would blame herself for whatever happened, and the shame of being wrong would further isolate her from social connections. This would be the path of depression, as the blame would be directed towards the self. Another typical reaction would be to blame someone else for being such an idiot, and the anger would be projected to the outside as a way to avoid the experience of shame.

Creativity in the psychological domain focuses on internal processing of personal shame scenes that relate to integration of rejected self-images.

Another woman was always fighting with the system, her boss, her family, social care. She felt she was a victim of more powerful forces. She was stuck in the social domain where creativity operates between the individual and the social system as a development of both parties. When one part becomes more powerful, wanting to control the other part, original creativity cannot take place, because there is no freedom to develop the relation to the inner self.

Another woman had dissociated a part of her consciousness from reality and lived her life in a secret spiritual dimension where *she* was the queen and where she felt the love and belonging she needed in order to function in daily life.

Creativity in the spiritual domain operates in the field between the human and the transpersonal dimension, attempting to create a dialogue instead of a separation.

The point is that the transformative process of change includes all four domains, simply because they are part of the exchange we have with life: a) first the affect must be activated as a motivation to express (balance), b) then we use the expression as an image of who we are (reflection), c) then we interact with those around us based on who we are (socialization), d) then we find a meaningful relation to the transpersonal self (individuation). From this perspective we can approach the concept of creativity from four angles depending on the character of the problems we have that need change.

If, for example, a person is stuck in being a victim in life, there may be no psychological reflections because the root of the problem is projected onto an outer, more powerful person. It may be a good strategy to include the psychological domain in order to work on the inner self-esteem. The methodology that is usually offered to individuals who have problems with socializing to outer norms is a behavioural focus, where the emphasis stays in the social interaction and shame is left un-noticed.

The purpose in choosing a creative method to unlock a fixation on a domain is important if the overall process shall continue its movement. In my last book, *Integrative Art Therapy and Depression,* 2015, I describe this methodology as an integrative art therapy approach. In the following section I briefly introduce the basic idea in this approach.

Art therapy and the four domains

1   Art-based therapy (process)
2   Art psychotherapy (person)
3   Behavioural art therapy (relation)
4   Analytical art therapy (self)

1. Art-based therapy (process)

This direction refers to a *biological* way of using the arts without therapeutic intervention. The therapy is considered to be a result of the expressive process. The client might experience a change based on the compensatory function of the creative activity, but the psychological pattern itself is not addressed, and the creative activity must be repeated in order to keep the body in balance. This way of using the artwork can be a preparation to the psychological exploration of the artwork.

2. Art psychotherapy (person)

This direction emphasizes a *psychological* use of the creative expression. There can be many different psychological ways of using the artwork related to different psychological orientations (person-oriented, psychodynamic, humanistic, Jungian, etc.). The main focus is to integrate personal inner rejected parts in order to come to accept one self as a more whole individual. The artwork is related to the personal and not the archetypal. This approach can prepare the individual for the social domain where new integrative parts are explored in a group dynamic.

3. Behavioural art therapy (relation)

This direction refers to a *social* orientation, where group dynamics and behavioural approaches explored through the arts are considered to be of main interest. The focus is on group interactions using the arts as a bridge to explore and develop new approaches to social behavioural patterns and identity. This approach can prepare the individual for a spiritual approach, where meanings of life issues are explored in a safe group environment.

4. Analytical art therapy (self)

This direction refers to a spiritual orientation, where the focus is on inner development, moving beyond personal life experiences. The transpersonal self is explored through symbols and imaginative dialogues exploring new aspects of the inner self that has not been experienced before. This approach reconnects the conscious and the unconscious in a way that completes a transformative process.

Comments on the four approaches

Using all four domains in an art therapy clinical practice or education is using an integrative approach to therapy as I define and use the concept 'integrative'. That includes a wide use of theoretical directions as well as different kinds of clinical methods related to each domain. The four approaches to art therapy (biological, psychological, social and spiritual) can be used with a focus on one of the domains, often based on the therapist's personality.

In processing shame I think we need to follow the client through all domains, as illustrated in Figure 2.3. If we leave the client after the psychological shadow integration, a stronger ego may come out of the process, but a true healing of

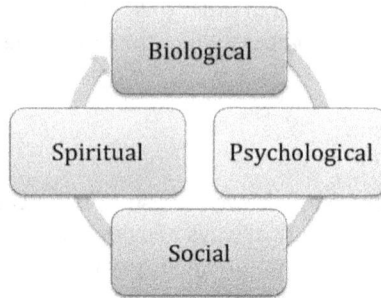

Figure 2.3 The four domains

the feeling function and of human relational compassion is left behind and inner strengths may never be manifested on the social domain.

Shame and bodily balance

The development through different phases in life starts with a biological body-mind union approach to life as the child expresses itself freely before psychological inner representations are formed in the psyche.

In art therapy a similar body-mind experience is re-activated through processes wherein the individual is invited to express him/herself freely from the body, without the shame communicated by inner judgemental voices. Of course this is not easy for most adults, who have identified with these shaming voices, but I have found that when confronted consciously, the inner judges lose their power to interfere in creative expressions. Instead of trying to avoid them, we should rather pay attention to their interference.

In my research I found that the inner judge appears in the artwork as part of the visual image, when he is ignored. The judge in us will try to cover up expressions that reveal the rejected images in order to maintain control of the ego. One woman painted the clarity she never felt she could express without her father's dominance. Later she said, "It was as if my father's voice came into my head while I was painting", and she began to make black lines and crosses covering up the bright yellow figure of her self.

Another painted her mother's hand in her head in a body painting, which later reminded her of forbidden spontaneity. When we pay attention to the inner judge during the art-making process, most individuals are able to 'catch him in the moment' when he interferes in the expressive process. I often suggest to my students to write down the judging voice on a piece of paper and then return to the art-making process. Stopping the inner judge from interfering in the art-making process is a mindfulness that will also support the ego in life when the shaming voice is activated. It shows that the patterns we live by in life and everyday creativity are similar to the patterns we activate in a practical art-making process.

The body experience of shame is sudden facial blushes, an instinctive need to get away from the situation and from the person who communicates shame, and a sense of dissociation from the moment followed by a loss of vital energy in the body. Working in the biological domain is less confrontational than working in the psychological domain, as there is little self-reflective process involved. The focus will be on the artwork and not on the psyche. The innocence of being creative without an explicit memory of shame can activate the two positive affects of joy and interest during the expressive process. As life energy, these affects facilitate hope, motivation and experiences of body-mind wholeness. Working in the biological domain without involving the psychological, social and spiritual domain can prepare for psychological processes, when regulation has been obtained (Skov, 2015).

Nathanson developed his 'compass of shame' as four reactions to shame: withdrawal, avoidance, attack other or attack self (1992). I find that it will be useful to add 'dissociation' as another reaction to shame, because it relates directly to the way consciousness reacts in the shame experience. When the mind dissociates, it can no longer maintain enough presence to make new decisions in the moment, simply because it has gone somewhere else. The dissociative state of mind is therefore one of the reasons why the shamed individual is unable to react with self-care when exposed to shame.

The pattern of creative expression

I became interested in the phase of creation that takes place in the body before the therapeutic dialogue, and wanted to see if there was any pattern in this process that could be considered important in relation to the more conscious dialogue afterwards. What would be the steps of transformation during the expressive process, if there were any awareness of this at all? Why do we feel better after the painting process, and could it be useful to know of these steps? Maybe the actual transformation takes place during the expressive process and not during the verbalization of the image, as we tend to think.

During the creative process our attention is more or less focused on the artwork. We are concerned about colour, forms and symbols as we try to express the inner self in the painting. We are looking for an expression that 'feels right' without intellectual explanation as we try to let go of the usual ego control in order to allow the flow experience to replace the controlling head. Maybe we forget to notice the transformative process because we are 'mindless' during this beginning phase of transformation? And if so, might this explain why our bodily felt change does not last for long – because the old patterns are stronger?

I invited a group of five women to take part in a little exercise. We had met seven times prior to this meeting, so they were all familiar with creative expression.

After some catching up from the last session, I invited them to express whatever their body wanted to express in a painting. I did not mention anything about the coming focus on the creative process, so as usual their focus was on the body–artwork connection.

When they had finished the painting process, I invited them to use their body to express their experience of the different phases they remembered during the painting process. After the movement exercise, they were to write down the steps. These steps are summed up in Table 2.3.

When we look at the first and last step in their descriptions, we find: awakening–curious, restless–self-confidence, being–determination, insecurity–receiving, concentration–flow. What we found was a self-regulative pattern for each participant. Without knowing or thinking about it, the body had an instinctive direction towards balance. I think this is what Jung refers to when he speaks of the self as having an instinctive regulative function. When possibility is there and the creative space is offered, the self will use that possibility to express its self as a counterbalance to any one-sided ego position. This may also explain why individuals say they feel better after the expressive process than before they started, because the inner tension is now projected outwards, leaving the body in a better balance.

In the process of self-regulation, shame can disturb the flow in art-making when the individual has idealistic goals concerning the outcome that cannot be fulfilled.

One client was painting with red and 'happy' rhythmic brush strokes, and suddenly she began to make some sharp black forms in the image covering the red background. In our dialogue she felt she blamed herself for just being happy and that it would be better to make some forms. Realizing how she had ridiculed her happy expression, she felt sadness, and I invited her to express her emotions in the painting without the inner judging voice. She then began to use her fingers as a brush being very angry and with her nails she was making marks into the paint. Finally she allowed her body to become involved in the art-making by following her reactions to the painting as a creative dialogue between the paper and the body. She was very pleased with the painting afterwards. This example indicates how the psychological domain needed to be activated in order to break a behavioural pattern of expression. As therapists, we can sometimes suggest new

Table 2.3 Patterns of creative activity

Person	Step 1	Step 2	Step 3	Step 4
A	Awakening	Moving forward	Protected	Curious
B	Restless	Searching	Calm	Self-confidence
C	Being	Connection up/down	Distance	Determination
D	Insecurity	Standing on both legs	Reaching out	Receiving
E	Concentration	Struggle	Surprise	Flow

possible ways of expression that support the change of a creative pattern, which will later become part of life.

Using the arts as a self-regulative process is important for personal balance, but also important as a way to counterbalance cultural pressure on the individual. In our culture we have lost that ritual space where individuals can regulate their inner balance in ways that do not hurt others and where the shame of letting go of control is transformed into beautiful artworks.

Shame and psychological integration

In the psychological domain we deal with personal experiences of shame. These early shame scenes are usually repressed into the unconscious and the implicit memory system, and therefore clients will share the *effect* shame has in their lives more than the shame scene itself. This is when the therapist can be useful as someone who verbalizes and guides the client towards the deeper understanding of shame. To verbalize shame by its name, sharing shame experiences with an empathic other, can help open the core complex of shame. I think this is a responsibility that therapists have, simply because the client has repressed the experiences of early shame. Levine says, "To break these negative 'complexes' (often associated with our parents) and enhance positive ones, we need to develop a capacity for self-exploration and reflective self-awareness" (2015, p. 31). The point he is making here is that biology alone cannot change our brains and minds. We also need to address the complexes that are kept in the unconscious in order to develop new patterns to live by. Jung also talks about complexes as tricking patterns in the unconscious that we cannot control even when we want to.

The bridge between the biological and the psychological domain is established due to the activated affects related to self-esteem. Schore says, "Self-esteem has been conceptualized as an 'affective picture of the self,' with high self-esteem connoting a predominance of positive affects and low self-esteem of negative ones" (1994, p. 362). The moments of vitalization during the creative process are perceived as moments created by the self and not by someone else. The client will learn to trust the self as a meaning-making function in the psyche, thus developing high self-esteem based on the positive affects of joy and interest.

From a developmental perspective it also depends on the client's ability to be 'away from mother' during the expressive process. The ego-self relationship in the client must be established in order for the client to feel safe during the process of creation, as there may otherwise be no sense of direction from inside and the client may feel lost and unable to begin the creative activity. In such cases the therapist will need to stay within reach, representing the good 'environment' mother while the client is producing the image. During the client's transition towards more independent psychological patterns, I personally prefer to leave the room while the client is painting in order to prevent a re-activation of a judging other.

The psychological domain is most typical in traditional verbal therapies, where the client discusses personal issues together with the therapist.

The professional art therapy identity has many faces where often one or two domains are preferred. My approach in this book is related to the process of individuation, and I have found that working on all domains stimulates the ongoing creation of the self. But the resources we need in order to process shame, like joy and interest, are not available in the shame experience, and that is the limitation in working in the psychological domain without including the biological, social and spiritual. That is also an argument for using all domains in the healing of shame because the experience of joy, interest and high self-esteem lies beyond the personal shame scenes.

Shame and socialization

One of the consequences of working through the affect of shame is that it can help us with social timing. Shame sensitivity will stop us from behaving in such a way that we risk exclusion from our social community, family or group. Being able to see our self from an outside perspective will inform us when we are on the border of becoming 'too much' for others to tolerate. This is one important function that shame, as an innate affect, facilitates for us in the development of social integration. Dissanayke (2000) has found that social belonging is one of our prime needs as humans, and without shame sensitivity, the process of adapting to a group can lead to an outside position and to a low quality of life. Looking at shame as a pattern behind 'anti-social' behaviour would lead to more innovative interventions centred on shame issues as an alternative to medical and cognitive approaches.

More and more individuals in our time have difficulties adapting to outer expectations at a young age, and feel that their individual needs are not met by parents or the social system. They may not know what they are truly interested in and they get no help to find out. Often they end up blaming themselves for not being able to live up to the ideal and they get stuck in the self-destructive spiral of shame.

Working creatively in the social domain in group settings creates an opportunity to explore a different social community, where individuals can develop the ego strength of knowing who they are through the interaction with others. Many individuals use a safe group setting to show new sides of themselves before they express these in their home lives. Using the arts to explore social interaction in mutual and non-verbal creative processing offers an opportunity to experience action-reaction behavioural patterns and to discuss them afterwards. These patterns are formed during early family life and are stimulated by what others do to us. This recognition in a group is an important step in changing social behavioural patterns.

The relationship between the individual and the group was of great concern for Jung, especially when he saw what happened during the Second World War, and he thought that the collective pressure would diminish the free will of the individual. Group therapy was therefore not a method that Jung recommended.

Having worked with groups for 30 years as a frame for art therapy training, I find it important to deal with group issues for several reasons – first of all to create a safe environment for the individuation process where no individual in the group should feel isolated or dominated by anyone else.

Secondly, it is important to learn about behavioural patterns that come up between the different members of the group, so students learn to work with projections and without communicating shame. When an individual is shamed in a group interaction, painted over or ignored, the reaction in the moment may not be released, but held until later, when it takes revenge through compensative behaviour. Therefore it is important to create different social expectations in the group, where individuals learn to share the shame that they unintentionally pass on to each other. Because we all have a mutual understanding of the self and include inner work in relation to the group dynamics, this is a frame that facilitates ego strength, self-esteem and group coherence.

Working on the social domain using the group as a holding environment makes the individual repeat behavioural patterns that were formed in early childhood. "You are just like my father"; "Nobody likes me, just as it has always been"; "You are not listening, just like my mother" or "You always think you are better than me, just like . . ." Projections of inner representations are played out, and can be transferred back to the original relationship and processed. This process of taking back projections creates a new space in the group that can be explored and used more on the premises of the self. New behavioural patterns can unfold according to the positive affects of joy and interest, and the 'pretend' persona can be replaced by a more authentic presence.

I find that group work is an important structure in working with shame because it makes it possible to recognize and process old patterns of behaviour when they are actually happening. Personally I like the flexibility that is available in a group where focus can change between the inner and the outer reality.

Shame and individuation

The stimulation of the spiritual domain creates a connection between the personal and the archetypal dimension of life. When this relationship is disrupted we lose the trust in our ability to rely on the self for change. We begin to control and categorize creative processes and the core of creativity is reduced to something that has no originality. The fear of letting go of control even for a short moment is an important challenge in every creative process, which is why chaos and trusting chaos must be part of the process of creativity.

Creativity is sometimes a feeling of control, as for example when we finish a process and just know what was not known before. At other times, when we don't have that clarity of knowing, our consciousness is chaotic. Without some trust in chaos, creative and original solutions cannot become known. Instead there is a tendency to think that we must return to the control that was once there and we miss the opportunity to develop something original out of chaos.

I think this is an important understanding of creativity that must be made less mystic. We cannot rely on the present world order as a general stimulation of creativity, because that world order relies on control being more worth than chaos. The collective attitude affects the individual to judge chaos as a more shameful condition than control, and the transformative process gets stuck in that void.

In *The Cambridge Handbook of Creativity*, a summary of theories of creativity presents ideas where the process of creativity is described as taking place between the individual and external factors resulting in a creative product (Kaufman and Sternberg, 2010). None of the mentioned theories focus on the inner relationship between the ego and the self as a core psychological foundation for creativity. Research in psychological creativity does not include the unconscious as a domain that can be investigated as a partner to the conscious mind.

Jung emphasized a connection between the instinctive and the spiritual nature of the self as represented in the affect and the combined image.

Using symbols and imaginative dialogues might seem irrational to the individual who has no connection to the spiritual domain, but often the experience of finding meaning in symbolic artwork, where they did not expect to find any, can help restore some trust in chaos and in the self. The meaning-making process occurs when the symbol becomes vivified by the affect. One student was about to write her essay after an art therapy course and she just could not get started. She went out to get something in her garage where she saw a blackbird nest. This did the trick! She suddenly knew the beginning of her imaginative story about the blackbird's life. She used an experience from the physical reality as a symbol of her inner reality and interpreted this synchronicity as a meaningful sign that released her creativity into writing.

The spiritual domain is connected to the transpersonal reality, where shame is experienced in relation to the self or in its extroverted form to God. The spiritual domain is accessible through the symbol, imagination and the archetypal world of the psyche. It should not be mistaken as personal but kept as a separate reality accessible to ego consciousness. This differentiation between the ego and the self or the personal and the archetypal is an important duality that makes conscious dialogue possible.

The problem arises when the self is experienced as a shaming other based on an early experience of a shaming mother. The ego will avoid contact with the self as a way also to avoid shame, leading to damaged self-regulation and inner guidance.

One of the participants in my research study was brought up in a very religious home. In the painting of her family, God's eye was dominating everyone in the family. She said that aggression was the most forbidden emotion in her family. To be angry with God for making such restrictions is not an easy task, and her parents did the best they could, she said, because God also controlled them. She had learned to turn her anger against her own self, so when her husband left her for a younger woman and she was furious, she felt an overwhelming shame related to her anger towards him.

The spiritual domain is powerful in its goodness, kindness, helpfulness, guidance and love as one aspect of the God polarity. In dissociated states it can become the archetypal loving and idealizing world, as opposed to the evil reality of shame. Using the spiritual as a hiding place for shame, it is also the place of initiation, death, rebirth and transformation. The creative challenge is to use the spiritual realm in relation to the other domains, so that it can function in the transformative process instead of being a hiding place.

One important function of working on the spiritual domain is to develop a spiritual attitude to the creative process, so that trust in the unconscious self can replace fear.

Summary of the integrative model

Using biological, psychological, social and spiritual methods in processing shame not only reflects the natural development through different domains in our lives but also reconnects us to our *ability* to transform and change.

To me an artwork becomes alive when we relate to it. It can happen during the creative activity and it can happen during the subsequent dialogue as different experiences related to the different domains.

The fear of the unconscious is in reality a fear of the affects that are attached to the image – the fear of being overwhelmed by these affects and that we will lose control and go crazy. The general understanding and approach to the affects are that they should go away. If repression does not work, then we have medical treatment as a plan B. We forget that when affects overwhelm us and we lose control of the body, the psyche, our social behaviour or spiritual guidance, it is merely a result of our own rejection of the affects. Outer expectations of how we ought to behave have taken control of our instinctive reactions to life. When affects finally explode within the individual and we see rage, terror, illness and depression, we make new rules and restrictions in order to control affects that in reality are uncontrollable. This road has a dead end. Working with affects through art can be a safe way to restore our relationship to the affects.

My point is that we can always compensate for what has happened to us in life through some activity that will keep the core of shame in the unconscious. We can compensate on all domains and get caught in patterns that exclude the feeling of wholeness.

Cultural patterns of shame

Each culture has specific rules and expectations of their members. The basic line for all cultures is how and to what extent the two positive affects of joy and interest are rejected during upbringing when we develop our personality.

Looking at mythological themes that tell us about shame related to the masculine and feminine archetype as images of the positive affects, we have to move beyond the patriarchal period in order to discover the qualities behind the shamed feminine. We have been told that Eve was born out of Adam's rib and so belonged to him, but not that his first wife, Lilith, left him for a life in freedom. We took for granted that men had more worth than women in all of life's domains, because that was the reality for most of us growing up in families with a father who was given the authority and dominant role of the patriarch.

In general it seems as if women have been victimized for centuries by being devalued and shamed when expressing their Lilith qualities, such as sexuality and freedom. Using a Jungian approach, it is important to point out that so have men. The feminine Lilith side of men has also been repressed and so kept men from using their freedom to express feelings without shame for not being a 'real' man. The split between head and body or between intellect and affect has been a reality for both genders and is part of the patriarchal culture. We repress the many shame scenes where we experienced this unbalance, and it operates from the implicit memory system as a Lilith reaction to a cultural shame.

According to Koltuv (1990) the matriarchal period before 2500 B.C. was a time when women were worshipped for their sexuality and their access to the dark mysteries. After the inception of patriarchal domination, her sexual power was demonized as a force of evil and she became the image of the feminine shadow. Even today there is a general understanding of the feminine as a passive principle and of the masculine as active, and we have identified these principles to be gender related instead of principles that live in both men and women. Lilith therefore represents a feminine aspect, born out of the passive womb, who refuses to project the masculine onto outer men. Koltuv (1986) says that Lilith is "the animating, instinctual natural level of being" (p. 8). This means that Lilith is our instinctive force towards individuation: "she wants the freedom to move, act, choose and determine. These are the qualities of the individuating feminine ego as it is born out of inert passive matter" (ibid, 1986, p. 22). She is an important image during the process of separating from the values of the patriarchy in order to find our own attachment to life. Her qualities are hiding behind her reaction to the patriarch's rejection, which are to be found in "images of humiliation, diminishment, flight and desolation followed by fiery rage and revenge as seductress and child killer" (ibid, p. 19). In her unconscious and un-integrated aspect Lilith relates to self-destructive patterns and suppression of inner needs, and as such she has a negative maternal function. This is her child-killing reaction to being rejected, and I think many of our cultural problems, such as addictions, eating disorders, depression, unhealthy lifestyles, suicide and terrorism, can be read as signs of Lilith's return.

When working with shame scenes, an instinctive reaction is often released in the client which is best characterized as rage and wishes of revenge. Like a pendulum these emotions become the counterbalance to the repressed position. Letting go of the emotions that have been withheld in the body does not break the shame pattern; it balances the shame experience by expressing the affect that was withheld in the shame scene. Lilith is a run-away archetype. She does not stay long enough to process her shame of being rejected for who she is. She reacts instinctively and withdraws to the desert and the Red Sea. It is told that God was on Adam's side. He thought she should have stayed and surrendered to Adam. Instead she became a compensative instinct to counterbalance suppression. If we look for Lilith signs in our modern time, it is only fair to follow the background for her activity.

One of the participants in my research study was abandoned by her husband, who had found a younger woman. Secretly he had bought a house and moved in with his new woman, leaving my participant in shock after 34 years of marriage. First she was scared of being alone, then sad and confused, and finally she became angry and cut his shirts to pieces. The rage of having spent her life focusing on his career while sacrificing her own was almost unbearable. But she managed to re-connect with Lilith without actually killing her ex-husband and started to develop a more independent personality, first manifested in her artwork.

There was no therapeutic debate between Adam and Lilith. She became invisible in the same way as we see in depression, and we have only her reactions as signs of her presence. In order to use her potential as an instinct towards individuation, we have to understand her reactive signs, not as images of who she is, but as images of what we have made her become. We have to allow her to react to the rejection she experienced from Adam and God. And what could be a better place for that than the art room? A space where affects can be unfolded freely and directly from the body. When there are too many restrictions, she cannot do that and she will flee again. When I visit institutions I always ask to see their art room, and usually I am referred to the cellar! Some small dark room that was left over and then used as an art room with little space to unfold affects. Lilith needs space and freedom in order to express her sadness, anger, shame and fear before she can function as a natural instinct in the original and creative development of the self. If creativity shall become free from the influence of patriarchal power needs, Lilith must first be redeemed. George (1992) says that freeing Lilith goes through three phases. The first is to confront the shame scenes from when she was rejected. The second is to release the emotions from the body and to recognize the patterns in our lives where we take revenge. Third is to release her true nature from captivity. This process guides us back to the empty void from where all true originality comes. The process of individuation is always original and free from patriarchal influence.

Whitmont (1983) addresses the use of ritual as a form of transformation and says, "Any affect or emotion which in its raw and unaltered form is too intense to be controlled by will alone may need its ritual" (p. 235). The ritual helps us to dis-identify with the affects through the process of sublimation and functions as a transformer for overwhelming affects. Whitmont combines the ritual as a frame for play, which he says "mobilizes and structures the powers of the unconscious psyche. It gives form to raw energy; it civilizes" (p. 241). The expression of repressed affects through the ritual of play becomes compensatory and balancing to the psyche, thus transforming the emotional condition of the individual. Stewart (1986) further suggests that play and curiosity "are related to each other in an on-going dialectical process that reveals. . . . two kinds of thinking, fantasy thinking and directed thinking, and the principles of Eros and Logos" (p. 190). The problem related to creativity arises when the feminine principle of Eros is devalued by the masculine principle of Logos. When play is based on rational terms, the positive affect of joy in playing for fun is repressed together with the free Lilith aspect of the feminine. The compensative process of creation will then always refer to the repressed affects and not to the manifestation of true originality. I find this unbalance to be a cultural issue that must be confronted in personal development as choosing a different approach in the art making process. To paint without having a precise purpose or a specific outcome, allowing impulses to be included in the creative process, is a choice that can be made conscious and lead to a discovery of the psyche's way of creating wholeness.

Summary

Lilith is the archetype that connects to creativity as a transitional archetype, moving from passivity towards a natural instinct to be original, expressive and free from patriarchal influence. Koltuv (1986) says, "To become conscious of the deep split in the feminine between the child-killing Lilith and the child-loving Eve, a woman needs to be connected to herself at a basic and instinctual bodily level" (p. 89). Integrating Lilith is not an original creative process but a process of working through shame scenes where she was rejected. Approaching this theme from a cultural point of view can support the individual in taking a personal stand in relation to the patriarchal values that influence us unconsciously when we are creative.

So how is this process different for a man?

Ayers (2011) says, "Being a sexually adequate male means not being loving . . . the highest expectations of masculinity and the development of power are to destroy any vulnerability to shame" (p. 110). Ayers's point is that men are leaving the mother much too soon and without keeping a connection to the mother realm of body, emotion and the unconscious. The opposite applies to women, who return to identification with the mother in order to get their gender identity established. This may explain why so many women struggle with a male partner who refuses to discuss emotions in their relationship. Such discussions throw them right back to the mother realm, where they are not supposed to be, as real men. When we work with emotions, the body and imagination, men therefore have a different self-protective system than women, which gives them another challenge in using symbolization and doing apparently irrational things, such as play. They want to stay separated and move forward, instead of being caught by the mother womb of fusion. The ability to symbolize using the right side of the brain is therefore more accepted by women than by men. I wonder how that cultural influence affects access to the imaginative reality differently for men and women. Do men feel threatened in their masculinity when being creative just for the fun of it? Is it more shameful for men to surrender to the affects because they are made feminine by a society that devalues feeling for rational thinking? As Ayers puts it, "The absence of the symbolic function means that true creativity is lost" (2011, p. 138)

Reactions to shame

The reaction to shame is more connected to the way a rejection is communicated from another than to the content itself. When left-brain rationalization is more powerful and true than the right-brain ethic, shame is most often activated in the individual. The difficulty of reacting to shame in the moment is that we have learned that content is more important than how we experience the communication of it. We do not confront someone who criticizes us, saying they should speak in a friendlier tone, especially not when we are two years old. Nor do we say that they hurt us by the way they address us. The most difficult shame to tolerate is the more subtle humiliation, where nobody else interacts and we are alone with the reality of being wrong. When such experiences are confronted, it is easy for the shaming other to deny them, because they may not exist in the physical reality where rational objectivity has the highest value. The psychic reality belongs to the invisible underworld and it is far from easy to come back from that dark domain of experience without some back-up from the collective to confirm that you are not entirely crazy. One example is the following.

A client was having a talk with a friend at a social gathering, when she saw another friend standing alone close by. She wanted to include her friend and invited her into the discussion, and a few minutes later her friend had taken over the dialogue completely and she herself felt left out. Later she told her friend about her experience of being excluded and her friend said that she would not protect others anymore as this was an old pattern of hers, so she did what she wanted because it was right for *her*! My client felt deeply hurt and shameful because she was rejected, not only in the discussion, but in her ethical behaviour and sensitivity to her friend's aloneness. She felt rejected in her feminine principle but not in her womanhood. The invisible action of empathy was used against her and she felt betrayed by her friend for not seeing that. Her friend's reaction activated her relationship to her narcissistic mother and the way she had learned to sacrifice her own needs in order to satisfy her mother.

The taboo operating here is that verbalization of the underlying pattern is not discussed in such a way that both realities are considered true. When her friend says that she is done with fulfilling others' needs and that she had finally learned to consider her own needs, she became just as narcissistic as the mother she wanted to be free from. This period in her development was anti-social because her own needs were more important than her relationship with her friend. She lost her compassion and her access to the psychic reality because of a personal mother complex.

My client could not express what that made her feel – that she felt left out and betrayed in the moment – because that would be considered weak and out of touch with the topic of discussion. She finally blamed herself for not being worthy enough to be included by both of them, and got stuck in the shame cycle.

In therapeutic processes we do need to be good mothers to our newfound inner children as a compensation for all the attention we learned to live without in our childhood. That is part of the integrative personal therapy. We also need to repeat new behavioural patterns in life until they are wired into the brain as part of who we are. This personal process does not necessarily include experiences of the underworld domain and the psychic reality. It includes personal scenes from life and rejected emotions related to the ego-shadow polarity. The psychic reality is the reality of the feminine principle of relatedness. When development gets stuck in the personal without the opportunity to process archetypal shame, we may also get lost in compensative ego-oriented behaviour as a fulfilment of earlier narcissistic needs.

When we experience shame and don't acknowledge the experience, we still react to shame in different ways, depending on our shame vulnerability and past experiences. Lewis mentions denial, forgetfulness, laughter and confession as ways to avoid shame experiences in single moments of shame because we can move the focus from the shame itself towards something else (1995). When shame is repeated over time it may not be possible to change the focus, because the shame experience can be overwhelming and activate other reactions like rage or depression, which Lewis refers to as pathological reactions to shame. Anger and sadness are considered normal forms of emotions and Lewis finds that they work as defensive reactions to a shame experience (ibid). If we recall the Blue Diamante model described earlier, sadness and anger can also be considered as opening affects in relation to the individuation process, because ego consciousness moves towards the self and not towards the ego as in the socialization process. Experiencing anger or sadness can lead to the deeper experience of shame when the sadness-anger relationship is established as equally accessible emotions.

In discussing reactions to shame I want to focus on the reactions we have when shame is not made conscious – that is, when shame is avoided and 'substituted' by something less painful, like sadness or anger, which Lewis thinks are the most typical reactions to shame. He also finds that anger is more typical for men, while women tend to be more sad (ibid). In therapy that would mean that in order to balance the sadness–anger polarity, men should be guided more towards sadness and women more towards aggression, which is also a confrontation with many gender-related aspects of socialization and the way we expect different reactions from boys and girls.

Sometimes shame is so subtle and invisible that we need to locate the shame scene in the subjective experience, as it may not make rational sense from an objective angle. Lewis makes the point that we often focus on the case or incident instead of the shame *experience* and then miss the opportunity to process shame (ibid).

Shame sensitivity

Considering the sensitivity to shame that many individuals have, it would seem natural that their shame sensitivity also picks up other people's shame. The mechanism of transference and counter-transference does not occur only in the therapy room between the client and therapist. Projection of inner shadow personalities to other individuals creates the affective bonds that keep us connected to each other. If the affects were not there, between us, we would have no interest in anybody and our vulnerability as a human race would be increased. Often we believe in the projections that other people see us through, and forget that we are more like, or maybe not at all like, these images. The shamed individual, who has no inner sense of dignity and self-worth, can easily become a garbage carrier for others' shame without knowing about it.

One student was sitting beside another student, who was going to present her family portrait within a few minutes. She could see that her fellow student was very nervous, uneasy and not very happy about the prospect of presenting her family to the whole group. Suddenly she felt that her own heart was beating fast and she also got nervous 'out of the blue'. When the presentation was over, she was back to her normal self again.

When we become conscious of our own shame sensitivity, we also learn to detect it from others and sometimes, when we resonate with someone, we might want to release them from the pain we know so well and we take into our bodies the pain that they feel because we have the 'instrument' to do so. It is part of how empathy operates sometimes on a deep, unconscious level, and sometimes the other person's shame stays too long in our bodies and we mistake it for our own. These are the small gifts that we bring to each other in the invisible reality where nobody sees the psycho-logical interaction that goes on. Becoming aware of our personal shame can help us let go of the shame we sense in others, giving them a possibility to work through their own stories.

The shamed personalities

The intensity of shame reactions that we have learned to live with becomes part of who we think we are, and they may stay with us for a lifetime; or they make too much trouble in our lives and we search for new understanding and change. I have located six basic reactions or personalities based on un-acknowledged shame (Figure 2.4). They should not be considered rigid character structures, but

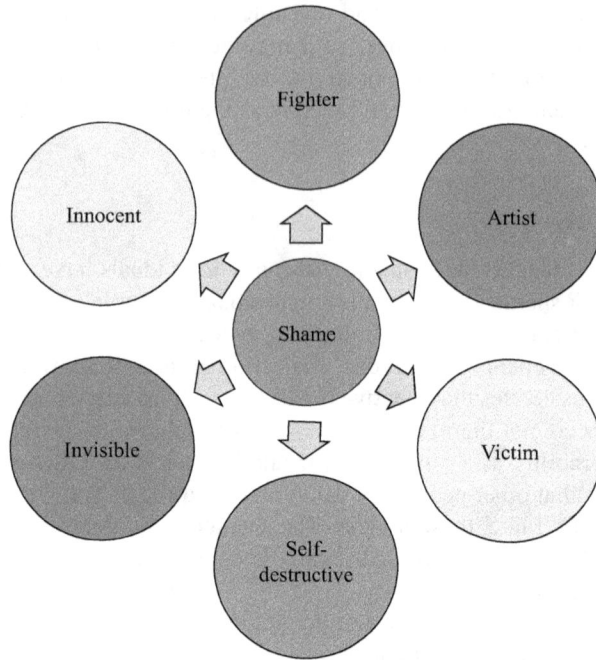

Figure 2.4 A personality model

possible reactions to shame experiences when the affect of shame connects with sadness, anger or fear.

The intention of combining different identities with specific shame-connections is to inspire the individual or clinician to find a starting point in working to change patterns of shame. As I have come to see it, there seem to be three affects that can be activated in an introverted or extroverted way as reactions to shame. It is fear, sadness and anger. Referring to the Blue Diamante model, they are the affects 'above' the shame affect, and all the other affects (surprise, joy and interest), are below the affect of shame and therefore reachable only through processing shame as a movement towards the self.

When sadness becomes attached to shame, the personality will tend to be identified as introverted, because sadness carries us towards the inside reality opposite the more extroverted nature of shame: anger. When fear connects with shame, the danger of becoming visible in life can be so threatening to the ego that only excessive visibility can protect consciousness from the experience of shame as an inner condition, or the opposite escape into invisibility.

I think these connections are like tricksters to consciousness. They bring attention to the *signs* of shame in order to avoid the more terrible experience of shame itself. They are like self-protective patterns and avoiding mechanisms, based on the experience that the wholeness of self is in danger. The affective connections are like survival mechanisms, activated instinctively and un-knowingly, leading to a way of living that means running away from the true potential we have as individuals. The individuation process is about un-covering the connection between the shame identity and the self in such a way that the self remains whole. Integrating the rejected shadow and other inner personalities can support such development of inner wholeness, before actually confronting shame. It gives consciousness the time and integration to meet the ugly face of shame without the risk of fragmentation.

Each personality in this model has a shadow side, shown as the opposite in the figure. The fighter is opposite to the self-destructive, the innocent is opposite to the victim, and the artist is opposite to the invisible. In un-acknowledged shame, the shadow in the personal unconscious is kept separated from consciousness, so they do not know of each other. I think a first step in recognizing shame is to identify the personality that we have grown into as a reaction to shame experiences.

In Table 2.4, I have shown the ego-shadow polarities between shame–sadness, shame–anger and shame–fear as introverted and extroverted personalities. The point is that we tend to feel safest in one or the other identity and therefore may need the skill attached to the rejected shadow side. When someone shames us, an extroverted personality will be useful in order to stop the abuse, while the introverted attitude will be needed in order to avoid *being* an abuser. The flexibility of having access to both the extroverted and introverted attitude is one of the cornerstones in processing shame. We need them both in order to live a life where shame does not control and define who we are.

The fighter. Extroverted identity. Shame binds with anger

The fighter avoids shame by fighting back before shame reaches consciousness. The fighter is an individual who tries not to sink into the feeling of being wrong and therefore becomes angry instead. When shame connects with anger, these two affects create a friendship whereby anger becomes the protector of shame as a self-caring system (Kalsched, 2013).

One client had a miscarriage early in her pregnancy and felt irritated and angry with her husband after the incident, and she did not understand why, because they

Table 2.4 Shame binds

Identity/Bind	Shame–sadness	Shame–anger	Shame–fear
Extroverted identity	Innocent	Fighter	Artist
Introverted identity	Victim	Self-destructive	Invisible

loved each other. So why did she push him away? When asked about her feelings related to the loss of her baby, she said she felt such anger. She was angry with her body for not being able to keep the baby and she was angry with her husband for every small thing he did, and she and her husband seemed to be drifting apart. Going a little deeper, she said that her husband wanted to play cards with his friends the night she came back from the hospital – as they had arranged long time ago. The rejection she felt from him, when she was still in shock after having lost their child, was devastating to her and she was right back in her childhood loneliness and rejections. They did talk about it for hours, but that did not change her experience of being rejected when she needed him most. How could he not sense her need for him that evening? I think many women live with such experiences of having been rejected due to our patriarchal culture, especially related to childbirth, family responsibilities and emotional exchange. Women are expected to tolerate men's rational explanations, such as "I work for you and the family" or "This was what we agreed on", and her 'right' to react to his rejection is ridiculed. The shame of being rejected is kept inside.

Shame-sensitive individuals are susceptible to these invisible rejections that hurt the inner woman and isolate her in her shame of not being worth the man's attention. My client already felt a deep shame about her womanhood, and her man's preference to be with his friends at *this* moment was just another piece of wood to the fire. It became more than she could tolerate, and the affect of aggression was activated as a defence against the deeper unbearable shame.

Referring to the Blue Diamante model (Figure 2.1), we follow the affect of anger as the masculine reaction to shame, leaving the affect of sadness as a feminine response to her loss. In order to work with the underlying shame, the balance between sadness and anger needs to be established, which means that her reaction to her loss must be processed. My client's reaction was similar to Lilith's behaviour when Adam rejected her. She left and came back as a vengeful witch full of anger. She too was reacting with the masculine affect of anger, ignoring the feminine sadness that can take us inward towards the empty void and shame.

In creativity the fighter is that part of us who does not give up – who keeps the painting process moving, in spite of all resistance, inner judges and outer business, until the artwork is finished.

The self-destructive. Introverted identity. Shame binds with anger

Destruction of one's own self is aggression turned inward instead of outward. We find it in addictions, depression, eating disorders, stress and all the many times we know what would be a good thing to do for our body and mental health, but still we go in the opposite direction. Then we make a promise to ourselves every new year that next year will be better. The self-destructive personality actively uses anger to destroy the good feeling of self-care. The voice inside who overrules the voice of the self is a voice that was once outside. We are not born to harm ourselves and therefore must consider the self-destructive behaviour as another sign of self-protection. We can also see the self-destructive personality as a protector of others, as one client said: "I just don't have the heart to say no when they need my help, even when it means that I don't have any time for myself". When we learn from 'shaming others' that we have no value and don't deserve their love, we turn that anger against the self instead of against the other as a way to protect the self from being shamed again.

The self-destructive activity is part of the creative cycle in which we destroy something we have painted because it did not mean anything to us. It was an expression related to the false self, made out of boredom and attempts to fulfil outer expectations for a nice painting, and it has to be sacrificed and painted over. In order to do that, as a search for the authentic expression, we must select carefully what is important to us in the image before we blindly destroy what we like most. This ability to select one colour or form from another is based on feeling and not thinking. There may be a rational explanation to the choices we make during the painting process, but they are not important to know of until later, when reflection takes us to a deeper psycho-logical understanding of the creative process.

The victim. Introverted identity. Shame binds with sadness

As an opposition to the innocent personality, the victim is projecting the power to someone in the external world. As a victim, you do not see your own role in activating the aggressor in the other person and therefore hold no responsibility to the abuse felt from someone else. Also there is no learning from the situation, because the creative cycle of projection and introjection remains incomplete. When the shame-sadness personality lives with a dominant introverted attitude, the path towards depression is wide open. Moving farther and farther away from the power that is needed to manifest in life, the victim may get caught by the inner empty void of the underworld. As opposed to the face of innocence, the victimized person is always on the run away from outer judgement and shaming others. The ability to set clear boundaries as a protection of the self is the most difficult challenge for the victim personality, because that would include some access to the *inner* aggressor.

The creative process is not easy for the introverted victim because the judgemental voices are directed towards the self. One client had felt victimized her whole life. In her family her four sisters and brothers had teased her as the youngest, and when she started in the art therapy group she never felt she had a right to speak up. She expected others to laugh at her or not understand what she wanted to say. Getting access to the power through the art-making process is a way for the victim to re-discover the power within instead of projecting it onto someone else as usual. Another client defined herself as a victim in a present conflict in her life. She was living in a collective with an unpredictable neighbour, who would shame her for being lazy and criticize her two children aggressively. In those moments she froze and felt unable to defend her self, and therefore she had decided to move to another apartment in the collective, in spite of her love for the apartment she was now living in. She felt stuck in the victim's role, and what should she *do*? It turned out that she had felt like a victim all her life, living in a family where she became responsible for the well-being of her mother, father and sister, as they were unable to support themselves. During these years, she abandoned her connection with her own needs and with her body, and managed to get rid of her abusive husband by gaining 50 kg in weight in five years, so she was sure he would not be attracted to her anymore. She used her body as a shield towards the aggressive other, instead of taking a stand and defending her self. The innocent shadow part of her was identified as her lack of consciousness about what was going on in her body. She was always there for others, but could not feel the un-expressed reactions to being rejected when nobody was ever there for her.

The innocent. Extroverted identity. Shame binds with sadness

When shame binds with sadness the connection to the unconscious is felt as a big empty void of nothingness and the innocent psyche is disconnected to the body and to other affects. The self-caring system is based on this dis-connection to the affects as a way to avoid the pain of shame. In the myth of Amor and Psyche, Psyche is living isolated from other people except those who worship her, as if she was the goddess herself. As an innocent princess living in a cage of protection, she is not able to take the initiative to process any of the affects by her own choice, and in the myth it is therefore her father, the king, who asks the oracle for advice and who initiates the process. He represents an inner masculine authority that trusts the spiritual voice of the oracle and operates from the unconscious and not from the ego. The innocent personality often uses a childish attitude of 'not knowing', looking for someone else to carry out the parental function in a relationship, therefore there is a stronger dependency pattern here than in any of the other personalities.

One student with such a personality had the following dream in the beginning of her training to become an art therapist:

> I am in the street and I feel very confused and do not know where to go. Suddenly my boss comes in a car and asks me to jump in. I feel very safe with him driving around, but after a while he tells me to get out of the car indicating that I am safe now. Back in the street I fall down hoping that someone will come to my rescue, but no one does, and finally I get up. . . . I am dragging a big and heavy wooden box and see my boss standing 100 feet away. I want to reach him, but know that he will be gone before I can manage to get there.

Obviously she had a good relationship to her boss and used him as an image of the supportive parent. She was struggling to make connection to the inner guiding parent who could help her find direction in life that was good for her. As a general rule, the beginning of a dream indicates the theme that the dream is presenting, the middle part the conflict, and the last part the solution. Looking at the dream from this perspective, we can assume that the transference of the good parent onto her boss is coming to an end. In the beginning it helps her to escape her fear of not being able to find a direction in life, but then he leaves her alone to solve this on her own. Why does nobody come to help her as she is lying in the street? From the perspective of the self, this is because she *is* able to support her self. She does not need to depend on others for support. It is a trick made by the complex. A behavioural pattern that no longer fits to her maturity. In the end we see that she is again trying to reach the idealized parent, but she is dragging this heavy wooden box. I think there is an allegory to Christ, who dragged the wooden cross before his crucifixion. So how can this be a solution to the dependency pattern? Christ is an archetype of transpersonal love but also of someone who consciously committed ego-cide. He decided to sacrifice his life in the name of love for humanity and as such also links to the archetype of the victim, which is the shadow side to the innocent. The dream can therefore be pointing towards an integration of the child (innocent) and the loving adult (victim) as two aspects of the self. One of the most important things for the innocent psyche is to take back parental projections from others as the inner child becomes strong enough to leave old patterns of dependency.

In creativity the innocent attitude supports the shameless and free expression from the body because there is no self-judgemental influence in control.

The invisible: shame binds with fear

When we want to be invisible in life it is because we find it dangerous to be seen by others. We can get hurt and rejected by others and as a self-protective system we hide in the dark.

One student, who repeatedly had been verbally attacked by her aunt during her childhood, still remembered how her body had frozen from the shock of the aunt's aggression with no possibility to defend herself. She was told that if she gossiped to someone about these incidents, something 'terrible' would happen. In her family she learned 'not to trouble anyone', and she developed an 'invisible' personality where shame was connected to the fear of being attacked by someone from outside, and in general she spoke very little in the art therapy group.

During one of the exercises in the music therapy week, all the students in the group were invited by the music therapist to 'fill out their private space' with their voice, and she experienced for the first time that she was able to let go of her self and discovered her voice as surprisingly powerful and playful.

The following night she dreamt: "I am in a room filled with people. My job is to serve coffee and to clean the place. I see a famous Asian singer in the room. She looks very calming and natural and she is giving interviews to some journalists.

She reaches the heart of other people with her singing. I know that she lives in a beautiful nature with mountains, water and animals. Suddenly she comes over to me and invites me to visit her in her private home and gives me her address on a piece of paper and walks away. I feel such warmth and happiness and know that she will become my soul mate. I discover that her address is already in my book, but I must have forgotten that I once wrote it down". The dream is making a connection between the invisible personality (the servant ego) and her artistic shadow potential (the famous singer) as a result of her letting go in the creative expression. Later she began to sing with her boyfriend, who plays the guitar.

Dreams may be a good support to the experiences we have in the creative process, because the feeling in the dream can confirm the feeling we have already experienced in the art making and make it more memorable.

Another student, who was frightened of churchyards, wanted to challenge her self. When she was a small girl, her father took her and her sister to the churchyard in the evening and scared them by hiding from them and then suddenly coming forward from behind a stone. So she went to the churchyard beside the school one evening and as she was sitting quietly on a bench, she felt she suddenly had no body and that she was about to faint. She got scared and ran back to the school. Later she painted a black darkness on a big piece of paper. Having looked at the darkness for a while, she felt the urge to put a picture she found in a magazine of the Virgin Mary in the centre. With crayons she made some white rhythmic lines moving forth and back from the centre and to the blackness. In that painting she found compassion in the middle of her darkest fear, and the integration of good and evil became transformative. It is an example of how the unconscious only becomes dangerous because we think it is, and when we have the courage to confront it, it will change.

The artist. Extroverted identity. Shame binds with fear

Individuals who have a shame-fear bind can use the art-making process as a reaction moving away from the shame experience. Projecting the unconscious to the artwork reduces the tension in the body and the pressure from inside is felt less dangerous. When the artwork is not reflected upon or worked with in a therapy setting, there can be a 'need' to be creative, as otherwise the fear becomes more conscious. The artist personality can then come close to the narcissistic need to be seen and admired by others in attempting to compensate for the invisible shamed shadow. Lewis (1995), who discusses narcissism as an increasing problem in Europe and the United States, sees it as a result of un-acknowledged shame, and he mentions creativity as one of the more mature defences to shame. When shame binds with fear, the true greatness of the self cannot be expressed through the art-making, because the self is experienced in its idealistic and omnipotent aspect. Even when the artist gets no admiration from the art world, the protection of the self can be maintained by blaming others for having no knowledge of true art. So when is art a narcissistic defence and when is it a true manifestation of the individuation process? For the narcissistic personality art therapy dialogues can be a way to reveal the shamed inner self, and therefore they may avoid the therapeutic approach, preferring to focus on the artwork and not the self. This is one of the core themes in many years of discussion related to the art therapy profession. Some art therapy approaches, like the expressive arts therapies, focus on the artwork more than on the self, while others focus on the self more than on the artwork (Skov, 2015). Different personalities may be attracted to methods that speak to their defences more than to themselves.

Summary

In this chapter the affects have been related to ego development as well as to the development of self, as presented in the Blue Diamante model. Approaching shame from a developmental view means to go back in time to remember how patterns of shame were internalized in the psyche through early relationships that resulted in present behavioural patterns. Recognizing those patterns with questions as to who we would like to become indicates the crossway between a regressive orientation and a more progressive one, where we move forward towards exploring and manifesting new parts of the self. Sometimes we move back and forward as an interchange between the personal and the archetypal parts of the psyche.

We also need to locate the main domain that shame operates on. Do we experience shame in the body as impulses towards compensatory behaviour where we lose control? Are we fighting with those inner judges who constantly remind us of our defects and humanity? Do we feel isolated from others in our social lives? Or do we experience life as meaningless?

In the integrative approach to shame we are working through all these domains in therapy using different theoretical orientations along with domain-related art therapeutic methodologies. Separating the different domains in processing shame makes it possible to approach shame in relation to the body, the psyche, the social relatedness and the spiritual belonging. Together and interactively they create the foundation to living that we refer to as quality of life.

Literature

Apuleius (2008). *The Golden Ass*. Oxford: Oxford University Press.
Ayers, M. Y. (2011). *Masculine Shame*. London: Routledge.
Cozolino, L. (2016). *Why Therapy Works*. New York: W.W. Norton & Company.
DeYoung, P. A. (2015). *Understanding and Treating Chronic Shame*. London: Routledge.
Dissanayke, E. (2000). *Art and Intimacy*. Washington: Washington Press.
George, D. (1992). *Mysteries of the Dark Moon*. New York: HarperCollins.
Grof, S. (1986). *Beyond the Brain: Birth, Death and Transcendence in Psychotherapy*. New York: State University of New York Press.

Hill, D. (2015). *Affect Regulation Theory*. New York: W.W. Norton & Company.

Kalsched, D. (2013). *Trauma and the Soul*. London: Routledge.

Kaufman, J. C. and Sternberg, R. J. (2010). *The Cambridge Handbook of Creativity*. Cambridge: Cambridge University Press.

Koltuv, B. B. (1986). *The Book of Lilith*. Berwick, ME: Nicolas-Hays, Inc.

Koltuv, B. B. (1990). *Weaving Woman*. York Beach, ME: Nicolas-Hays, Inc.

Levine, P. A. (2015). *Trauma and Memory*. Berkeley: North Atlantic Books.

Lewis, M. (1995). *Shame: The Exposed Self*. New York: The Free Press.

Miller, S. B. (1996). *Shame in context*. Hillsdale, NJ: The Analytic Press, Inc.

Nathanson, D. L. (1992). *Shame and Pride*. New York: W.W. Norton & Company Inc.

Neumann, E. (1954). *The Origins and History of Consciousness*. Princeton: Princeton University Press.

Neumann, E. (1973). *The Child*. New York: Harper & Row Publishers.

Rosen, D. (2002). *Transforming Depression*. York Beach, ME: Nicolas-Hays, Inc.

Schaverien, J. (1999). *The Revealing Image*. London: Jessica Kingsley.

Schore, A. (1994). *Affect Regulation and the Origin of the Self*. New York: Psychology Press.

Schore, A. (2012). *The Science of the Art of Psychotherapy*. New York: W.W. Norton & Company.

Skov, V. (2000). *Be-coming Creative*. Vejle: Marcus Publishers.

Skov, V. (2015). *Integrative Art Therapy and Depression*. London: Jessica Kingsley.

Stevens, A. and Price, J. (2000). *Evolutionary Psychiatry*. New York: Routledge.

Stewart, L. H. (1987). Affect and Archetype in Analysis. In: Schwartz-Salant, N. and Stein, M. (editor). *Archetypal Processes in Psychotherapy*. Wilmette, IL: Chiron Publications.

Stewart, L. H. (1996). The Archetypal Affects. In: Nathanson, D. L. (editor). *Knowing Feeling*. New York: W.W. Norton & Company Inc.

Tomkins, S. S. (2008). *Affect Imagery Consciousness*. New York: Springer Company.

Ulanov, A. B. (2013). *Madness and Creativity*. College Station: Texas A&M University Press.

Whitmont, E. C. (1983). *Return to the Goddess*. London: Routledge & Kegan Paul.

Wilkinson, M. (2010). *Changing Minds in Therapy: Emotion, Attachment, Trauma and Neurobiology*. New York: W.W. Norton & Company Inc.

Plate 1 Knowing shame

Plate 2 Self-protection

Plate 3 Birth of self

Plate 4 Sadness and anger

Plate 5 Release of instincts

Plate 6 Woman with snakehead

Plate 7 Meeting Ereshkigal

Plate 8 Dancing skeletons

Part 3

Healing shame

Clinical approaches to healing shame

In this last chapter, healing shame is referred to as a therapeutic process, where fragmented parts of the psyche are integrated and made whole. In Jungian terms, I suggest that healing processes refer to the attempt of re-connecting a broken ego-self axis. Healing shame is therefore part of the preparation to individuation, which is based on a living dialogue between ego and self.

After many years of repression and shame taboo, the interest to define and understand shame is increasing and a few structured procedures for healing shame have been published. Some of these are self-developmental in orientation, which means that the individual living with shame is invited to follow a step-by-step procedure without much preparation to do so. I think this can be difficult when the memory of shame and the instinctive need to get rid of the affect, is working beneath the threshold of consciousness. As Gilbert (2011) says, "The experience of being alone, beyond rescue, with no one to help is central to the shame experience" (p. 331). Working alone with one's shame is therefore part of the shame pattern itself and may keep the individual caught in isolation, unless the ego-self relationship has already been established.

Processing shame needs preparation. First we must define the goal of such a journey, which in this book is connected to the individuation process. Then we need to understand the collective aspect of shame, that we all have experienced shame, and that many of our behavioural patterns are built on these experiences.

Following this consciousness of a wounded self-image and knowing that it is only the top of an ice mountain leads to a practical orientation. What is there to do about it?

Most of the clinical suggestions to heal shame are based on the relationship between client and therapist with the transference relationship as the healing agent. According to Jung the individual is able to work without the transference on an outer therapist to hold and trust the process, because the relation to the inner self as a guiding function in the psyche to some extent has replaced the need for outer guidance.

I think many individuals have prepared themselves for healing shame through years of therapy but now need a practical tool to heal shame itself. Using art therapy methodology in this process means that the image will come to replace the transference onto the therapist for those individuals who are able to do imaginative work on their own. For others who have no or little experience with the unconscious and with the use of art in therapy, some preparation is necessary before confronting shame.

Brown, Hernandez and Villarreal (2011) start the shame resilience program by suggesting that sharing shame with others is an important first step in the healing process. They define shame resilience as "a person's ability to recognize and understand shame, move through it constructively while maintaining a basic level of authenticity, and increase his or her level of courage, compassion, and connection as a result of experiencing shame" (p. 359). She has made a 12-step psychoeducational procedure based on this definition. Apart from the teaching aspect of the procedure that follows each step, helping the participants to reflect on their own shame and vulnerability, the basic methodology is to learn to practise empathy in relationships. Brown has contributed to the normalization of shame through her TED talks, research and books.

In Compassion Focused Therapy (CFT), which is another psycho-educational approach to the healing of shame, there is a similar focus on affect-regulation, and "the idea is to create experiences in which clients can engage with problematic aspects of themselves, but through the eyes of the compassionate self" (Gilbert, 2011, p. 345). In these programs they use imagery as a method to replace the negative shaming voice with a compassionate one and through practice make a change. Both Brown and CFT emphasize the importance of training the compassionate attitude to one's self as well as to others, referring to research that shows how empathy and compassion reduce shame (Gilbert, 2011). At the same time Gilbert asks the question, "Can we teach people how to practise and generate a particular type of self-to-self relationship that is based on self-compassion?" (ibid, p. 341). I think this is what Jung refers to as the process of individuation, based on his understanding of the ethical aspect of the self-archetype.

Kaufmann, who was a pioneer in the study of shame, was more concerned with power issues in family, work and romantic relationships and thought that shame was tricked by powerlessness (1996). He developed a 15-session psychoeducational group program, and suggested this be combined with individual therapy. His program contains five units: a) stress, b) self-esteem, c) identity, d) affect management and e) interpersonal relations. His purpose was to give individuals the tool to transform shame but without the therapeutic relationship, which is emphasized in most individual approaches to shame (1996). He wanted to re-educate the self by using affects, images and language as basic instruments and emphasized writing exercises between sessions as a creative way to increase consciousness. He said that "when competency can be learned, it can also be taught" (1996, p. 247).

Methods to avoid being overwhelmed by shame are part of the general purpose in psycho-education and one of them is to normalize shame as part of humanness. Another de-shaming method is to validate the client's experience in order to strengthen the self-care system and decrease the inner judgemental voices (ibid). Instead of following the inward spiral of shame, Kaufmann suggests we keep our attention on the shaming other while we question the intentions behind the person's behaviour (1996). We can ask questions directly, like "Why do you speak to me in that way?" or "I feel you are trying to make me feel small, why is that important to you?" The point is to push the attention back to where it comes from with a curiosity more than a judgement of the shaming other. At the same time, this is also the *result* of having processed shame and can hardly be accomplished by individuals who are caught in unconscious reactions to shame.

Kaufman further suggests that identification with the therapist can be a way to reduce shame, because he thinks that equal power in all relationships is one of the goals in shame work. De-shaming methods are useful in situations where shame might otherwise overwhelm the individual, but cannot be considered transformative as such, because of the intention to *avoid* shame.

I think this is an important issue in dealing with shame. Do we want to get rid of it because it is such a devastating experience, or do we want to transform shame and change our core identity and sense of inner dignity? According to Brown, Hernandez and Villarreal (2011), Kaufmann (1996) and Gilbert (2011), the goal is to transform shame, but none specifies a tool to access the affective power in doing so, and this is where I suggest art therapy has something to offer. Practically, they all use writing as a tool to activate consciousness but propose no tool to use in relation to right-brain processing, not to mention the important bridge between the two sides of the brain. The use of imagination in CFT becomes compensatory instead of transformative because it is induced by will more than through the coming together of affect and image. I do believe that training of mental competencies is useful during the overall process, but I also find that the most important *transformative* part of that process is archetypal and cannot be held in rational language only, especially when we work with core shame that was internalized before language and is therefore reachable through the visual more than through words. I do not think we can induce love and compassion as a wishing attitude by *wanting* to do so. It will become a superficial survival need attempting to avoid shame more than a true result of a transformative process.

What the educational parts of these programs have in common is to prepare the individual living with shame to approach shame through new knowledge and personal reflections. I think they overlook the important function that release of affects plays as part of transforming shame.

In artwork the affects are often too powerful to be represented by personal representations. Therefore, when shame scenes are remembered and expressed in a painting, something *more* that has no personal associations is often added to the image. One of the most common symbols that illustrates the affect behind shame is the snake, which illustrates the underworld power of Kur.

Working with the image

Through my use of creativity in therapeutic processes over the past 30 years, I have witnessed how therapeutic use of images has turned fear of the unconscious into trust and interest. When the client discovers that magical voice of the self that comes out of the image hanging on the wall, we both know that this is a voice coming from their inner self. It does not come from me – the therapist – or from anyone else in the outside reality. It is their own discovery of an inner source of wisdom and guidance and it helps them prepare for the integration of more painful experiences like shame.

One woman artist painted an image of a female face. She had no emotional connection to the image when we started to talk about it and had just enjoyed making the painting. When we sat in front of the image, and I asked her who *she* was, she first said that she looked like a woman from Egypt. Then her body began to vibrate and she felt moved into tears. She said that by looking into that woman's eyes, a much bigger world opened up for her, and she felt she had access to all experiences. She said it felt as if the woman in the painting had been waiting for her for the last six months. In her outer life, the woman had left her husband six months previously and had felt like she was in a dark hole ever since, without being able to paint. This image reconnected her to her feminine power and to the origin of creative inspiration. Just as the eyes can be shaming and destructive, they can also open up to that dimension in the psyche that is hiding behind shame. I think this example shows that it is not only the kind eyes of a therapist that can wake up the self behind shame. The image can in some situations allow the more independent client to create a new connection to the self, where the therapist becomes a witness.

Another client painted a boat with a sail and said that an invisible woman was on board, lying in a glass coffin. She didn't know whether she should let the boat drift away or try to revive the woman. In other words, should she avoid the shamed feminine part of the self by letting it go back to the unconscious, or confront it? This is the question coming from many women in our time. What to do with that shamed inner part when it becomes conscious and before it is transformed. How to endure the pain and lack of dignity long enough in order to transform it?

When therapists use art in therapy they must be trained in doing so. There are so many ways where a therapeutic way to use an image can go 'wrong' in the sense that it can re-activate rejections from the therapist that can increase shame in the client. All suggestions to heal shame that I have come across emphasize that the therapist must have processed her or his personal shame in order not to pass it on to the client. The same is true for the therapist using the arts in therapy. We must know how art can be used as a mirror of the unconscious and develop methods to take back these projections in a way that fits to the individual's defences and possibilities.

The therapist must have experienced the art media related to their personal unconscious as well as having processed their personal shame. If the un-trained therapist ignores the image or communicates that it is not as important as the rational psychotherapeutic dialogue, the self within the client will not be reached properly. The challenge is to use imagination in relation to the artwork without reducing the image too soon to just mean something personal. Trusting the self to do that job inside the client is crucial for later integration, because the transcendent function must be activated first. We all want rational answers to our problems and questions in life and sometimes this eagerness stands in the way of getting them. The amount of time it takes to move from an imaginative experience of a symbol towards a personal association cannot be generalized, because it depends on the individual's self-protective system and the intensity of the affect.

The art-making process is an outgoing and extrovert activity, while the subsequent therapeutic dialogue relates to the inner life. I think this outside-inside movement of attention illustrates the potential ritual in art therapy where the physical and the psychological become equal.

Throughout this book I have referred to ways of using images without going into details about working methods. I do not think there is only one way of using the arts in therapy or in processing shame. As therapists we can all dip into that creative space where sudden intuition and 'know-how' breaks into consciousness, depending on the strength of our own ego-self axis.

My experience is that no matter which directives or original initiatives the therapist offers, three qualities remain characteristic for the art therapy method, which are the *projected* image, creation of *symbols* and *imaginative dialogues*. I also find a Jungian paradigm to be the most supportive understanding of these processes due to Jung's concept of self and the archetypal nature of the images that evolve in the artwork.

When I have wanted to use the myth of Inanna as a structure for processing shame, it is first and foremost to show the archetypal nature of healing shame, which we can use as clinicians. The archetypal nature of shame psychology brings shame out of the isolated and personal connotation, indicating that there is a procedure, which we all can follow by using Inanna as a guide, since she was the first to travel to the underworld and to come back to life as a transformed individual. She created the pattern of transforming shame .

The symbol as a bridge to personal change

When working with images I have come to see a pattern where the archetypal and the personal come together during the dialogue.

When both client and therapist are sitting in front of the image after the expressive process has ended, the attention must be on the image and the therapist's curiosity should initiate the imaginative dialogue related only to the image. In this first period we try to activate the image as a psychic constellation in the unconscious *before* the affect is felt in the body. It is a way to prepare the ego for the affective experience without overwhelming consequences. When individuals have little imagination, as in depression, they might return to personal associations during this first part of the dialogue, reducing the images to personal life experiences. The therapist should look for openings to return to the image with new curiosity, attempting to stimulate imaginative thinking in the client. When the client has described the image in detail, the therapist knows how the client perceives the image and they share a mutual understanding of the different elements in the artwork during the subsequent procedure.

Images are not always symbolic in their language. They can be both chaotic and rhythmic, and the beginning dialogue may be more about colour and emotion than about memories.

I think one of the biggest challenges for the therapist is to stay in the imaginative exploration of the image without reducing it to something specific before that association is made by the client. Also, asking all those irrational and 'crazy' questions, as children do when they play, can be a challenge, and as one student said after her first imaginative dialogue, "I haven't done this since I was a child". Most adults have forgotten how to play and to pretend in order to discover something new, because our minds have become rationalized by collective expectations and therefore a training of imagination is part of the preparation to process shame.

Through the dialogue with the image we can explore the archetypal content. How do the different figures or colours move? What do they say? How do they feel inside? Where are they heading? What are their identities? How is their relationship with each other?

At a certain point many clients begin to associate to symbols. They bring forward memories that they had not thought of during the art-making process. This is the place in therapy where the affect of surprise is activated as the image is related to scenes from personal life. If the client cannot make that bridge to the personal life by her/him self, the therapist can ask if anything that has been said calls forward associations and in this way support the connection between the imaginative and the personal part of the psyche.

Moving away from the imaginative exploration of the image indicates a possible shift of attention. Instead of keeping a focus on the image, we can now move into earlier object-relations that are activated from the symbol and the imaginative dialogue. This is a useful match between unconscious shame and the method itself, as shame becomes available through the projected image, when it is not available in memory. Therefore shame scenes from life can appear 'out of the blue' during an art therapy dialogue, indicating that the memory was able to pass the self-protective system.

Cultural perspective

The many behavioural patterns that we take for granted in our culture or consider 'normal' are more than often not reflected upon by the individual, which is part of the reason why we pass on shame to the next generation without knowing about it. Knowing about cultural and collective shame is one way to gain a more objective perspective to shame when it attacks us personally. Cultural shame is connected to the moral matrix that each culture lives by, communicated through the family systems.

In an international art therapy group, there were some students from Estonia, Spain and Japan. What turned out to be a different shame codex compared to the Danish culture was the individual's attachment to parental expectations related to future education and work. It seemed to be more shameful in those cultures to follow a different path than the one chosen by the parents.

One woman was an engineer like her father, but after one year of work she left her job because of depression and came to Denmark with the longing to work with art and to get away from her parents' disappointment in her choice. Confrontation with cultural values is part of the personal integrative process of freeing the rejected shadow. When we are working with shame in therapeutic processes, I think the cultural aspect is important because it makes it easier for the individual to avoid putting all the blame on the self.

Since objectification can be one of the ways we communicate shame to our clients, the therapy room becomes a vulnerable place to communicate knowledge of cultural shame patterns. The interaction between working with personal shame scenes and education in cultural shame dynamics is difficult to introduce in individual work. It is much easier in groups, where it brings the taboo out into a more open and collective space. Another advantage of working in a group setting is that the participants can practice their communication skills with one another as part of developing new communication skills free of shame.

In Brené Brown's 12-session psycho-educational shame resilience curriculum, the focus is on the cognitive training of knowing shame. The curriculum contains training in developing a more empathic attitude as a replacement for shame identity (Brown, Hernandez and Villarreal, 2011). In step number 9, which she names 'Practical Critical Awareness', she addresses the cultural aspects of different shame categories and invites participants to use a critical awareness related to the link between personal experiences and social systems (ibid). I find her approach to be a good cognitive preparation to the therapeutic and archetypal experience of shame processing where the affects are more directly involved through the use of creative modalities.

When it comes to the healing of shame related to the individuation process, which I have suggested comes after a therapeutic integration of shadow images, we cannot use the very system that traumatized the individual in the first place. We need a different paradigm and a different way of thinking about a social system wherein some of the basic ethical principles are based on equal rights between the masculine and feminine principles. The problem is that we do not know how such a collective system functions when shame does not disturb the interaction between those two principles. We only know a system based on repression of the feminine in both man and woman. Following Jung's psychology we might find such a role model for a new paradigm in his description of the individuation process, since this process is a result of the interaction between the feminine and masculine principles in the psyche. Some individuals judge this process to be selfish and anti-social by nature and cannot imagine that an individual would ever want to return to society after a longer period of self-development and inner search. I do not think that is true. I think, with Dissanayake (2000), that our social instinct and need to be together as a group will bring us back together after such inner confrontations.

For 30 years I have been drumming with students every morning as a ritual before teaching. First we all drum a rhythm, which I introduce. Then they are invited to be selfish and anti-social and just express whatever they like on the drum. If I give no further instruction, it is merely a matter of time before we all play different rhythms together as a group. Nobody wants to be alone for the rest of the drumming time. They all want to be together and to contribute with their special beats on the drum. Some go back to the first rhythm as a safe place to be, and others move forward creating new contributions to the group sound. I have always found these moments of coming together valuable, because they are based on individual choices of wanting to be together and to contribute something special. So I have come to see 'anti-social' behaviour in self-development as an attempt to catch up with past repression. Allowing these periods to take their time according to individual life history and needs becomes even more important as otherwise the 'new' socialization of self will lack the authentic relation to the inner emotional life of the individual.

Rejection of the feminine principle has many different faces in different cultures, but the bottom line shows the same unbalance depending on religion, economy and power. Therefore I will address cultural shame as part of collective shame when I later include the myth of Inanna as an archetypal procedure to process shame.

One of the main purposes of processing shame is to change our behaviour when we experience shame, to avoid the typical signs of shame, like moving away from the situation, dissociation, isolation and low self-esteem. We want to avoid the impact that a shaming other can have on us by becoming stronger in order to stay in the moment with our conscious awareness. We need an inner good mother available in the psyche to protect us when we are most vulnerable to life. But self-protection is not enough when we also want to *act* differently. The good mother may tell us that we are good enough inside, but she alone cannot act in the actual shame scene. In Jungian psychology this dynamic activity is related to the inner masculine part of the psyche, and therefore it is important to develop a new inner masculine side as well as a good mother. If the inner man is not available in the psyche as a response to the woman, the energy to act in the moment is not available either, and all the typical signs of shame will take over, leaving the inner woman overwhelmed, rejected and hurt. Therefore the process of healing shame is not only related to the process of healing the wounded feminine. It also includes the communication between the feminine and masculine principle in the psyche.

Meeting between the personal and the collective unconscious

As a preparation to Inanna's descent, I discovered a story in the Sumerian genesis which I would like to share and use as an image illustrating the meeting between the personal and the archetypal unconscious. This mythological story gives an understanding of Jung's struggle in his discovery of the collective unconscious as a different layer in the psyche than the personal unconscious. I also think this story can illustrate how the symbol came together with the affect in the first place, as two sides of a coin. I find the story interesting because it seems to illustrate the activity that takes place before human consciousness is even born. In that respect it is the story of how the self was created as a foundation to ego consciousness in the very beginning of life and before we knew of ourselves. I suggest that the same procedure takes place whenever original creativity is operating in the psyche, shown in the story by the meeting of two different waters. When something original is created, it is often described as a mystical process inspired by nature, muses, gods or something else outside the personal domain. This story may be the myth of deep creative processes preparing consciousness for change that is to come.

My reference builds on Jacobsen's presentation of Mesopotamian religion (1976).

Creation of the Sumerian world

It all began with two different waters coming together. The 'mingling' of the salt-water, represented by the first great mother, Tiamat, and the sweet water from the 'fresh waters underground', Apsu. This watery fusion between Tiamat and Apsu gave birth to the first two gods, Lahmu and Lahamu, who then gave birth to all the 'newer' gods and the creation of the world.

The world of the gods, referring to the creation of the self, came into existence through the name-giving process. I think this first fusion between the small water and the big ocean is synonymous with a fusion between the personal and the collective unconscious. Characteristic of the union was that the old gods, who existed before anything else, wanted rest and inactivity, while the new gods wanted movement and action. One must therefore assume that the fusion happened by chance and without approval from Tiamat and Apsu.

Translated into psychological language, original creativity cannot be planned. It happens as we name the sky, the Moon, the Sun, the heaven, and all the archetypes that are created through symbolization. During the therapeutic dialogue, consciousness of self is born. The resistance to put words to images is, according to this old story, caused by a deep avoidance of becoming conscious of self, creating instead a pull towards psychological death. I wonder whether this pull towards psychological death is activated by shame experiences as an attempt to avoid consciousness of shame. Do we have a conservative instinct deep inside, in the collective unconscious, that resists change unless we accidentally bump into a life experience that sets the creative inner struggle in motion? It might also indicate the value of naming shame as a first creation of consciousness.

If our self has been shamed, we may not want to know about it unless *other* and more positive self-experiences can be added to the consciousness of self. These can be explored through the activation of joy and interest in the art-making process, often described as 'flow' experiences. The word 'flow' has an association to water, and a thought is that when we can let go of some control in the expressive process, the two waters mingle and create something original and new.

From the salt that occurred in the meeting point between the two waters, the creation of the world/self was initiated.

I recognize this image in the creative process as that magical outcome we see in the artwork when we discover content that is not made by conscious will. It is that mysterious aspect of the creative process that cannot be explained in rational terms – the surprise we can experience, which links us to the original creativity of the self that we do not know exists until we give it a name.

The meeting between the two waters created an activity that wakes up the archetypal self. We may also speak of this as a meeting between the symbol as a form and structure without life, representing the old gods of inactivity coming from the underground, and the affects representing Tiamat and the big ocean/collective unconscious. The symbols and affects create an activity in the unknown part of the psyche before consciousness is created. The basic wish to remain unconscious, symbolized in the old gods' wish to sleep, is an image of the resistance we all have in relation to the unknown. Part of us wants to be passive, because being conscious of self has consequences.

In the story, the contradiction between the old gods and the new gods leads to a conflict between the two forces. An unpredictable happening then took place as all the newer gods began to dance as an expression of that conflict. The transcendent function had created a solution to the inner tension between the two waters, which was expressed in the dance. This was the very first creative activity where the inside was expressed in an outside activity as a natural (and irrational) response to the conflict. This activity had consequences and prevented the old generation from getting their sleep and they did not know what to do.

The dance made the conflict more conscious, but did not solve it. Apsu was very disturbed by the dancing and suggested to his wife Tiamat that they should kill their children in order to get their rest, but Tiamat refused to kill her own children. The young gods heard about the plans, and "at first they ran about in wild confusion, and even after they quieted down they could only sit speechless with fear" (Jacobsen, 1976, p. 171).

The representatives for all creativity, movement and actions are traumatized by the thought of their own death. It could very well be the first description of an archetypal image of a fear that we feel is not human in its affective power, indicating a recognition of a change that will come. The death of the old ego is 'heard of' before it actually happens and the ego dissociates and becomes inactive.

Then Apsu was tricked by Enki, who 'recited an overpowering spell' so he fell asleep and was killed. Enki is a masculine aspect in the psyche, representing wisdom and water, and he does not surrender to fear. Therefore he becomes the link to further activity when the psyche is traumatized. Jacobsen (1976) points out that "the myth moves on a primitive level of social organization, of virtual anarchy, in which dangers to the community are met by individual action by one of the more powerful of its members" (p. 172). I suggest that Enki symbolizes the power of original creativity as an instinct born to initiate change. Could he represent the transformative function itself?

According to the genesis, the instinct to change does not come from *multiple* parts of the psyche or society, but from that single voice which can act independently from any outer collective expectation. I wonder whether this refers to Jung's approach to change where he suggested that individual change comes before social change, because the collective is paralyzed in fear of the unknown and therefore cannot act heroically? The hero myths also point towards the individual as a saviour of society. Recall the hero Perseus, in the story of the killing of Medusa, who escaped traumatization only by using a mirror-shield instead of direct confrontation.

In the genesis, the power in need of change clashes with the power to resist it, and the solution to this in its very origin is to kill the resistance/Apsu! There was not much negotiation in those days!

After this episode, Enki builds a temple on top of the sweet underground waters, and from there he controls "the original watery form, thus allowing forms other than the liquid one to come into being, creating the possibility of the present world with its multiplicity of forms" (ibid, p. 172). These 'other forms' can only refer to the archetypal structures in the psyche, which is our foundation for all symbolic creation.

Continuing the story, Enki and his wife Damkina had a son, Marduk, who was very close to his grandfather An. An gave him many toys and said, "Let my grandson play" (ibid, p. 173). This activity disturbed the old gods even more and they still could not sleep during the night or rest during the day.

Finally Tiamat was accused of being an unloving mother. "You are no mother . . . and we, who cannot go to sleep, us you do not love!" (ibid, p. 173).

So those who wanted to sleep accused the big mother of being unloving because she did not nourish their needs, and this accusation activated Tiamat to give birth to an army of monsters. The affect of rage had been born as a reaction to being shamed for not being a good enough mother. Tiamat gave her new husband, Kingu, full authority over her army of monsters to attack the younger gods, her children.

Again Enki heard the news and this time he did not know what to do. He contacted his father, An, who suggested giving Marduk, his grandson, full power to act on his own, and he managed to kill Tiamat. Later Kingu was also killed, and from his blood, man was created.

So in the end, the principles of creativity, movement and activity won the power in the unconscious psyche, which can be associated to the drive in the self towards individuation. Three generations of masculine creativity – An, Enki and Marduk – were operating in the psyche before consciousness/man was born.

In psychological language Apsu and Tiamat represented the feminine passive principle, while Enki and the younger gods represented a masculine and dynamic force. Marduk became the king of all the gods, and it was said that the new world order was "humanly satisfying: Ultimate power is not estranged from mankind, but resides in gods in human form who act understandable" (Jacobsen, 1976, p. 191). Therefore, Marduk's leadership should not be confused with the patriarchal paradigm, which is more associated with the old gods' fear of change. Another point is that Marduk was stimulated to play by his grandfather, which refers to the interaction between joy and interest, the life-force in the psyche. Is there a connection between his heroic and creative ability to solve the conflict and his access to the two positive affects? Tomkins said that we lose the ability to transform negative affects later in life, when the positive affects are not stimulated 'enough' (2008).

This ancient story also points towards the importance of a masculine wholeness and rational order as a foundation for healing feminine shame.

Introduction to the myth of Inanna

Inanna is one of the oldest moon goddesses from the old Sumerian culture, dating from about 4000 years B.C. The story was first published by Kramer in 1942, as he collected the last clay tablets and almost completed the story (Kramer, 1961).

Diane Wolkstein worked together with Kramer and made the story available for the public. She chose Inanna as the most important moon goddess because she encompassed the many different aspects of the goddess. She was the new moon, related to spring and to the girl archetype. She was the full moon, related to summer and to the archetype of woman. She was the old moon, related to winter and to the feminine archetype of hag (Kramer and Wolkstein, 1983). Inanna was born to the moon goddess Ningal and the moon god Nana. She was the queen of heaven and Earth. She was responsible for growth of plants, animals and "fertility in human kind" (ibid, p. xvi). We hear of the young Inanna and her many affairs with different men. We meet a woman who enjoys her feminine sexuality and power, and finally learn the story of her mature descent, death and return from the underworld. It is this last aspect of the archetype which I want to focus on here as an image of shame and shame recovery.

Experiencing shame is in many ways a death experience, and often we do not know how to recover from this loss of soul and thus get stuck in the underworld. We learn to live with shame about who we are because we have no role models for transforming shame. Inanna holds the key to a return from such experiences. She comes back stronger and more whole as a woman, and therefore she has something to tell us about transforming shame.

I have divided the story into five parts, where each part is connected to specific affects as they are experienced during the process. This is when the affective steps shown in the Blue Diamante model (Figure 2.1), moving from ego towards the self, come together with the scenes in the myth.

The combination between the mythological steps and the different affects is for me an experienced wholeness in shame processing where affect and image come together through the creative process and dialogue. Using expressive media as a tool for this coming together of symbol and affect is for me an instrument of magic which cannot really be described in rational terms only. I have the advantage of having used the arts in therapy for many years, and some readers may not be familiar with creative methods as a practical therapeutic tool. I can only hope that the reader will gain some inspiration from this book to work creatively with shame.

In this book, the myth of Inanna's descent to the underworld is an archetypal story of healing shame, which is why we can use it as psychic images that bring meaning to the overall transformative process. My main literature on the subject is Jacobsen (1976), Kramer and Wolkstein (1983) and Perera (1981). None of them connects the story directly to shame, and I suppose this is a result of the collective rejection of shame in psychotherapy at the time. Neither do they see the story as a healing of an inner *relationship*; rather, they merely focus on Inanna's integration of her shadow sister, Ereshkigal. Lastly they do not emphasize the experience of *rejection* as an activator of the process, maybe because it is not directly expressed in the story as something of great importance.

When we recall the affect theorists' emphasis on shame as a result of being rejected by an important other, I hope to clarify how Inanna's experience of being rejected by her husband, Dumutzi, becomes the activating scene that finally leads to a new integration of the masculine and feminine, followed by a new world order. If we ignore experiences of rejections that we have had in our lives, we cannot reach the shame underneath such experiences either. They become our possibility to change.

I have separated the story into five steps: 1) preparation, 2) descent, 3) death, 4) rebirth and 5) new world order. My purpose is to describe a way to use shame without repressing the experience of shame to the unconscious, but instead to free the reaction to shame so it does not get stuck inside as an ugly emotion.

As a presentation of the main personalities in Inanna's descent, see Table 3.1.

Table 3.1 Overview of personalities in the Inanna myth

Name	Symbol	Psychological aspect
Enki	God of wisdom and the waters	Masculine spiritual and creative authority Self-related
Inanna	Goddess of heaven and Earth	Passion, wilfulness, love and war
Ereshkigal	Goddess of the underworld	Shamed, unloving, unloved and cold
Dumutzi	Earthly shepherd/king and husband to Inanna	Patriarchal animus
Ninshubur	Inanna's helper	A helpful aspect of the self
Geshtinanna	Sister of Dumutzi	Compassion and feeling
Gilgamesh	Earthly hero	Bravery, action
Kurgarra and Galatur	Asexual helpers Professional mourners	Mirroring attitude, positive mother
Gugalanna	Ereshkigal's husband	Abuser, negative animus

The story of Inanna's descent

In my retelling of the story, I will begin before Inanna is called to the underworld, because it helps to understand the background for her descent. I refer to this as part of her preparation. Then I will talk about the myth as psychological steps in healing shame and introduce the different persons in the myth as inner voices operating in such a process.

The actual confrontation with shame is connected to Inanna's death in the underworld, but I think the other phases in the myth are equally important for the overall process as well.

Step 1. Preparation

Years before Inanna's descent, Enki, the god of wisdom and water, travelled to the underworld to visit Ereshkigal, who was the queen there, and "from the encounter between the God of wisdom and the queen of the underworld, a tree comes into existence" (Kramer and Wolkstein, 1983, p. 140). This is the Huluppu tree, the first living thing on Earth.

The tree falls into the water during the big flood and Inanna rescues it and plants it in her garden for 'cultivation'. In the trunk of the tree lives Lilith, in the crown the Anzu-bird and by the root the snake.

When the tree has grown strong, Inanna wants to use the wood to build a throne and a bed from the wood. Inanna is sad and full of fear, and she calls her earthly brother Gilgamesh to help her cut the tree. With his big axe he kills the snake; Lilith flees to the desert and the Anzu-bird flies away.

From the wood Inanna makes her throne and bed and thereby confirms her authority and her womanhood.

Inanna decides to go on a journey to visit her grandfather Enki, the god of wisdom and water, a great shaman and ruler of Earth. At their meeting, Enki gets drunk and gives Inanna all the 'me tablets', which consist of "that set of universal and immutable rules and limits which had to be observed by god and man alike" (Kramer and Wolkstein, 1983, p. 123), and she now has the power to rule Sumer.

She marries the shepherd Dumutzi, who becomes king of Sumer. After some time, Dumutzi wants to be 'set free' from Inanna (indicating that the honeymoon is over).

Step 2. Descent to the underworld

Inanna hears a call from Ereshkigal in the underworld, and decides to visit her. She prepares for her journey by letting go of her worldly cities and instructs her servant Ninshubur that if she has not returned within three days, Ninshubur shall seek help for her rescue.

When she reaches the first gate to the underworld, Ereshkigal's gatekeeper asks her why she has come. She says she wants to participate in the funeral of Gugalanna, Ereshkigal's dead husband.

Ereshkigal decides that Inanna can pass the seven gates, and by each gate she must let go of some of her clothes and jewels until she stands naked in front of Ereshkigal like any other visitor. According to Jacobsen (1976), she is found guilty because she tries to dethrone her sister Ereshkigal. She is killed and hung on a butcher's hook to rot.

Step 3. Death

After three days have gone by, Ninshubur tries to get help from Inanna's father's father, Enlil, and then her father, Nana, but they are both angry with Inanna for having chosen a different path in life and refuse to help her. She then contacts Enki, who creates two small, asexual creatures, the Kurgarra and Galatur, from the dirt of his fingernails. "He endows the creatures with the artistic and empathetic talent of being professional mourners, capable of mirroring the lonely queen's emotions" (Kramer and Wolkstein, 1983, p. 160). Ereshkigal is now suffering labour pain, while Inanna is dead and the two professional mourners, sent by Enki, mirror her pain with compassion. Ereshkigal is moved by the empathy of the two creatures and agrees to return Inanna's dead body on the condition that someone else must take Inanna's place in the underworld.

Step 4. Return

Inanna is brought back to life when the two helpers give her water and grass, and she returns to Earth looking for someone to replace her. When she sees Dumutzi sitting on his throne without mourning her death, and expressing no signs of joy when he sees her, she picks him to take her place in the underworld.

Step 5. The new world order

First Dumutzi tries to escape, but finally he is caught and sent down through the seven gates. His sister Geshtinanna decides out of love for her brother to take his place in the underworld for half of the year, and Dumutzi is therefore together with Inanna for the other half, and they rule Sumer together as equals.

The myth and the affects

When using the different steps in the myth as archetypal phases guiding the transformation of shame, I found that each phase had a certain affective quality, as if we were at the same time moving down from the ego position, shown in the Blue Diamante model, towards the self. The overlap between the mythological *image* as a psychic representation and the *experience* of the image as an affect brings wholeness to the process whereby mind and body work together.

In Table 3.2 I show the parallel between phases in the myth, activation of the affects and psychological themes.

I consider all the innate affects to be important stepping-stones in the healing of shame. Not only do they connect the lived experience with the spiritual image of transformation, but they also bring a different perspective and meaning into the process of individuation.

In order to bring the affect and the image together, we need the creative process as a dynamic activity that makes it possible. The challenge is to initiate these activities through methods which keep us on the track towards the positive affects of joy and interest as a stimulation of the self and the individuation process. I come to think of Odysseus, who had to be tied to the mast on his ship in order not to be seduced by the sweet songs of the sirens, those seductive voices of the negative feminine. Had he not been warned about the danger and planned what to do, he might not have completed his journey home, because the seductive voices of the sirens would have kept him captured and isolated on the island. Outer expectations test our will to complete the challenge of healing shame. We might prefer to live up to those siren songs from society and be seduced to follow more primitive satisfactions as a replacement for the individuation process.

Table 3.2 Comparison between mythological phase, affect and psychological theme

Phases in the myth	Activation of affects	Psychological themes
Preparation	Fear	Trust in the unconscious
Descent	Sadness–anger	Letting go of parental inner voices
Death	Shame	Aloneness
Rebirth	Surprise	Manifestation of new inner wholeness
New world order	Joy–interest	Masculine and feminine equality

Finding a starting point

Not everyone can identify with Inanna and her joy in sexual activity. It was said that she could make love 50 times a day, so we must imagine that she is a woman who represents many of the values that we have learned to reject in our patriarchal culture. At the same time there might be a longing in consciousness together with some vague memory of the positive affects of joy and interest that were once a living reality, and this memory can become a motivation for change in men as well as women.

It is so easy to blame men for not wanting to see women in their full Inanna identity and not giving her the attention that *she* expects in her immature personality. Experiences of being rejected became the starting point of Inanna's descent to the dark goddess Ereshkigal and the hidden complex of shame. As the story tells us, women need to do their own healing before equality with the masculine can be obtained.

Perera (1981) considers Inanna's journey to the underworld to be a story of a woman's integration of the dark goddess. In Jungian terms this is also the development of the inner feminine in a man. Women may be more conscious of shame because of identification with the feminine principle of relationships, while men who have identified with the masculine principle have less access to that inner realm of the Inanna–Ereshkigal polarity. It is there in the psyche somewhere, but as a more archetypal level to reach by consciousness.

Some individuals may recognize part of themselves in the figure of Inanna, the innocent young woman with so many talents and possibilities who ends up feeling rejected by the man she loves, all because he has better things to do than to be with her.

Inanna can be identified as the innocent, the fighter and the artist personality in the identity model presented in Chapter 2 as reactions to unconscious shame, while Ereshkigal, the dark goddess, is related to the self-destructive, the victim and the invisible personality types. The shamed individual who has identified with Ereshkigal already lives in the underworld, hiding in the dark without access to the positive shadow qualities that Inanna represents.

We find these individuals in depression, addictions, and other states known by the psychiatric system, living a life of unhappiness and psychological pain. They do not have a Ninshubur or inner good mother who can find help for their rescue and they seem stuck in the underworld. They need therapeutic processing with the help of an outer therapist, who later becomes the inner good mother. Much too often this is not an offer made by society, which offers medical treatment to Ereshkigal instead.

In this chapter I also address individuals who do have a Ninshubur aspect available in their personalities as a witness to their inner process. In practical terms this would refer to the individuation process, where individuals have some familiarity with active imaginative work without the need for an outer therapist.

For all personality types, the motivation to process shame is based on experiences of being rejected by some important other. I think the moment of rejection of the self always is a rejection of an innocent Inanna attitude to life, and when the experiences stay un-healed in the psyche it becomes part of the Ereshkigal domain, splitting the psyche in two.

In the following I will go through each step of Inanna's journey: 1) preparation, 2) descent, 3) death, 4) return and 5) new world order. From an affective angle this process is associated to experiences of 1) fear, 2) sadness–anger, 3) shame, 4) surprise and 5) joy–interest.

Step 1. Preparation

Fear

Preparing for the descent is a process where we must come to trust the unconscious enough to let go of old patterns without knowing what will come instead. Trust in the process that is to come replaces the control we usually have in life in order to live it without too much chaos and fear. When Jung describes the self as an inner guiding principle in the psyche, it is not easy just to let go and trust that he was maybe right. We need to experience the truth in that statement in smaller doses as a gradual build-up of trust. Using images is a method that allows surprises without getting overwhelmed by their affective force as long as we keep the separation between the image and the ego.

Lilith somehow made a home inside the Huluppu tree. What does that mean? Why does another shamed aspect in the feminine archetype find a resting place there, of all places? Lilith is connected to Ereshkigal because she also experienced the shame of rejection and she too reacts with rage and instinctive fury. She is closer to Inanna than Ereshkigal at this point. She actually lives in Inanna's garden, reminding Inanna of the process that will come. Is Lilith an archetype that we need to understand before we confront Ereshkigal and the affect of shame? She is certainly connected to Dumutzi, who also wanted his freedom, so she may be that intuitive voice within us that keeps pushing us towards independence and individuation.

The image of Lilith, the snake and the Anzu-bird are all symbols of primitive affects, but Inanna does not actually *experience* the affects until later. All she experiences is fear. This is a good illustration of the role that fear has in the individuation process, being very close to the ego, as shown in the Blue Diamante model. It signals a beginning intuition of the unconscious and a need for more time to prepare the journey. The challenge at this point is to keep on moving and not get too attached to the affect of fear as a defence against the unconscious. We must find Gilgamesh inside, as the masculine hero who takes action. This would be an argument for including expressive methods in psychotherapy as a way to wake up the Gilgamesh archetype of physical activity.

In art therapy, individuals create images that later become emotional experiences during the therapeutic dialogue and the conscious attachment to the image. The image needs *attention* in order to become meaningful to us personally. We need to focus on images with interest and attach to them with feeling. Otherwise they are merely psychic forms without vitality and bodily-felt meaning. In this way images can be used as a 'smell' of the affects before the 'real' experience occurs when these two things come together in the dialogue.

As an inner drive towards freedom, Lilith keeps us moving, because she herself is a runaway bride. She cannot stay and talk things through. She just takes off as the untamed instinct she is and leaves the more cultivated process of working through shame to Inanna. She is after all the goddess of heaven and Earth. Inanna has accomplished success in the outer world and has something to offer in her later descent, which Lilith has not. Lilith has only the rejection and shame, and no social worth. On the other hand, she has direct access to the rage of being rejected, which Inanna does not have, according to the text. Therefore it would be correct to understand Lilith as a premature aspect of Inanna's dark sister, Ereshkigal.

Abduction of Ereshkigal

According to Kramer (1961), Ereshkigal was abducted right after heaven and Earth were separated in the Sumerian genesis. She was taken to the underworld as queen of the dead "perhaps by Kur itself" (ibid., p. 79). *Kur* is referred to as another word for 'netherworld', but also to the 'monstrous creature' often represented as a large serpent which lived at the bottom of the underworld (ibid, p. 76). Following the rape of Ereshkigal by Kur, Enki travelled to the underworld "to attack Kur and avenge the abduction of the goddess Ereshkigal" (ibid, p. 79). There is some uncertainty how the battle between Enki and the great sea monster proceeded, but Kramer is convinced that Enki won the battle and therefore became the god of water and wisdom. Enki is associated to the water god Poseidon in later Greek mythology, who we know raped Medusa who then became the archetype of shame, terrorizing everyone who looked at her. In a later version, Kramer says about Enki that he "sets sail into the underworld, penetrating Ereshkigal . . . who reacts by storming, throwing up stones, devouring, and roaring", and from this encounter the Huluppu tree was created (Kramer and Wolkstein, 1983, p. 140). So there seems to be an uncertainty whether Enki also abducted Ereshkigal or whether he wanted to confront the unconscious as an initiation to wisdom. From the story we know that Enki and Ereshkigal are the 'parents' to the Huluppu tree, the first living thing on Earth. Also, Ereshkigal was already taken by the time Enki decides to visit her domain, so I don't think we can accuse Enki of having created the complex of shame. He may be responsible for its activation when he, the wise water god, confronts the complex and becomes initiated himself, referring to the rage coming from Ereshkigal in return. Enki has already taken the journey that Inanna is preparing, and this explains his creative ability to help her return to Earth later.

In so many ways Enki reminds me of Jung. Jung also travelled to the under-world and broke with all traditions (and with Freud), and experienced that dark, archetypal domain of instinctual life as no one else before him had done. He too has helped individuals to make the journey, and his theories and trust in the collective unconscious has been a wise part of preparing for the descent.

When we use the affect theory to understand how Ereshkigal came to the underworld in the first place, I suggest that the big sea monster refers to the affect of shame that overwhelms the innocent feminine affect of joy, leaving that part of the psyche traumatized in the unconscious. It is the most archetypal image we find of a shame scene in the Sumerian tradition, but as a healing image it is too powerful to use, because Ereshkigal was not able to return – she had to stay in the underworld. Therefore we can associate the figure of Ereshkigal as that part inside that cannot return to the upper world by her own forces. The key to transformation is in the hands of Inanna.

The activation of shame happens when Dumutzi says that he wants to be set free. He chose the masculine affect of interest (to be a king) against the feminine affect of joy (to be together) and created a deep split in the archetypal relationship between the masculine and the feminine in the psyche.

Processing shame is therefore not only related to the feminine but also to the healing of the masculine–feminine polarity.

When the Huluppu tree is going to be cut down, Lilith must flee when Gil-gamesh comes with his axe, because it is not yet time for Inanna to confront her rage. Inanna must first establish her power and her female authority before she confronts the dark aspect of her soul.

One client had the following dream the night after she painted a shame scene in a workshop:

> Looking at the ocean I see a fishing boat surrounded by a giant yellow snake. When the boat is emptying the day's catch, the snake just keeps coming out from the boat. I am completely unprepared. A fishing man is standing next to the boat. The snake first looks friendly, but suddenly it raises and it seems as if it will attack the fisherman. I get scared and think that I might be next. I wake up without knowing how the dream ended.

In the dream the snake illustrates the instinctive raw energy coming up from the unconscious/ocean. It is connected to the roots of the Huluppu tree and to Kur. The dreamer watches the snake from a distance, which means that she is not yet in direct contact with the affect. The image is known before the affect is actually experienced in the body, which I think is an important part of preparing the psyche so re-traumatization can be avoided. The dream also indicates the collective layer behind personal shame as a much more powerful energy.

I am wondering whether the animus, represented by the fisherman, is associated to Gilgamesh, the active principle in the psyche, who has been fishing (through the activity of painting a shame scene) and who caught access to the power of the collective unconscious. In my client's dream, Kur has been activated as the power deeper than the personal unconscious memory of shame and has brought the big snake up and into the daylight.

Living with a fear of the unknown can keep the ego in a stressful position, because running away from the unconscious often means living a one-sided, extroverted life as an attempt to avoid the inner Kur. This dreamer had stopped running. She had chosen to confront shame after years of preparation through art therapy training. The dream is collective in its symbolism except that the dreamer is in the dream scene as an observer. Everything else is unfamiliar to the dreamer. It is an archetypal image of the raw and unpredictable energy that lies beneath the personal experiences of shame, and the dreamer is warned in the dream. Will she be next?, she wonders.

Ereshkigal is the unconscious shadow to Inanna and is seen as "the prototype of a witch – unloving, unloved, abandoned, instinctual and full of rage, greed, and desperate loneliness" (Kramer and Wolkstein, 1983, p. 158). Her marriage with Gugalanna was also a story of rejection, and he is now dead. The two sisters have something in common and they both know about being rejected by their men.

The Huluppu tree almost disappears in the unconscious during the big flood/ overwhelming emotions, but Inanna manages to save it with a plan to use it to become stronger as a queen and woman. The tree, as the first living thing, is a representation of the conscious experience we have of the original self. Kramer says, "The tree embodies the dual forces of the universe: Enki and Ereshkigal, consciousness and unconsciousness, light and darkness, male and female, and the power of light and the power of death" (Kramer and Wolkstein, 1983, p. 144). By cutting the tree, Inanna shows that she is not yet ready to contain the polarity that she needs in order to establish inner wholeness. First she must create her ego-strength by manifesting her throne and her womanhood.

Compared to Eve from the Christian tradition, Inanna shows interest in the body and sexuality, while Eve was interested in knowledge related to the head and the patriarch who created her. Inanna is an earlier archetype of the feminine not yet shamed by patriarchy, and her shame is purely related to Dumutzi's rejection.

We may understand her fear of the unknown as a warning against the forces from the unconscious that are building up along with the growth of the Huluppu tree.

Jung also considered a grounded and socialized ego to be the best foundation for the individuation process, and this is all part of Inanna's preparation.

During a training week where we worked with the affect of fear, one student dreamt the following: "I have cut a lot of trees in my garden in order to get more light and in one of the big holes that is left from an old tree, I am going to plant a new tree. The new tree has been in water for the roots to grow, but they have grown so much that I need to cut some in order to get it out of the pot and into the ground".

This was her last week of a four-year training program, and she was going to start a new job as an art therapist. She had felt isolated in the dark, where the old trees had kept the light away from her garden and therefore she had not yet established her feminine authority and power in the outer reality. Coming from a depressed and introverted position, she was now more than ready to become visible – the roots of the new tree had been in water for longer than necessary. Just like Inanna, she saves the tree and plants it in her garden as a beginning of a new cycle of development.

When Inanna decides to visit Enki, the god of wisdom and water, she 'tricks' him into giving her all the *me* tablets when he is drunk, and she thereby gains the power to rule Sumer. In the text it says that Enki wants the *me* tablets back when he wakes up the next morning with a hangover, but I think it is an outside manoeuvre. He is after all the god of wisdom, and sometimes wisdom comes in disguise and can only be understood in its consequence. Again we see Enki as a positive animus helping Inanna to prepare her descent.

The *me* tablets are verbal naming of rules that do not change, which helped to keep some order in the Sumerian society. In relation to shame, the *me* tablets represent the objective structure and order in the transformative process of shame. They belonged to Enki, the wise initiator, but are now transferred to Inanna, who gains access to the inner spiritual masculine principle of language and order.

If we translate this part of the preparation phase into psychology, it suggests a verbalization of basic rules or rituals before a descent to the underworld can be trusted. We need more than intuition, sensation and feeling for this journey. We also need thinking as a rational set of world order. Time, I think, is another aspect that can create more trust in the psyche. Perera also suggests that the seven gates in the underworld represent a need for time as we are getting closer to Ereshkigal and to the complex of shame (1981).

In practical shame work it means that we define the overall process before we let go. There are rules to follow that are not changeable, which is the rational frame and procedure for the work. This is part of the educational aspect of knowing shame and the steps in the journey as a preparation to the descent.

Jung spent his life describing ways to approach the unconscious and how to return to normal life again based on his own confrontation with unconscious content (Jung and Shamdasani, 2009). We can use his experience, like Inanna used Enki's, to trust the unconscious laws by getting to know them through the words already written. I think this is the true reason why Inanna visits Enki and was able to trick him into giving her the *me* tablets. It gave her the control she needed to feel safe enough to later confront the unknown.

Following Inanna, we can also look for someone in our life who trusts our potential to become more whole if we do not already have that voice within. Someone, like Enki or Jung, who believes in the greatness of the self and the psychic reality, before we know of it ourselves. The literature is full of books written by such pioneers, who can make us see the world from different perspectives.

They all contribute to wholeness, adding pieces to an objective understanding of the psychic reality.

When I start a new group I sometimes begin by inviting the participants to make a figure in clay, which they use to introduce themselves. And when they present their figure in the group I ask if they can see their past, present and future self in the figure. I cannot remember anyone who could not see a future image of who they would like to become in their clay figure. Not that they thought about it when making it, but when asked, it was there. This is making contact with Enki during the process of creation and the use of imagination. He gives us the trust to become so much more, at least while he is drunk! When sober he tries to get his authority back, but it is too late. Inanna is protected during her journey back home in her heavenly boat and Enki must accept the transition of power. This is the danger in the initial relationship with the spiritual. It is a vulnerable position, because it is only in the mind and not yet in the physical reality. Negative inner father voices, as the shadow side of Enki, can make us doubt what we have just discovered during the creative process, but Inanna passes the test.

When we use a spiritual approach as an opening of the journey, it can lead to an inflated state of greatness in the ego as we come to know new aspects of the self that have not been shamed. This is all part of getting access to the resources in the psyche and the challenge is to maintain a separation between ego and self, in order to have a neutral Ninshubur as witness to the process. It also means that part of our consciousness stays in the physical reality: goes to work, takes care of family life, does shopping, cooking and washing and all the ordinary things that we need to do in order to stay connected to the physical and the collective. Maintaining our daily duties during the transformative process keeps us rooted in life and out of psychiatric care.

The call from Ereshkigal

Inanna decides to marry Dumutzi, an earthly shepherd, and she makes him king of Sumer.

It was said that Inanna heard Ereshkigal call her from below, "a sudden desire of Inanna for the netherworld", according to Jacobsen (1976, p. 55). According to Kramer and Wolkstein (1983), "Inanna takes on the voice of *the* woman. She proclaims what she will be. What once flowed so freely and naturally between man and woman is 'declared' and 'determined' " (p. 153). The roles between the two have changed, and Inanna here steps forward as a mature woman who knows about her self and the direction she wants to take in her life. As a consequence he says, "Set me free, my sister, set me free. You will be a little daughter to my father. Come my beloved sister, I would go to the palace. Set me free . . ." (ibid., p. 153).

Dumutzi sees her as a 'sister' and he wants to be 'set free', because he now has more important things to do. Inanna is rejected in her *mature* womanhood and Dumutzi's detachment from her shows that he could not combine being her husband with being king and chose power over love. His humanity against her divinity is a polarity that Dumutzi avoids when he changes his perception of Inanna to be his sister. Inanna is *not* his sister, and they do *not* have the same father, so why does Dumutzi reject her as his lover, wife and goddess? Also, he speaks to her as if she was a child/little daughter, and by doing so, he devalues her true divine self. Does his sibling transference on Inanna express his attempt to humiliate her true identity, in order for him to separate from the feminine and become a 'real' man and king? Ayers (2011) found this to be the case in a boy's rejection of his mother when his gender identity was developing, and the same seems to be the case for Dumutzi in his claim for independence and freedom, carried out through the sister transference.

The sister–brother relationship has been explored by Abramovitch (2014). He says, "'Sibling transference' occurs when a person transfers the emotional aspects of the brother/sister relationship to a person who symbolically resembles that sibling" (p. 97).

Dumutzi's sister is Geshtinanna, who represents compassion and love, and their relationship is strong. Abramovitch also calls the sister–brother relationship the "warmest and least complicated relationship" (ibid, p. 71). From this moment Dumutzi no longer sees Inanna as an individual, but as a little sister needing his protection and care. In the transference of his inner sister/ Geshtinanna, he is projecting his compassionate, loving side to Inanna as a step towards his own masculine identity. Is this how men in general maintains their masculine ego, by transferring the qualities of love and compassion to women, thereby robbing them of their individual competencies and unique power? I think this is an important image of the deep polarity between the feminine and masculine principles today. The rationality and lack of compassion for the individual in the patriarchal system illustrates how the feminine has disappeared from the masculine world of rational doing and is called by the underworld a reaction to shame.

Did Dumutzi become scared of Inanna's new strength as a woman and her ability to name her own needs and identity? Did he realize that he too must find his masculine identity (as a king) in order to match her strength and stay 'on top' in the relationship?

Is this not what has happened for so many women and men when men were expected to choose their jobs and women to sacrifice theirs in exchange for marriage and family life? Dumutzi got caught in the power game and need for social recognition, and women got caught in dependency patterns, fearing a life like Lilith's. The role model for women became Eve, because Lilith was long gone, as was the consciousness of shame. Though times are changing and more women are integrating their masculine potentials, becoming leaders and academics in society, we all still play by the rules of the patriarch. Some women become *like* men, being able to reject their needs for intimacy and relationships like Dumutzi, while other women become strong in their own values like Inanna, and verbalize their self-knowledge and needs, but are then considered dangerous by men because of their independence.

One client described how she was going to meet her partner with the expectation of having an intimate night since the children were out. When she got to his house it turned out that he had already drunk half a bottle of wine and smoked marijuana, so she felt he lacked the awareness and interest to be with *her*. Instead of leaving, she stayed and wanted to discuss some practical matter regarding what she thought was his lack of responsibility with their son. Her disappointment at his rejection of her vulnerable feminine Inanna side turned into anger at him for being an irresponsible father. They had an argument, and then she left. She chose the path of Lilith instead of Eve in her angry reaction, except that she did not make the connection between anger and rejection of her womanhood. Instead she directed the anger towards his fatherhood. Had she followed the inner voice of Eve, she would have surrendered to the situation and held the shame inside, leaving him 'on top' of the situation.

Instead of expressing her disappointment about the choice he made for their evening together, she kept her sadness to herself. She did not even experience the shame until we discussed it in therapy. Instinctively she tried to pass the shame of being rejected onto him as a way to avoid the experience inside her-self. This may be the way many women react to their rejecting husbands, when shame is not acknowledged, and so he blames *her* for being the irrational and aggressive partner, and they forget to share the experiences of rejection that lie behind.

Inanna's parents reject Inanna when she decides to visit the underworld against their wishes. When Inanna is dead and Ninshubur seeks help, they say it is her own fault and that she could have stayed in the upper world. The collective acceptance of shame patterns goes back many generations as normal personal behaviour expected by social systems. This is an image of the priorities we make in our society to this day, when power and economy have replaced love and empathy in so many ways. All the silent choices we make in life where we forget the value of caring for humanity. Fear of isolation and loneliness become the affective drive for women who choose a life like Eve's, because Lilith cannot surrender and chooses freedom instead.

From the text we don't know how Inanna actually felt about Dumutzi's request for freedom. We only know that the call from below came immediately after. The two positive affects of joy and interest in Inanna's life were then separated and left Inanna isolated from her masculine side and her man. With Dumutzi's rejection followed the immediate activation of Ereshkigal as a complex of shame, and Inanna left Dumutzi like Lilith left Adam. They both represent the archetype of feminine freedom pointing towards integration instead of surrender. I suggest that this moment in the story, when Dumutzi claims his freedom, is the key activator of the archetypal complex of shame. And also the turning point in life, as we decide to pay attention to the inner world, because we are wounded in the outer.

A conscious decision

Inanna is a woman who consciously decides to confront shame. It is not something that happens to her. She is not a victim of shame in the same way as Ereshkigal, who was dragged to the underworld by force, as was Persephone in the Demeter myth. Inanna is following an inner call, and I think that we can do the same. Instead of waiting for the affect of shame to take our life energy and creative originality, as in depression, we can decide actively to do something while our masculine side is still awake and before we forget about the rejections we have experienced in life. When women have the bravery to actually feel these rejections from their partners who want to be set free like Dumutzi, the possibility for initiation is also present and needs to be heard in order to accomplish the journey. The decision must be made consciously, because otherwise the witness to the process, Ninshubur, is not instructed to get help when needed and therefore Inanna will not be able to return.

Working with the shadow

One student, 'B', expressed how she felt wounded in her feminine identity when her husband wanted to be set free after seven years of marriage. They had both wanted children, but she could not give birth and felt a deep shame about her body. Finally she had all her female organs removed in an operation because of illness. She felt no support from her husband and found out that he was unfaithful to B with another woman. Finally he filed for divorce. During B's art therapy training she managed to return from the underworld with a new feminine identity starting with the peeing woman shown in Figure 3.1.

The image represented the bodily freedom that she felt was denied by her parents and husband and illustrates the shadow side of a well-behaved woman. When she was two years old she was beaten by her father for being too interested in self-stimulation and she learned to think of her sexuality and her bodily pleasure as something forbidden. Exploring the shadow through the creative process is a safe way to become familiar with those rejected aspects of self. Part of this process is to let go of inner judges and to choose one's own path, allowing a more free expression. The function of peeing (and shitting) is to get rid of the waste that the body does not need. It is a cleaning activity and psychologically speaking it is similar to the function of projection. This woman had felt victimized in her marriage, and as a victim you are not free to express whatever emotion you carry inside, so you turn your anger towards the self and the body. The shadow does the opposite; she turns her emotion towards the outside with some aggression to compensate for the self-destructive ego. So when the ego is introverted, the shadow is extroverted. The image of the peeing girl shows the extrovert aspect to a shamed ego.

When we live with shame, we survive by projecting the unwanted shadow onto others, so the pressure inside decreases. This is an unconscious and un-willed

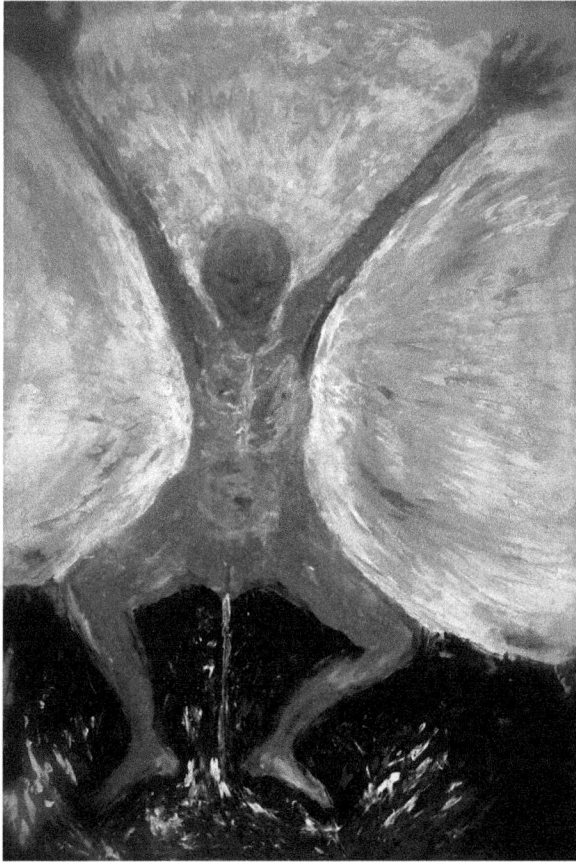

Figure 3.1 The peeing woman

activity and often it becomes part of 'the other reality' that is kept secret from others. It contains our true feelings related to those who hurt us. All these shameful experiences from B's marriage were held in her body, and with this image she came to experience the pleasure of cleaning her body through the art-making process.

This is another advantage of using the arts as media in transformative processes. We can express what we fear most in a safe environment and get the opportunity to discover and explore the content in the projected material, which in this case became sensual and joyful.

Inanna's protection and nourishing of the Huluppu tree became a protection of unconscious shame, which only became stronger by housing the snake, Lilith and the Anzu-bird. Calling Gilgamesh to help her cut the tree confirms the thought of an extroverted attitude as a solution to fear, because the attention moves away from the inner complex of shame. By moving out in the world, we are using our inner Gilgamesh, which becomes familiar to us through the art-making process. Moving out activates aggression, while moving in activates sadness. If sadness dominates the psyche leaving no access to aggression, fear will become too overwhelming in the confrontation with shame, dragging consciousness towards an overwhelming inner condition without sufficient preparation. Having worked through some of the personal experiences of loss (sadness) and restrictions (aggression) shows its benefits here in this scene, where we are to cut the tree. Without access to our inner hero Gilgamesh, fear would prevent individuals from even starting the art-making process.

Working with the anima/animus

Moving inward in the psyche we reach the anima and animus at a deeper level than the shadow. In projected forms we find these through the romantic partners we meet in our lives. What are we attracted to in the other? What is it that 'hits' us when we fall in love, and how do our relationships typically end? What is the connection to our first love affair, our mother or father, and are we seeking to fulfil needs from our partners that we did not get from them? One female student had a father who was always busy with his academic research and expected her to become rational and 'easy' as a child. She learned to withhold emotions and disconnected from the body to avoid the feeling of rejection and shame. She later chose partners with whom she could remain more or less invisible, but eventually felt a longing to be more whole and started in therapy.

A male client came into therapy because he felt inferior in his present relationship with a woman who had a stronger masculine side than he had. His need for intimacy was often rejected and he did not know what to do. He had experienced his mother as cold and distant and never felt accepted as the person he was inside, and therefore became the person he thought she wanted him to be. That pattern continued in his relationships, and no matter how hard he tried to please his partner, it did not seem to get him any closer to her. In some sense he had married a woman with the expectation that she was like his mother. She was the one who taught him how to behave when he wanted attention and love but also the one who taught him what to expect from life. Recognizing the pattern that repeats itself in his romantic relationships became a first step in paying attention to his own needs and to the process of finding a good mother within himself.

Part of the confusion in our time is that there are a lot of absent fathers (and mothers) in the families. Fathers who, like Dumutzi, reject their partner in order to gain social rank. They communicate to their sons and daughters that they love work and power more than they love their children. What does that mean in relation to the descent of Inanna?

When girls grow up and find their own partners, they will attract men like Dumutzi, who will be present during the falling-in-love phase, but who will then choose social kingdom over family life. Women learn to live with that rejection and keep it safe in the other reality, where Lilith is to be found in the Huluppu tree. When first the tree is cut down there is no return. This is the moment when women must make the most important decision. Do they want to be free or are they too scared of being alone and independent? Is the time right? Do they have the integrity that is needed to confront many years of shame, or have they projected the inner masculine strength onto an outer partner remaining helpless in relation to their own needs?

When women begin to feel the void inside with little connection to the body, then shame is coming closer to consciousness together with the sadness of having wasted so many years. When not taken seriously, it may lead to depression as a result of an unacknowledged shame. From this point of view, depression is an act of self-regulation and psychological ego-cide, but is often misunderstood to be a weakness of the soul.

The reverse method

I want to suggest one method, the reverse method, which stimulates symbolization (Skov, 2015). It can lead to experiences of a transpersonal reality associated to the greatness of self and is therefore often recommended to individuals who feel they have lost this connection. I learned it from a Jungian analyst, Jes Bertelsen, almost 40 years ago and have worked with it since then. It can be used in relation to dreams, but also as a way to regulate emotional conditions, in supervision or, as I suggest here, to prepare individuals to process shame.

Materials are A-3 copy paper and oil crayons.

As a starting point for the first picture you choose a theme that you would like to know more about. It can be an emotion, a scene from a dream or an experience from life. The important thing is that you have a question in mind and that you trust the self to comment on this question by not trying to solve it intellectually.

When you have made the first drawing, you put a new piece of paper on top of the drawing and transfer the lines that you can see through the paper to the new paper. From these lines you imagine a new image and finish the drawing. You can make another reverse drawing on this picture until you have a series of drawings. In the end you name them all and put them in the order you made them.

As a reflection you may think of the last picture as 1) a regulation of the emotion expressed in the first picture and 2) an 'answer' to the question you had in mind when you made the first picture.

The method is first of all useful as a regulative method as it visualizes the emotion in the last image, which is absent in the first drawing. If there is sadness in the first image, anger might show in the last picture as a compensative image.

The method is also useful for individuals who work alone, or in between sessions, when experiences from life are overwhelming. One woman from my research group said she used this method to work with her anger towards her husband and that she felt able to 'calm her self down'.

Working with fear

Personally I prefer the educational and the practical part to be interactive, in order to create a flow between the head and the body through the *experience* of theoretical concepts. I think this structure prevents fear from building up, because the affects become known through the attachment to images. When we work with inner personalities the art media can make this process fun, imaginative and vital as well as serious and painful, which means that the resources and positive affects of joy and interest become part of the process connected to the inner rejected child.

Through the experience of connecting head and body we can transform fear into trust. Repetition of such meaning-making processes will slowly wire the brain to look for meaning when there seems to be none.

The first step in processing shame is to become familiar with the language of the self through creative processes and psychological understanding. The purpose is to turn fear into trust, preparing the conscious mind for the descent that will follow.

Verbalizing the artwork is an important part of the transformative process as it moves the experience of the image from right to left hemisphere.

As a general rule, the following phases in the art therapy dialogue are suggested in all steps, inspired by Abt (2005). They are described in more detail in my last book (Skov, 2015).

1   Describe the artwork as you see it.
2   Tell the story of the artwork using your imagination.
3   Make associations to your personal life.
4   Find the themes and behavioural patterns as you recognize these in your life.
5   What does the image tell you about the direction in your overall development?

As a summary to number one we use the creative processes in order to experience the inner personalities in the psyche, the shadow, anima/animus and self. We learn to trust the symbolic language of the self through the use of the artwork and as a new way to approach the psychic reality. Parallel to the art therapy experiences there are teaching themes that introduce new learning related to the inner reality, which is often not reflected upon by individuals who live a more extroverted life. The psychology of the unconscious is suggested in order to bring meaning and rational understanding as a preparation to the steps that follow.

Step 2. Descent to the underworld

Sadness–anger

When we decide to confront the unconscious, we need an inner witness to the journey. We need someone inside (or outside) who trusts that we can endure the journey and who will be there to keep us connected to the physical world of functioning when part of us is in the underworld. This is the role of Ninshubur, Inanna's servant and helper.

As a self-representation, Ninshubur is that part of our consciousness that knows about shame from earlier therapeutic processes and who remains grounded during Inanna's descent. It is a consciousness capable of seeing the self objectively and without her; we would be stuck in the depressed position with no one to save us. Ninshubur can therefore be seen as a result of the preparation suggested in Step 1, where we learned to reflect upon self instead of just living it.

Gugalanna's death

When Inanna was asked to explain herself and to name her reasons for entering the threshold to the underworld domain, she said that she wanted to participate in the funeral of Ereshkigal's husband Gugalanna. Gugalanna is known as the "great bull of heaven" and Perera identifies him as the dark side of Enlil, who "was a rapist banished to the underworld for his violence" (1981, p. 51). Gugalanna is identified as having "bull-like passion, raw desire and power, sadistic bull-dozing violence, demonic bullying" and described as the "archetypal patriarchal shadow" (ibid, pp. 51–52).

It was said that Gugalanna was the only one amongst all the gods who did not stand up in respect for Ereshkigal at a meeting, and therefore Ereshkigal wanted him to come to the underworld so she could kill him. Another story is that Gugalanna left Ereshkigal after having made love to her for six days, and Ereshkigal then threatened all the gods by saying that she would not be able to do her job as the underworld queen because of the wound he gave her. All the gods were scared and sent Gugalanna to live with her in the underworld, where he dies.

This could mean that a pattern of unconscious abuse represented by Ereshkigal and Gugalanna has been broken, and Ereshkigal is therefore calling Inanna to help her to become more whole as a woman. From being the cold, angry and un-loving aspect of the feminine archetype, she now has a motivation to develop her inner shadow, represented by Inanna, because the abuser Gugalanna is no longer active.

Just as Inanna's descent is motivated by her loss of Dumutzi, so has Eresh-kigal lost her man, and this is what brings them together. Perera (1981) trusts Inanna when she says that she comes for Gugalanna's funeral, but I think it is an excuse for confronting her own deeper shame as well as to heal Ereshkigal. Why would she die for attending a funeral of her sister's abusive husband? A sister who wants her dead! I think Inanna wants to know more about shame. She is already a goddess of heaven and Earth, so why not include the underworld as well, while Dumutzi takes care of social affairs.

It is true that she wants to be part of Gugalanna's funeral, but only as a symbol of the emotional death of her own husband Dumutzi. It is also true that she wants to explore her shame of being rejected because she has to follow the call.

We cannot really know what her consciousness about the descent is at this point, but we do know that she prepares her own death and return before she descends and therefore she knows more than what it seems from the text.

There is a significant parallel between the father–daughter relation in our time and the rejection Inanna experiences from her husband Dumutzi. The personal part of this journey is about transforming the wounded father–daughter relationship, while the archetypal part is about the masculine–feminine polarity.

A client came with the following issue. When she experienced shame in a relationship she would either pretend that she was strong enough to listen to the shaming other, or she would become angry and attack the other person. After such an outburst she felt a terrible shame and expected the other person to punish her later.

She had identified with Inanna and in her painting of the shame scene she painted herself as a slim white teenager opposite an abusive masculine part that she associated with her father's brother. In my client's childhood and adolescence she experienced many meetings with her father's brother where he had shamed her in sadistic ways, and at the same time others admired him as a free Enlil spirit of the upper world. The shame was communicated indirectly and disguised as justified reason through the collective moral of right and wrong. As an un-initiated Inanna, my client was not prepared for this underworld attack of rational power. The painting illustrated a meeting between Inanna and a very alive Gugalanna! The repressed masculine abuser of feminine innocence was operating from the other reality and my client was dragged to the underworld with no time to prepare her self for the journey. In our story, this dark aspect of the patriarchal Sun energy must die before Inanna can start her journey. Perera further describes how a woman's idealized father projection falls apart as a disappointing experience, symbolized in the death of Gugalanna (1981).

The mythological mystery is to understand the importance of the dead Gugalanna as a beginning of the descent. Was my client ready to accept the disappointing news about her idealized father/uncle, in spite of the collective opinion of him? Or did she need to protect *him* by shaming her self instead of 'killing' him?

Both Gugalanna and Dumutzi are referred to as the great bull of heaven. They both rejected their partner, creating a wound of inner suffering, and now that Gugalanna is dead, a self-destructive pattern in the unconscious psyche may have ended. Instead of blaming one's own self, as is typical for shamed individuals, it is time to pay attention to the shaming other and the Gugalanna power operating behind.

The seven gates

Part of Inanna's descent is to let go of her many responsibilities on Earth. Her authority is slowly minimized and her earthly tasks are left to others. She withdraws from her offices and outer duties because she needs all her attention to the inner journey ahead. In Jungian terms this means that we let go of the persona and the self-image we have developed as a result of outer mirroring and now choose a more introverted approach to life. This turning point is described as the 'ego-cide' phase in Rosen's model of change (2002).

Letting go of the social mask means that we are vulnerable to the inner reality because we do not know what is hiding there. Who are we when we no longer identify with the mask we show to the world? What will other people think about us, being passive in a world where active engagement and fast running has high priority? Can we choose a 'depression' without being caught in the collective moral and way of thinking about it, knowing the purpose of this 'irrational' behaviour? This is a point where our preparation for understanding the process can help us avoid getting stuck in self-judgemental thoughts, because we already have an image or intuition of the outcome that we can hold on to while we let go of the attachment to outside obligations.

Inanna is dressed like a queen when she knocks on the door to the underworld and Ereshkigal gets furious. Why is that? Why is she so angry because Inanna wants to visit her, considering the fact that she has called her herself, and what does that mean in psychological terms?

Inanna's arrival at the first gate activates the shame–anger affect in Ereshkigal as a first emotional consciousness of the hidden aggression behind shame.

As Inanna gets closer to Ereshkigal, it is not only Inanna who makes sacrifices. Ereshkigal experiences the pain of becoming self-conscious, while before she was merely a repressed and hidden memory of an old familiar shame.

Kramer and Wolkstein (1983) describes Ereshkigal as "unloving, unloved, abandoned, instinctual, and full of rage, greed, and desperate loneliness" (p. 158). The pain of getting to know this part of the self is described as Ereshkigal's birth pain, while consciousness (Inanna) is dead/not functioning.

Inanna must leave a part of her divine identity at each of the seven gates, and ends up naked in front of the seven underworld judges.

Perera (1981) suggests that the ritual of letting go of one part of persona at a time is to make sure that this process takes the time necessary. Moving from an innocent Inanna identity so full of love, sensuality and creativity towards the dark inner rage and shame is a major step for Inanna and the process needs time. I think this is an *individual* timing that should be considered related to change.

Those who have lived a life in the dark through identification with Ereshkigal will also need time to become conscious of shame instead of just living it. In therapy this means that we take one step at a time and one relationship before another. We do not attempt to compensate, as when the client says, "I feel so shameful," and the helping therapist says, "But you have so many resources", or when a more innocent client says, "They are all wrong and I have no responsibility" and the helping therapist begins to talk about projections and how they belong to one's self. Also, we should not generalize this slow descent through the gates by explaining and theorizing archetypal wisdom to the client. That belongs to the preparation phase, which took place earlier. Perera (1981) explains the seven gates as a descent through the seven energy chakras in the body. Moving from the highest energy at the crown chakra toward the lowest energy of the root chakra, Inanna falls from spiritual heights towards psychological reality.

Psychic reality

I think it is important for an individual at this stage of the process to be in an environment where the psychic reality is experienced as true, otherwise the upper judges and inner parental voices hold their shaming influence against the more and more vulnerable ego consciousness as we let go of the 'divine' identity associated to the figure of Inanna.

Individual therapy can of course take place in such an environment, where the therapist is able to trust the psychic reality of the client, without attempting to reduce its invisible character to the logic of the physical reality. I prefer working in a group setting, because the other group members, and the mutual support between them, makes the objectivity of the psychic reality more convincing. It becomes a shared and trusted space as we confirm each other's symbolical inner worlds. I also find that the freedom to express without shame becomes easier when more individuals work in the same room. It feels as if the collective energy from more individuals affects the archetypal level of the individual process.

The perspective of the underworld judges is a reality most individuals learn to mistrust during upbringing, because it is connected to our own individual wholeness and truth. We learn to trust the collective outer moral and to reject our inner truth as a condition for belonging.

During this phase I like to use rituals, such as symbolic sacrifices of the persona we let go of, by using creative expressions as representations for the 'dying' ego. We may use drumming as a rhythm of seriousness and group cohesion and/or fire, where images are burned.

Working with sadness–anger

Working with the sadness–anger polarity as a next step towards the affect of shame means that the conscious ego must accept both emotional states as possible expressions in life.

Individuals who feel more comfortable using sadness as a reaction to shame will need to work with aggression as a withheld reaction towards the shaming other and opposite for those who are more familiar with anger as a reaction to shame. The potential in those emotions is that sadness connects to the inner life while aggression is energy moving outwards.

There are many ways to work with this polarity in art therapy, but first of all the therapist needs to pay attention to openings that may arise during the initial therapeutic dialogue with the client. For example, when the sad client shows signs of aggression in the body when talking about her abusive husband, the therapist can support further attention to that emotion and invite the client to express it in paint, clay or some other material. The movement from body to art-making to dialogue is a process that takes the client from the unconscious right-hemisphere experience towards the left-hemisphere understanding by using the image as a focus for imaginative and associative dialogues.

One client artist, diagnosed with cancer, came to therapy because she had lost her interest in painting. She just did not have the energy to paint any more in spite of the good prognosis the doctors gave her, as the cancer was no longer developing. Getting the diagnosis two years earlier was for her a complete shock and she could not think about anything but death.

One of her paintings showed this dilemma. In the centre was the black 'death/ desperation'. At the left was the green 'hope', and to the right the pink 'love and energy to live life'. From the pink there were branches moving towards the green hope, and she said there was a power struggle between the black part and the pink. When looking at the picture, the only dynamic colour able to move was pink, as it was reaching *across* the black to meet the green hope. Normally I think hope is a good thing to have in any crisis as it makes us believe in change and in future, but in this case hope was preventing her from living her life in the present. When I covered the green hope in the painting with a piece of paper, and only the black and pink was left to see, she said that the pink would become more active and stronger in relation to the black. Following this pattern, where hope would steal the energy from living life, she first came to think of a period in her childhood when she was two or three years old, and her mother had locked her up in a room to sleep where she could hear animals being killed in the butcher's shop downstairs. She remembered how she had screamed every evening when she was placed in that room, but nobody ever came to her rescue. Another memory appeared from the time she got pregnant and the father to the child left her and did not want to be involved. She was 20 years old. For two years she lived in the hope that he *would* come back. She could not believe her reality because it was too painful. But when he still did not return, she finally moved to live with her religious mother until she married another man some years later. Her brain was wired *not* to expect that her dreams would come true. She had learned that hope would lead her to give up her life energy and her healthy aggression to be creative, because hope and death of the self was associated with each other. She had repressed the shame of not being loved enough to be heard. And when her cancer was diagnosed, creating another shock in her life, hope took over as her self-protective system and survival of trauma. Living in hope was easier than confronting the possibility of death.

If we refer back to the Blue Diamante model (Figure 2.1), she was stuck in the affect of sadness and had given up her aggression, because she had learned that it was useless anyway. Getting back the power that was left with her rejecting mother and partner would be a challenge in further therapeutic work and needed for her art-making process in the future.

Approaching the inner child with an empathic attitude can happen through the dialogue with the artwork, where the child image becomes affectively alive. It becomes more than a figure hanging on the wall, when the emotional attachment to the child in the image is felt as an attachment to the child in the psyche. When the rejected child appears in the painting, the client can be invited to explore the inner life of the child using a good mother's attitude. What are the needs of the child? Where has she been all those years? What are her longings? And how does the client experience the connection with her? In this way the inner relationship between mother and child is being re-established, leading to a new pattern of self-compassion.

In the other psycho-educational programs mentioned earlier, an attitude of compassion does not seem to relate to the inner child, but seems to be a new education of ego consciousness. Verbal exercises between participants are meant to train the participants to replace a shaming approach to life with an empathic one. The vulnerability in this more cognitive approach is that the shame scenes remain dissociated from the 'new' compassionate consciousness and therefore continue to operate from the unconscious when stimulated by rejections.

Summary

The purpose of the descent is to let go of the self-image that feels un-authentic or no longer meaningful. As we move through the seven gates, we make a new sacrifice at every gate. We just cannot transform our relation to the deepest parts of our inner self in one go. We need time to focus and to reflect on the many aspects of our self-understanding that we used as protection from shame, remembering that the shadow to the shamed individual is an inner shameless Inanna who is hidden in the other reality. The descent refers to Inanna's sacrifice and to Ereshkigal's pain. As we move through the gates, one after the other, we lose our inner spiritual self-worth that has been speaking to us from the other reality in order to keep us alive. One student had a Mother Theresa image of her self when she was working with a client. She was convinced that her healing power was almost divine and forgot to pay attention to the power that was hidden in the client. In this way the client became 'one of her children' who needed help.

Another student would talk to her inner angels in order to survive the humiliation instead of confronting the person who shamed her. Such patterns maintained the dissociation in the psyche that were preventing the shame behaviour from changing. In the Inanna myth we therefore hear about the (birth) pain in Ereshkigal as Inanna comes closer to her, unprotected and naked. The shamed part of the psyche is revealed and experienced through the symbolical death of Inanna.

Step 3. Death

Shame

Psychological judgement

When Inanna stands before the seven judges from the underworld, the judges "perceive Inanna's hidden, split-off parts and condemn her" (Kramer and Wolkstein, 1983, p. 159). She is killed by Ereshkigal and hung on a peg to rot.

Standing naked in front of Ereshkigal and the seven judges is a vulnerability that "permits us to be penetrated by the reality of the other, the full force of the affects, without defending ourselves with our professional persona" (Perera, 1981, p. 60). This is the trauma of shame in its most devastating power. Whenever someone shames us in life, we are sentenced to death. We dissociate, and part of our conscious mind splits off to the underworld, where Ereshkigal and her seven judges are waiting. Inanna lost her protection from shame by letting go of her identification with all her material values. She became weak in her persona and in her defences.

Individuals who have developed a persona strong enough to avoid shame can function well in society. They may have good jobs and are admired by others for their social rank and rational strength. Jung assumed that the beginning of the individuation process took place during midlife when engagement with outer reality became more and more meaningless and the inner calling stronger. In our time there are so many individuals who do not have a strong persona. They may not have a job, or the job they have is stressful, demanding or without social value. This vulnerability in not having a strong social mask is a social vulnerability to shame. It corresponds to the image of going through some of the gates in the underworld, but with nothing to sacrifice because you are already naked.

A client came to therapy because of a bad relationship, which she had finally just ended. Her partner had convinced her they would have a glorious future together and insisted how much he loved her, but as time went by, he began to humiliate her more and more, blaming her for destroying their relationship if she did not adapt to his needs. She felt confused about her own experience of being humiliated and whether he was right in his judgement of her. Was she a destroyer of relationships like her mother? This was the third relationship that had ended in this way. Was it all her fault? Who should she trust? Her mother was an unpredictable narcissist who would threaten suicide one day and be nice the next. My client's hunger for love was so strong that she could not see the man from the underworld perspective until very late in their relationship, when shame became unbearable. She was vulnerable to shame because she felt unloved and with no social dignity that would compensate enough for the inner loneliness. She was attracted to a man who had the same narcissistic personality structure as her mother, and the compulsive need to repeat a trauma in life had now taken place three times, so she knew she had to change something in her self.

Compared to the story of Inanna, my client was confronted with shame involuntarily in her relationships to men. She fell in love with men who convinced her that she could get the love that she never had from her mother. So when he separated from her, making her an object to humiliation, the rejection activated the shame complex related to her mother and made her mistrust her own feelings.

In a way she had two sets of judges, one from the upper world and one from the underworld. And they confused her because they were both true from their own perspective of truth. If she should follow Inanna, she would need to let go of the upper judges and confront the shame related to her mother and the inner child, but was it too fast for her? Did she need more time to let go of the accomplishments that she had fought so hard to get in order to move away from shame in the first place? In her painting my client depicted her inner child reaching out for love, and when I asked her how she felt about the child, she said that she did not like the child's neediness. This is to me a sign that her inner child–mother relationship needs to be more loving before she confronts the complex of shame directly. She will need to find that inner positive mother who can support the shamed child as otherwise her own ego consciousness will become one of the inner shaming judges, leaving her without a Ninshubur as witness of the further process.

When Inanna is dead and Ninshubur seeks help, Inanna's parents refuse to help. It is her own fault, they say, because she chose to disobey them. Therefore they became part of the upper judges blaming her for her death/depression.

This image is still alive in our time, when we view depression as a failure to achieve outer expectations. We say it is the individual's own fault, and that they should 'pull themselves together' using their conscious will to become more active in life. We shame the depressed individual for not being able to stay in the upper reality as expected by treating depression as a weakness in the individual, just as Inanna's parents did to her. Using the language of the myth, we need to seek help to get out of depression from other sources than our inner parental voices, and Ninshubur finally gets help from Enki, who is Inanna's grandfather.

He takes some dirt from under his fingernails and creates two small asexual helpers. They are so small that they can enter the underworld and reach Ereshkigal unseen.

Ereshkigal is in 'birth pain' while Inanna is dying, and the two helpers, sent by Enki, are non-judgemental mirrors of Ereshkigal's pain. They repeat her pain as if it was their own and so they suffer *with* her, using a mirroring attitude. They don't try to analyze or change Ereshkigal's pain to make her feel better, but endure the process with active communication, letting her know that they see and hear her.

These helpers in the story show us what we need when confronted with the affect of shame. As therapists we have to let go of our ambition to help our client using our therapeutic methods. Nothing will work anyway, as long as the painful experience of shame is killing ego consciousness. No cognitive tricks or compensative painting exercises can re-orient consciousness to a more joyful place. We have to be present, professional, mirroring, neutral and non-directive during the death of Inanna and Ereshkigal's birth-pain. In creative expression this is when the body is a director of the painting process, expressing whatever needs to be expressed, and the artwork becomes the mirror of the affects.

One student working with her shame painted the image shown in Plate 6 (see plates between pages 112 and 113). Her comments on the image were the following.

> It is a naked Indian woman and instead of a head, there is an opening to a volcano combined with a green snake. Water and smoke is coming out from the body. The tongue of the snake is touching a girl, standing by the right hand of the woman. The girl is about seven years old. She is the shamed girl in me.

She came to understand that she could not solve her shame using her thinking and self-reflection, and that the instincts needed to take over.

Readiness for this process of 'killing' consciousness can be found in the attitude to the symbols and her trust in the spiritual and guiding principle/self, which she felt from the figures in the painting. The snake was friendly, the girl felt safe and the red (Indian) woman was powerful and birth giving. This image can be associated with Ereshkigal, who is expressing the affects of shame when consciousness reaches her in the dark and primitive realm.

I think this phase in the transformative cycle is the most difficult part of the journey for the individual who wants to *do* something to make a change. The depressed individual is not able to do anything since the inner masculine – animus – is dead. Gugalanna is dead and Dumutzi is also 'dead', so there are no active masculine partners close to either Inanna or Ereshkigal, except Enki. Enki understands because he was once in the underworld himself. "Enki is the generative, creative, playful, empathetic male . . . he includes the opposites . . . he is the culture bringer, not the preserver of the status quo. His wisdom is that of improvisation and empathy . . . and having a bisexual breath . . . he can penetrate into any necessity. . . . He is also the creative sculptor god . . . of the original form, archetype . . . endlessly he improvises to create what the moment needs" (Perera, 1981, pp. 67–68). Enki is not a patriarch but has a 'bi-sexual' character, which means that his balance between the feminine and the masculine makes him flexible to penetrate both the physical and the psychic reality. He can see what is needed for change and acts without consideration to collective morals, so he is not part of the upper group of shaming judges. He is a true original creator and does not follow the path of tradition but the path of the moment. The two passionate figures created by Enki from the dirt under his fingernails are sexless, and again it seems important not to identify with either the feminine or the masculine principle when we confront shame directly, because that will only maintain the split between the upper masculine world and the feminine underworld.

Enki's ability to hold an opposition without projecting one or the other is a function in the psyche which Jung has described in relation to the transcendent function. The transcendent function is activated when a polarity in the psyche can be held long enough to create a third solution to a problem, and this is exactly what Enki is doing here. He creates a magical and original solution to bring Inanna back to life by using the dirt that has no material value. And he can do that because he is able to hold the inner tension long enough to discover what needs to be done.

And what does that mean in the therapy session? When Enki, as the active principle, is projected to the therapist, the therapist must act independent of tradition and therapeutic training, trusting the inner original self. The solution therefore depends on the therapist's own ego-self axis and the original creativity that 'fits the moment'. This special moment is the time of not doing anything but instead *being* with the client in pain.

When we see Enki as an *inner* spiritual centre we know that this pain cannot be compensated for by something that brings attention away from the actual moment of pain. Freud's sublimation theory must be avoided while we stay within the whole body–mind experience of shame.

When the two small professional helpers mirror Ereshkigal's pain, she too becomes more empathic and wants to give something in return. The two helpers insist that they want to take Inanna's dead body with them back to the upper world, and Ereshkigal finally gives in. Ereshkigal has changed. She has become kinder and less cold and angry, as a consequence of being seen.

The self-caring system is restored as a new body–head integration based on a right- to right-brain communication between the shamed part (Ereshkigal) and the good mother (the professional helpers).

The helpers give Inanna water of life and she returns to consciousness as they hurry back to the upper world.

Using images as voices from the self

In an art therapy process, the Inanna–Ereshkigal polarity is symbolized as a death–rebirth theme, often with affective intensity during the expressive process. This is when imagination is experienced as a bodily felt presence creating a new integrative consciousness of wholeness. The following example illustrates this.

One participant in a shame workshop who had felt shame 'her whole life' visualized her inner Ereshkigal in a painting (Plate 7; see plates between pages 112 and 113). Being a victim of shame, she did not know much about the power behind, except when she was expressing her self through a creative medium. Early in her art therapy training, she discovered her ability to let go of control when she was painting, as a contrast to her life. In life she felt she was a victim and that she did not live her full potential in her job as a teacher. About the image, she explained that Ereshkigal's rage, shit and power would be right in front of her when she stepped into the empty feet painted on the floor of the image (inside the green). She was able to breathe some of that power into her body as a replacement for shame and that felt good. She felt she could step out of the image when she wanted to and in this way she could keep some control.

The image and the affect have become one, and the creative process holds that integration, being both physical and psychic by nature. Using the image as a projection of the rejected feminine does not always show as symbols; as in this painting, it is merely rhythms. During the integrative phase the energy is often more raw and instinctive, and it comes out with physical power indicating its bodily nature. Of course an individual needs to be prepared for such expression in order to trust the process at this crucial moment of tolerating the emotional tension in body and mind. Allowing the raw energy to become visible in the upper world (the art studio) is another way to understand the symbol of Ereshkigal giving birth. The instinct is no longer fused with the underworld reality where no one can see it, and the separation between Inanna and Ereshkigal is healed through the visualization.

I think there are two ways to understand the importance of the creative process during the death–rebirth phase. One is the experience of wholeness as the image and the affect come together. The other is the experience of Enki as the archetype of that part within one's self which is capable of creating this integration. The self-confidence in knowing that original creativity is part of our own psyche replaces the shamed self with a more modest attitude to the greatness of self. This experience can communicate to the ego that the body can be trusted after all, and by listening, waiting and mirroring, new integration *can* happen.

Perera (1981) refers this integration to an "inner-outer" fusion that takes place in the transference-countertransference field where the therapist represents the two empathic helpers sent by Enki. She refers to Enki as "the God of therapists" (p. 73). She describes the transformative integration as a result of the therapist's empathic identification with the client's pain, as in the early relationship between mother and child. This has also been described by Schwartz-Salent (2007) as the "fusional complex" operating in therapy as an archetypal identity between client and therapist, which makes it possible to understand the pain of another from the therapist's own inner somatic experience. Schwartz-Salent's point is that we need to dis-identify with the client again in order to avoid a counter-transference reaction leaving the client with no possibility to heal from within.

I think this is an important discussion related to integration of the feminine polarity.

First of all we have to question whether integrative processes can take place when part of the energy needed for that development is projected onto someone outside. Is it possible to heal the feminine Inanna–Ereshkigal polarity when Enki, the archetype of wisdom, is projected and experienced as a quality that is attached to the therapist? In the beginning of therapy clients expect the therapist to be wiser than the client, able to support a personal development because he or she is an (Enki) authority in the field. (Otherwise they would not come to therapy in the first place.) But as clients, we also need to learn that we can take care of ourselves in all the decisions we make in our daily lives. That we can listen and mirror our own needs without seeking affirmation from a therapist whenever we hear Ereshkigal calling from below. The process of internalizing the attitude of Enki replaces the negative inner mother with a more empathic voice. I discussed this process earlier as a *preparation* to the healing of the feminine. We do need new role models who can see us through the eyes of Enki and teach us to care for the psychic reality as well as the physical in order to trust that the descent has some meaning after all. But the integration of an inner good mother is not the same as an integration of the Inanna–Ereshkigal polarity. First of all, the mother archetype has nothing to do with Inanna or with Ereshkigal. They are both archetypes of the feminine connected to the original self and not to the caregiving mother archetype.

Secondly we must remember how it all began with Inanna being rejected by Dumutzi, and this indicates that it is the inner polarity between the masculine and feminine that needs healing as well as the mother and child relationship. Inanna is hurt in her womanhood when she decides to visit Ereshkigal. She is not a child looking for a new mother/therapist. She organizes her own transformation by instructing Ninshubur, her inner grounded self, to rescue her when she has not returned within three days. If a therapist cannot *see* this independence in the client but acts as a mother would with a dependent child, a shame reaction in the client can very well be the result. I think Perera is talking about the *therapeutic* process and not the process of individuation, even though it can sometimes be difficult to differentiate. One of the signs of individuation is the independence of the client and the ability of self-knowing, which is often absent at the beginning of a therapeutic process. Remember Inanna's ability to define herself as a mature woman, just before Dumutzi said he wanted to be set free? She knew already who she was and she wanted to know more.

The benefit of including a creative process is that there is always some independence in creative expression. There is a time during the expressive process when the client is free to unfold without directive from the therapist and where the client must have access to some vitality in the body. Otherwise there is no movement when we approach the process from Inanna's perspective, because she is dead. From Ereshkigal's perspective the feminine is very much alive, expressing the pain of giving birth. The masculine and dynamic part of the psyche connected to the affects behind shame is now becoming conscious as a new understanding of a more whole self. I suggest this to be Enki operating inside the client as a guiding principle connected to the self. If Enki is still projected onto the therapist at this point, an inner basic trust will be missing within the client and the affect of shame for being wrong may replace the potential of original creativity.

As therapists we can hold many different roles for our clients. Sometimes we fuse and mirror as a good mother would do, and sometimes we give analytical or spiritual advice like Enki the father. Other times we act like Ninshubur, making sure that the client doesn't lose connection to outer reality. From a Jungian perspective, these roles are all professional parts of a therapeutic function that we us, when they are not integrated parts inside the client. The different roles we have as therapists make the therapeutic situations more complete, but might leave the client fragmented when maintained.

When the client becomes more independent and the individuation process begins to take over, we cannot use any of the parental roles with our clients, but must use our own self as a creative instrument. The challenge for the therapist is therefore to spot the signs of independence and challenge it with more stimulating 'surprises' in the therapy, based on the therapist's ability to act in the moment.

A shame scene

A client made the shame scene shown in Figure 3.2. In the painting she is about five years old in a situation where she is helping her grandmother to iron her grandfather's shirts. She feels very proud. Suddenly her grandfather comes

Figure 3.2 Shame scene

into the room and shames her for not doing it well enough. She lies down on the floor and cries, and they just let her lie there alone. The snake in the painting feels dangerously close, but the child in the image does not see it, so fear is not activated. When we later dramatized the image through movement and included the imaginative good mother in the scene, the child and the snake began to play, initiated by the trusting mother. The snake became a creative potential that would stimulate the positive affects of joy and interest, indicating a replacement of being overwhelmed with shame. Here the power of Kur, the underworld snake, shows a more playful potential initiated by the protection of the good mother. What is also interesting is that the scene from the client's personal life became more archetypal when it was painted. The big snake was added to the personal scene as if the shame experience could not be expressed in any other way than through the symbol of the snake. I think it also indicates the power that links to shame as an affect that goes beyond personal reference, and therefore symbolization is an important part of understanding the depth in shame experiences.

Chaos, rhythm and symbolism as expressive styles

In my therapy and teaching room, I have drums, big rolls of paper, paint, crayons, clay, a box with plastic animals and other things that can be used as transference objects.

As children, we all have experiences of chaos, rhythm and symbolism as we socialize and finally end our artistic development with a naturalistic orientation. These are expressive styles that we can use freely in therapeutic processes. Sometimes we can begin with chaos just to get started. Then we can look for rhythms in the chaos that we would like to explore further and the body can begin to repeat these movements until some kind of form appears in the rhythms and we move into the symbolic phase. Some prefer to stay in the abstract style, and only in the subsequent dialogue does the image make more meaning.

During a training course where healing of shame was the topic, one directive for painting was to use these first three types of expression that we know from children's drawing development; chaos, rhythm and symbolism. The student begins the artwork by using colour to express uncontrollable movements on the paper. Of course this is not easy, as we have learned to control our body with our conscious will, but small tricks can be used, like using the left hand (if you are right-handed), closing your eyes to increase body sensation or using fingers instead of brushes to gain more direct contact with the paper.

In the next rhythmic phase some of the movements from chaos are chosen and repeated on the paper until the rhythm is felt within the body.

The third phase is more imaginative, as you are looking for forms and images in the rhythm, trying to make them more visible in the painting.

One example is shown in Plate 8 (see plates between pages 112 and 113).

The image shows a couple of dancing skeletons in a fire. The woman associated the image to a freedom that she felt was missing in her childhood, yet she felt it during the forbidden bodily pleasure of painting. She started with chaos, moved into rhythm and finally discovered the two skeletons as symbols in the image. In her imaginative exploration of the image, she allowed the skeletons to speak: "We have no fear. We burn everything that keeps us hidden from life. We welcome desire, sexuality and the power of freedom. We are not responsible, we surrender and we are eternal". Associating to the voice of Ereshkigal, they speak directly to the ego in a voice of strength, passion and power. Using these three steps as a method of painting can allow for more unpredictable images to be revealed in the artwork.

Working with shame

I suggest that individuals start with a focus on shame patterns from present life situations. They can relate to a partner, a boss, a colleague, a son or daughter, parent or friend. Scenes from newer experiences of shame often activate the memory of earlier unnoticed shame, and the process can move in a regressive direction, attempting to integrate basic shame scenes from different domains in life. On an archetypal level, it can be the shame of being a woman exploring the history and rejections related to romantic relationships in life.

I remember a woman in a group who painted herself as a three-month-old baby with her physically abusive father. She did not actually remember the incident where he hit her in the kitchen, but had been told about it by family members. The next day she was ill with fever and unable to continue the course. The body sometimes has its own way to avoid meeting with affects that can destroy the vulnerable self. This woman had an extra sensitivity to all wireless networks and the whole system in the house had to be closed down while she was there. I don't think she was prepared enough to process shame, because her sadness–anger polarity was still unbalanced. She felt like a victim of the invisible, aggressive rays from the network that left her powerless and wounded. She taught me to be more aware of the preparation phase, as well as the choice of a first shame scene.

Sharing the shame scene with an other

When a shame scene is painted it is important that it is shared with someone else, a therapist or fellow student. The other person should not try to solve a problem or feel sorry for the individual, who may be sharing this experience for the first time, but rather just listen and contain the experience with an attitude of kindness. This attitude refers to the two small helpers who calm Ereshkigal in her birth pain.

One purpose of using an image in the sharing process is to avoid being looked at directly. Both people must focus on the image and not on the shamed individual. The individual who is sharing shame will take the initiative of looking at the other person when safety has been established during the investigation of the image. There is a 'shame-free' zone in this structure, where the individual is protected by the image during the sharing process.

The listener can ask questions of the image as an expression of empathy and interest and should hold personal projections back until later sharing.

Discovering the voice of the shaming other (negative introject)

When the sharing process has ended, the voice of the shaming other from the image should be located in one sentence, such as, "You are no good", "You don't deserve to be loved", "You are too stupid, fat, ugly", and so on.

The purpose of locating the shaming voice is to separate the voice from the ego, as they are often fused into one identity. The separation between ego consciousness and the inner judging voice is preparing the object-relational experience of shame as an experience involving a shaming other before the shaming other was internalized. One of the points made by Kaufmann (1996) is that we need to get the power back from the shaming other, which is only possible when the shaming other is recognized as an other person that we know.

Painting the positive mother into the painting

Relaxing music can be used to find an imaginary positive mother.

The personal mother should not be used as an image here because she usually also has negative aspects, having not been there to protect the self/child. It can be an archetype like the Virgin Mary, Demeter or a friend's mother, a neighbour and so forth.

The positive mother is invited into the shame scene and painted into the painting.

Sharing the 'new' shame scene with an Other

The image has now become more imaginative, because it includes a good mother. Again questions can be asked in order to explore and verbalize the image, and the good mother is given a voice: "I will never leave you", "You are lovable", "I am always here for you", and the like.

With this ritual the death phase has ended, because the good mother voice is reducing the shame by activating a compassionate self-attitude.

We now have two sentences: one from the negative shaming other and one from the imaginary good mother. The opposition between the good and the bad is a way to activate the transcendent function in the psyche, which Jung has described as a condition for change, but at this point they are only felt as an inner tension, and the original self has not yet been born.

It is important that the inner voice of the positive good mother is used repeatedly in coming shame scenes as a replacement of the judging voice.

Eventually it will become part of the new ego-self connection and a result of self-compassion.

Step 4. Return

Surprise

In a depression we feel stuck in life because we cannot find a solution to our problem using the rational way of thinking. We are stuck in a one-sided attitude, and the solution to this is to integrate some of Enki's water quality and freer way of thinking. When we allow Enki to influence us, we are able to find solutions that 'fit the moment' because it also includes the underworld perspective. This is experienced as sudden moments of enlightenment where we feel vitalized as we discover new, previously unknown aspects of the image. The positive affects of joy and interest are activated by the grace of untraditional thinking.

These moments show that the affect of surprise can function as a stimulation of creativity instead of being overwhelming traumatic experiences of shame coming from the outside.

The surprises we have from working with images come from the inside. They are projections that we make, not induced by anyone else unless a reductive method is used without considering the client's experience. I remember one client who was afraid that the dark man in the painting would jump out of the picture to catch her, and I had to clarify one important ground rule: that it was *she* who was in control of the image and not the other way around. That seemed to calm her down and we could continue exploring the image. Sometimes when defences are vulnerable, we can support the power of the ego in order to keep the dialogue moving. As a therapist I can intervene, as a good mother would do, when something becomes too powerful for the client.

The good mother makes sure that we are not re-traumatized, and therefore we need her inner voice as it came up during the death phase. The inner mother was not present for my client in the example above, so I had to step in and set some structure as a way to maintain a separation between the two realities.

When working with depressed individuals, we often find very little imagination and few surprises in working with the artwork, because the self-protective system blocks the entrance to the self. In the individuation process, the archetypal self is more available for the ego to explore, because the ego-self axis was restored during the integrative therapeutic process.

The challenge in the return phase is to bring that creativity to life in the external reality.

Moving from the art studio to the 'real' world is often a transition the client makes alone, based on the development of supportive new inner voices. The transition from death to return involves a change in attitude, returning to a more extroverted orientation. The point is that some connections to the inner world must continue, which is why Ereshkigal demands that someone needs to replace Inanna in the underworld.

When Inanna returns home she finds Dumutzi sitting on his throne, and even though he thought she was dead, he shows no emotional sign of being happy to see her again. Inanna sees him with cold underworld eyes and she chooses him as a replacement for her-self in the underworld. Dumutzi tries to escape, and asks Gilgamesh to help him transform into a snake in order not to be found, but finally he is caught.

Who is the new Inanna who returns from the underworld, and why does she choose Dumutzi to replace her?

First of all, Inanna comes back to a Dumutzi who "clings to his new role of kingship and refuses to acknowledge the ties of feeling and love that once bound him to his wife" (Kramer and Wolkstein, 1983, p. 162). Again Inanna experiences a rejection from Dumutzi, but this time she is more prepared. She sees his lack of love but does not get trapped in the complex of shame. She acts according to a more objective view and does what she needs to do in order to save her marriage – she sends him to Ereshkigal.

I find this to be a theme in present-day relationships, where the woman does not feel the love she needs from her partner and thinks, with her rational mind, that he just needs more time and maybe if she was more slim or feminine or understanding. . . . Eventually she comes to therapy with a shame of not being loved and with many scenes from life where she silently ignored the shame of being rejected. Some women feel a shame of being stronger than their partner but cannot find the strength to leave him, because how would he survive without her? Others stay with a partner they do not love for the sake of the children and end up lonely and shamed by not having used their potential in life. Finding and accepting the inner Ereshkigal can give women a different approach to this kind of relationship where they can make decisions of their own, without falling into the 'mother-trap'. They can decide what is 'the right thing to do' based on both the upper and lower judges and make a decision, which is not coloured by shame, of who they are and what they were told to deserve. Using the myth as a guide, this integrative attitude from the woman would send her partner to therapy, so he can learn to see life through the lens of shame.

Maybe men do not hear Ereshkigal calling from the underworld since they have identified with masculine values? Maybe women in general are closer to the realm of shame simply because of a long history of being shamed in culture as well as in personal relationships? And maybe we do have a responsibility, as women, to take this journey to the underworld so that the world can change into a more creative and balanced place for all of us? Maybe men are more vulnerable to guilt as an emotion related to wrongdoing when the realization of shaming the feminine becomes more conscious?

Dumutzi tries to escape his descent, and his starting point is therefore different than it was for Inanna, because she chose the descent by free will. Inanna did not reject Dumutzi and therefore he did not hear Ereshkigal call him. His conscious position was related more to shamelessness than to shame, because he had identified with his high position of being a king and forgotten about more human affairs such as love and relationships.

First he reacted with fear of confronting the underworld, and when he finally realized that he could not escape, "his heart was filled with tears" (ibid, p. 163). The affect of sadness is described as his first experience of the inner life and the feminine, and he then seeks his family home because "he has lost his strength and vitality and can no longer provide for them. Alone, without power, comfort, or direction, he turns inward and dreams" (ibid, p. 163). In order to understand the dream, Dumutzi goes to his sister Geshtinanna, who represents compassion and love. She is the one who tells him to hide, but he is finally caught and begins to prepare for the journey to the underworld. Out of love for her brother, Geshtinanna decides to take half of the time in the underworld and thereby releases Dumutzi to spend only six months away from Inanna. The other six months he is side by side with Inanna as king of Sumer.

Kramer says of Geshtinanna that "her offer is of such magnitude that the mind can scarcely grasp its meaning. The instinct to live, to survive, becomes secondary. Love transcends life" (ibid, p. 165). Compared to Inanna, who has passion and wilfulness, Geshtinanna has compassion and feeling. Inanna is touched by Geshtinanna's offer and her "words awaken her nurturing, compassionate side" (ibid, p. 166).

In this final part of the story another integration of the feminine archetype is completed, leading to a more compassionate approach to life. From wholeness in the feminine follows the rescue of Dumutzi, who can now be with Inanna for half of the year.

I find this to be another important outcome from healing shame. To include compassion in the many choices we make in life might lead to more compassion and equality between man and woman, especially because now they both know about shame.

The ability to show compassion is not a typical motherly quality but contains a feminine aspect as well. The mother in archetypal form will always think of others before she cares for her own needs. Often a mother does not know what these needs are in her self until her children have left home and she experiences the inner empty space. Geshtinanna does sacrifice her own life for half the year but not for the whole year. She keeps half of her life dedicated to her own self and so she avoids the trap of sacrificing her inner wholeness.

I recognize the theme in many of my students' lives. When they become familiar with painting they want to paint when the need comes between their training courses. They want to have a place to paint in their home, but all the rooms are filled with family activities, so there is no private space where they can do their artwork. For many it takes a long time before they insist on having such a space. Rather, they sacrifice their own needs for the needs of the husband and family in order to avoid being 'selfish' in wanting something for themselves. Many of these women think that they need permission from their partner in order to follow their own needs, like a child who has been shamed for being creative and joyful now waits for permission to play again. Geshtinanna is a good role model to mothers. She shows us that we can be both loving and compassionate as well as self-supportive and independent. We do not have to make a choice, and so the image of the self-sacrificing mother is also transformed through the healing of shame.

Working with surprise

Expressing the affects behind shame

Based on the dialogue between the child/shamed part and the good mother, the frozen affects in the child become alive as emotions that were not expressed before. With the acceptance from the good mother and a self-caring attitude, this is the process of release. It moves from the inside to the outside, the reverse of the shame response that takes us to the dark underworld. It is a process of rebirth, as this energy can be felt as a new and vulnerable expression that can become part of future living. It may start with aggression related to the shaming other, but as the creative flow continues, it usually becomes a process of satisfaction and surprise as the artwork becomes filled with power, expressing new inner life. The point is to direct the aggression towards the shaming *other* instead of towards the self, and therefore the relationship must be held in consciousness to avoid the shame spiral of going inward.

This was also what Inanna did when she returned and saw Dumutzi sitting on his throne. She saw who *he* was in his shameless behaviour and was able to avoid dissociation and the spiral of shame.

In the creative process, as in life, the challenge is to prevent the shaming other from taking control. If the judging voice appears in the art-making process, it should not be avoided but re-directed.

This is the time to recognize the shaming voice that was found during the death phase as a sentence and to train the awareness before it takes control of the creative process. The voice of the positive imaginary mother, also found in the death phase, should be remembered and held within during the continuation of the art-making process.

I often suggest that the voice of the shaming other is expressed in a different painting, maybe in another room, or written down in a book. The important thing is that the shaming voice does not interfere directly in the art-making process, and the only way to avoid that is to be mindful when the voice enters the field of consciousness.

One student who found her inner child isolated behind bars in her painting helped the child find the courage to express her emotions by keeping away the negative judges from her painting process. It turned out that this child had a special gift for working with colours, and to her surprise she made the most beautiful painting. The discovery of beauty in what was thought to be an ugly emotion of shame is in itself a transformative experience and supports the further connection with the positive affects of joy and interest.

When the painting is finished, the dialogue should first of all be imaginative and not personal, exploring the potential new aspect of the self. I think it is important not to reduce the image to something familiar until the moment when it just happens. When the individual suddenly associates the symbol to something known, the dialogue becomes more personal and connected to present life issues. These are different moments of surprise that can happen during the therapeutic dialogue. One is more imaginative and related to the archetypal self, while other surprises are experienced when the symbol connects to personal life issues.

It feels as if the archetypal image gradually comes closer to ego consciousness as the dialogue continues, and it finally reaches a moment of recognition. These moments are integrative and transformative, because the consciousness that we know of suddenly expands beyond its own limit and becomes more than it was before.

When the art-making process becomes joyful and interesting, the shaming voice is no longer directed towards the self. Consciousness related to the *expressive* process is based on the positive affect of joy related to the feminine, while the *verbal* exploration of the artwork stimulates the affect of interest, related to the masculine. Bringing these two processes into balance is a challenge to the art therapy profession.

Summary

Here it is important to experience the power in the body as a creative energy that one becomes familiar with through the art-making process by repeating the procedure. The affect of surprise can be explored in expressions where we risk destroying a 'nice' painting by following an impulse we experience in the body. We let go of control expecting a disaster, but might instead create an artwork. The same may be true in relationships, where we hold something back because we don't want to destroy the relationship, when in reality it can make the relationship grow and deepen.

The function of the underworld judges is a result of the feeling function that evaluates experiences. When our feeling function is healed, we do not need to hide from the other as a result of being wounded, because we understand the wound in the other as well. We may decide to leave the situation, say stop or respond in ways where shame does not control behaviour. The underworld judges are on our side. They do not take outside expectations into consideration when they make their judgement but refer only to the self. The ego becomes stronger and more stable when listening to the underworld judges because it also indicates that the ego-self axis has been re-connected.

Step 5. New world order

Joy–interest

Healing shame is more than healing the wounded feminine. It includes the masculine part as well in order to develop a more creative orientation in life based on the affects of joy *and* interest. Compassion seems to be the key to do this, and as Kramer points out, Geshtinanna's sacrifice to her brother is almost incomprehensible to the rational mind (Kramer and Wolkstein, 1983). What is the rationale in choosing death? Our affective system is stimulated to keep us alive, and here we are dealing with a love instinct more important than physical survival. Can humanity survive without compassion? Have we forgotten the one thing that we do not 'need' but cannot live without? And is this the true potential in working with shame? It certainly is the last thing we hear of in the story and also the main theme in most shame healing programs.

When Inanna comes back from the underworld she sends Dumutzi as her replacement. But what does that mean on a psychological level? Is that a sign of compassion? I think not. It seems to be an act of feeling more than an act of compassion. But when we look at the consequence, it makes more sense. The compassionate attitude is activated in Geshtinanna's generous offer to her brother *after* Inanna's decision. This is one of the magical things about mythology. We cannot split up a story into its details and deduce a solution from one image in the story. They all play a part in the plot, and when one part is taken out of the whole story, something will be missing in the end. So healing of the feeling function comes before the activation of the compassionate attitude.

Inanna sees that her husband shows no sign of joy when he sees *her*. Instead of choosing the easy way, which would be getting a quick divorce, she saw his shameless behaviour, lack of compassion and love, and she decided to work on the relationship. Though it seems as if she sends him to death, the consequence of her action is that she wins him back. When women see their husbands in this manner, they sometimes close their eyes and wait for them to change, or they learn to live with their shame of not being loved, developing depression, addictions or other reactive patterns. But Inanna has changed. She is no longer the naive woman who sees what she wants to see. Her vision has expanded and now includes the psychic reality as an objective reality to trust, and she acts upon it.

This is the feeling function that works as a true evaluator of relationships without getting emotionally involved. Her love and hurt in relation to Dumutzi did not disturb her ability to see *him* and to act accordingly. To understand Inanna's consciousness at this point in the myth is important, because her action is based not on her personal complex but on her evaluation of something missing.

The new consciousness of self that develops from processing shame has many parts, and I think one part leads to another, so they all seem connected.

First we have the integration of the Ereshkigal–Inanna polarity. This new consciousness is related to the acceptance of the dark goddess and the qualities in the feminine that we have rejected as a collective. Freeing the emotional reaction to rejection that is held in the body means a willingness to let go of the relationship in order to act in new, self-supportive ways. It means a development of a new potential in the feminine archetype, based on an acceptance of the wounded feminine Lilith/Ereshkigal and the innocent Inanna. Through this integration, we may find that not only our own self-understanding will change, but so will the relationship we have to others.

Inanna's descent gives us an idea and a method for this integration as she prepares to confront and change through her meeting with Ereshkigal. Allowing the feminine wholeness to become part of life without giving in to the collective attitude to the feminine needs strength and first of all an acceptance from within. I think the integration of the Inanna–Ereshkigal polarity relates to this *inner* wholeness in the feminine before any action is carried out in life. The conscious attitude to life is still introverted by nature after this integration and the transition towards the outer life is vulnerable.

One couple came to therapy because the woman felt that her partner abandoned her when she needed him most. He said that he was there for her but he could not guess her needs, and if she could express those verbally, it would help. The problem was that she could not *ask* him to choose her. She needed him to choose her from his own heart. In one situation he left her in a vulnerable position where he knew an aggressive neighbour would attack her at a meeting. He chose not to be there beside her and wounded the relational bond between them. He chose his own well-being and left her alone and she was devastated inside and 'just wanted to die'. These are the many silent moments when Dumutzi's coldness sneaks into a relationship. Inanna confronts him, directly mirroring his coldness, and when he finally understands that he made the wrong choice, his 'heart began to cry'. This also came true for this couple. When he understood her angry accusations of having left her by choosing his own escape, he was confronted with the objective truth and reacted instinctively by leaving the room. 'I cannot take it anymore', he said. When he returned one minute later, he was ready to hear her out, and from that moment he chose to listen to the inner voice of 'we' instead of his usual voice of 'me'. I think he became aware of the risk of losing her and that she was only expressing her reaction to his action.

In another relationship it was the man who was living the 'we' and the woman was the princess. She gradually came to feel strangled in the relationship, because she felt that his happiness depended on her. He had almost lost his connection with his own needs and put the relationship before anything else. He felt guilty when he spent an evening with old colleagues or when he went bicycling by himself, as if he had betrayed her. So the challenge for him was to address his guilt of thinking about his own needs before thinking about the relationship. The story was that in their early marriage, when their two children were small, he was in the army for eight years working abroad. He did not ask her if she wanted to raise their children alone and live with a ghost husband all those years he was gone. She silently accepted this lifestyle and she became independent and strong from raising their children on her own. Now retired, he is compensating for those years of choosing 'me' instead of 'we'. When she one day told him that she was going on a holiday with a good friend, he became upset because she did not invite him first. She said, "But you never asked me when you went traveling". Her long-forgotten feelings of being rejected still underlie her independence and she compensates by pushing him away now that he tries to be there for her. Of course he cannot change the past, but recognizing the wounded feminine by giving her a voice, both inside himself and from his partner, might be a first step towards letting go of personal guilt of having chosen outer expectations instead of the relationship to his family at the time.

In shame courses, I see the strength appearing in women as a newfound sensuality and joy explored through the expressive process. I have also seen how this process repeats itself when women come back after two to three months feeling that nothing has really changed in their lives. Why is that? How can they let go of this power that felt so good and return to the old collective expectations, where the voice of the feminine goes back to the invisible underworld? Integrating the shadow is obviously not enough to change outer reality.

Another new consciousness comes from the interaction between Inanna and Geshtinanna. Two strong characters in the feminine that combine feeling with compassion.

Geshtinanna does not claim anything in return for her sacrifice. As Dumutzi's sister, she relates to his anima, who is helping him to spend only half of the year in the underworld, averting a lifelong depression. Geshtinanna's action not only helps Dumutzi and influences Inanna, but most importantly heals the relationship between them so they can be together for half of the year as equals. Geshtinanna therefore connects to the consciousness of 'we', because she is activated by love itself.

Related to creativity, the balance between being in control and surrendering to the body is part of the original self-creative process that makes life joyful and interesting. This is one of the benefits of including creative media in psychological transformation. In expressive processes we constantly control and let go of control as the image takes form. We follow the affects as impulses to change direction, colour and form in the flow of creativity, and the masculine and the feminine principle here operate as equal partners.

Perera suggests Geshtinanna to be a result of Inanna's descent (1981): "she conveys the possibility of an incarnated capacity to serve both the goddess and human life" (p. 92). In Jungian language she represents the connecting link between the ego and the self, a loving principle born out of transforming shame. Geshtinanna is therefore the third solution to the polarity between Inanna and Ereshkigal and a result of the transformative function in the psyche that was activated by the meeting between the white goddess and the dark goddess. She is the unpredictable outcome to the healing of shame.

Healing of the masculine and feminine polarity is the deeper consequence of Inanna's descent, and I think this needs to be part of the overall understanding of the myth. If we see the myth only as a healing of the feminine, we may miss the deeper understanding of Inanna's transformation. She transforms her own self-image during her descent, and is ready to confront her partner because she has the strength to stay present in the moment instead of hiding. She is not afraid to appear cold, angry and fearless in her integrated feminine power. When Inanna later realizes that she has lost her loved one, she is mourning her loss together with Geshtinanna, who has lost her brother. The affect of sadness is activated in both women on a personal level as a result of having lost the masculine vitality to the underworld. In psychological terms, it is the longing for human love that sets the last scene in action.

Inanna's decision to send Dumutzi down was not emotional. She did what was needed according to human balance and without considering her personal loss in that moment.

Women of today who return to daily life after their descent to Ereshkigal may find some satisfaction in being stronger and more independent than before in their relationships. They no longer need a man to fulfil their needs because they are self-supportive, and maybe this is enough for a while. This is what we might call a 'me' integration and a healing of the lost connection with the dark feminine. Our attention is related to our own needs first of all.

In the healing of collective shame, our attention includes the other and the need to nourish the relationship as a gesture of love. There is a great difference in awareness here that affects the balance of the collective. In the myth this awareness comes after Inanna has sent Dumutzi down and she feels her loss on a human and personal level. I see this reaction in Inanna (and Geshtinanna) as an illustration of future development of the feminine. At some point, when we as women have regained our own balance enough to be able to feel the longing for equal comradeship with a partner, the need to let go of the 'me' orientation half of the time will create a more collective consciousness in behavioural patterns based on compassion and love.

I think the fear that arises in many strong women today is connected to the risk of losing everything with no return possible.

A new paradigm is shown to us in Inanna's descent and return as an archetypal image of reconnecting to that original creativity where woman and man are equal.

I suggest we can do this by focusing on two things. First of all we need to repeat the creative cycle of healing shame scenes as a way to increase the connection to the self. New pathways created in the brain need to be used repeatedly in order not to be forgotten, just as a pathway in a forest will fade away and become part of the forest when the path is not used. Secondly we need to be present in those moments when the old judge tries to take control in situations where we are confronted with a shaming other. Our ability to be momentarily present depends on how much unconscious shame we have hidden in the shadow part of the psyche, since shame makes us disappear from these moments when not recognized. The transition between the invisible and introverted personality living with an unconscious shame to a more creative and extroverted self-expression happens gradually the more we come to understand and tolerate our shame sensitivity.

Working with joy–interest

Activating the affects of joy and interest in art-making processes stimulates the ability to use imagination as an equal partner to rational thinking. When these are separated from each other, original creativity has lost its humanity, indicated by the split between Eros and Logos, art and science, affect and image.

The issue here is how we as individuals can use the art-making process as a method to develop and strengthen this new world order within. How can we trust that a shame experience can lead us to joy and interest for long enough to stay in the moment and act within the relationship?

The most difficult thing for many individuals is to use imagination as a language for the psychic reality. It is even more difficult to write about it because we read the words with our rational brains. Using imaginative methods alone can also be challenging and may need some training ahead of time.

The interaction between the inner woman (joy) and man (interest) is responsible for the birth of new parts of the self and therefore holds the key to the individuation process. Therefore, the ego should not affect any of them with the learned personal value system. The function of the ego needs to be neutral, like a Ninshubur function, in order to facilitate the processes that can change the relationship between the inner woman and man. This is the reason why a teaching program is useful together with practical work on shame scenes. It is a re-learning process for the ego that helps part of consciousness to remain neutral during confrontation with shame scenes.

While part of the masculine-feminine polarity is related to our experiences of mother and father, there are other aspects of the feminine and masculine archetypes that have never been activated and known to us personally because they were not stimulated in our lives. They could have been so, under different circumstances, but they were not. Therefore we do not know of any other way to engage in life than through the patterns we internalized earlier, unless we consciously confront these patterns later. Changing the inner dynamics between the masculine and feminine is more than learning to accept what is already there based on our upbringing and personal development. I suggest that this is when association stops, and imagination begins when we work with images. Association leads us to past experiences, while imagination creates something new and original.

The last step

The last step in transforming shame emphasizes the development of all four psychological functions described in Jung's typology. Stewart (1996) suggests that each of the four negative affects refers to one of the four psychological ego functions and says that a) sensation is related to sadness, b) feeling is related to shame, c) thinking is related to aggression and d) fear is related to intuition. When we change our relationship to the affects, we therefore also stimulate the way we understand reality.

Working with shame has been discussed throughout this book as a healing of the feeling function, leading to more empathy and compassion. When we also want to use sensation, thinking and intuition as psychological approaches to life, we no longer focus on shame and the feeling function alone, but look for ways to integrate feeling with the other ego functions in order to create wholeness in consciousness.

One of the ways to activate the psychological functions is by seeing each of them as a polarity containing a feminine and a masculine part. Stewart (1996) does not connect a feminine-masculine polarity to the crisis affects, but I suggest that the crisis affects refer to states of imbalance in the inner masculine and feminine relationship. The inner man and woman are just not on speaking terms and do not work together in order to allow the specific psychological function to serve consciousness.

The purpose of the creative process suggested here is to use active imagination as a dialogue between the man and woman, giving them a space where they can develop and change. The function of ego consciousness is to be a witness to this process and a secretary who writes down the imaginative dialogues between them.

Suggestion for an active imaginative ritual

1   As a starting point, two clay figures are created. One represents the feminine and one represents the masculine as two different sides that you know of. Place the two clay figures in relation to each other as you feel they connect in the moment. Do they look at each other? Know about each other? Like each other? What is the story between them? Imagine that they come to you for therapy and you must try to avoid alliances with either of them, staying neutral, friendly and interested in their relationship. You may recognize parallels to personal life issues as you get to know them. They may remind you of your mother and father, ex-husband or ex-wife, but just make a note of these personal associations and continue their imaginative dialogue. Your focus should stay on the figures and not on personal experiences.

2   Let them speak to you and invite them to respond to each other in words that you write down. This is an active imaginative dialogue. Allow them to move

as the dialogue continues, so you update the figures and how they physically relate to each other. Also be aware not to get trapped in a fantasy of compensation and what *you* would like to happen. Fantasy is often more related to the ego than it is to the self, and it functions as an activity of escape and dissociation more than a true original act of creation. You may have to question the neutrality of the ego before moving on, and often the alliance with the woman or the man goes back to childhood experiences of being more attached to your father or mother.

3 Repeat the ritual as you have the time. It can be once a week or once a month. Each time you may need to change the figures as they transform during the dialogue. A plastic cover can keep the clay wet and workable for a longer period. If you do not have clay, you can choose one object in the room as representative of the woman and one as the man.

When individuals create the inner couple for the first time in clay, they are usually and surprisingly able to recognize their mother and father in the two figures, though the instruction was to create their experiences of their *own* masculine and feminine sides. In the development of ego identity we internalize not only mother and father as inner voices in our mental structure but also the way they communicate and relate to each other. The dynamic between them becomes a role model for the dynamics in ourselves as we creatively engage with the outer and inner reality. Unless we make a conscious contact to the inner couple, this pattern will function as an instinctive and automatic pattern in the psyche below the threshold of consciousness.

Some women entering therapy today are unhappy in their marriage and unable to take the step to leave. They may have felt rejected by their partner for years, and when they finally come to therapy, they blame themselves for not being the perfect wife, mother and lover to their husband. Or they stay for the sake of the children, hiding their aggression towards their partner. They reach a limit that either sends them to therapy or into depression. Fear of being alone after many years of living with someone else, or the idealized thought that their partner will eventually become more loving, can postpone important decisions and a better life. The rejections are not taken seriously enough to be acted upon, and shame for having failed in marriage together with economic bonds often prevent consciousness from facing the issue. As one client asked, "Can it really be true that I am afraid of my own power?"

How does a man experience a crisis in a relationship? He may want out of the marriage because his mother appeared in the woman he fell in love with. His experience of 'a woman', based on his mother as a role model, may not have changed, and unconsciously he expects his woman to become like his mother, as the woman expects her man to become like her father. Relationships are based on countertransference reactions and mistaken for love. Taking back these projections from each other may indeed lead to separation, as we do not really know whom we married in the first place. On the other hand it can also lead to deeper connection and true love.

In creative expression, we need to connect with a masculine Gilgamesh archetype who has the bravery to express without fear. He just acts. In depression we see the opposite – no or little courage to express and very often the imaginative and symbolic function is more or less passive. The depressed individual might experience an inner richness of ideas and thoughts but has no fool to carry them out in the physical reality. The fool is the unconscious hero, a masculine archetype who acts from intuition more than from rational understanding. Sometimes, when we think for too long, the moment passes, and the timing gets wrong. Like Gilgamesh, we need to trust that spiritual feminine voice of Inanna without questions and rational argumentations in order to bring the inside and the outside together in the right moment.

Individuals who have been involved with the inner world for a longer time often develop a spiritual identity that becomes stronger and stronger as they come to know more and more parts of the self. If they leave the masculine part, Gilgamesh, behind in such a development, they may end up feeling isolated and not understood by others in their inner greatness, and therefore keep the self inside as a self-protective pattern.

In art therapy the expressive process is a fool's activity, and as such it makes sure that the inner world is exposed to the outer world without permission from ego consciousness. The vulnerability of being misunderstood and reduced to someone smaller is the risk in any visibility of the self.

Healing of the feeling function

Healing of the archetypal feminine means that the psychic reality becomes as valuable and present as the physical reality. With this balance in mind, we can confront the shaming other, avoiding the compensatory reaction that belongs to the spiral of shame. Hillman says, "The feeling function is that psychological process in us that evaluates. . . . [A] prerequisite for feeling is therefore a structure of feeling memory, a set of values, to which the event can be related" (1971, p. 90). These sets of values that we bring into a relationship affect our feeling function, as we see reality through the lenses of these experiences. Healing of the feeling function therefore means that these fundamental values need to be addressed, reflected upon and maybe changed with a new set of values that are more objective and less biased.

One of the main characteristics of the psychic reality is its objective character as a reality we cannot actually see, but only perceive through the feeling function. In general we tend to identify feeling with emotion as if they were the same, and therefore we do not really know about the true function of feeling. In personal therapy we work with emotional ties to our life experiences, attempting to decrease their influence on our lives. We could also say that we try to regain access to feeling, because the objectivity of experience has been reduced to be only subjective and emotional. Someone with more power or rank convinced us that what we were feeling was not true on an objective scale but merely a fault of perception within our own self. This is basically how shame is communicated, leading to mistrust in what we experience as true.

Even when an experience or behaviour seems completely out of present context, there still is a rational explanation hidden in the psychological invisible reality. This is why the feeling function is defined as rational as well as the function of thinking; we just need to include the invisible reality in order to understand it.

When we work with an image in art therapy, we can explore the image through the feeling function. We may experience that a symbol has certain characteristics which are not defined in the actual visual representation but merely defined by the client's imagination. A tree can for example suddenly speak to the client, or a crystal become identical with a new value in the self. An animal can appear as a guide, or a child may appear with special gifts. Imaginative explorations have a life of their own when we step into that feeling reality. Such experiences can affect us in emotional ways when we bring our personal associations into play. We may discover the sadness of having left the child alone for so long, or anger can come up when we think about earlier experiences when we were hurt in relationships. But the evaluation of the symbol as a felt reality of truth is not in itself emotional. The imaginative child is a felt reality while the attachment to the child can be emotional.

I think this is the difference between the use of the feeling function and emotional reactions to what is actually felt to be true.

The last part of Inanna's story is that a new ritual is suggested, which also led to the new paradigm, namely that both Dumutzi and Geshtinanna are introverted (in the underworld) as well as extroverted (back on Earth) and thereby combine the two attitudes to life in a new balance.

Women have a choice when they feel rejected and shamed by their partner or by the patriarchal influence in our culture. They can do as Inanna did and use the rejection as a motivation to heal their inner feminine wound and, as a result of that, their relationships.

Our collective system does not consider the importance of a 'we' culture. It has become either our own needs or the needs of others. There is no time for family needs to be satisfied, or for a couple to nourish their relationship, because the working life takes all the vital moments, and the family has become a place to recover instead of a place of creation. As a collective we accept this imbalance because we are caught in the economic cycle of life and death, unable to confront the system with rational arguments for change.

Abt (2005) has used Jung's typology as four different approaches to the image, making the analytical process more whole and less reductive. I also find his method useful as a creative approach to life based on the four different paradigms of life experiences.

In our time, when thinking is more valuable than feeling, we may think we can 'figure out' how to fix problems, but in my understanding this only creates a deeper wound in the feeling function, which again is not trusted in its potential. The myth of Inanna becomes a story of healing shame as well as healing the feeling function. We cannot replace one deep wound in the soul with a fantasy of its solution as a true healing agent. We need to fully understand the consequences of a collective rejection of our most vulnerable part in being human, the self. And also to find ways to relate to the greatness of the self, using shame as a pathway to humbleness and kindness in order to avoid inflation and compensative behavioural patterns.

When Inanna comes back from the underworld as a heroine and sends Dumutzi down, she forces him to become a hero against his conscious wish. He too must journey to the underworld as a counterbalance to his shameless behaviour so their feeling relationship can be based on empathy instead of shame.

One client was taught that everything *she* did in life would affect her parents' lives and social reputation. First she would feel proud of her own creation and independence, but shortly after, all the inner judges would shame her for harming her parents, sometimes for several days. As we discussed her situation we talked about the 'underworld judges' as a different judgemental perspective to her creative activity in life. They see things from the perspective of the self and the psychic reality, while her parental judges have a perspective based on outer collective values. When Inanna is confronted with the underworld judges, they sentence her to death because her life until then had been based on outer morals without considering the inner reality. She was guilty of having rejected her own self, and that identity was killed. My client thought there was only one kind of judges, namely those she had known for her whole life, starting in childhood. With a clearer understanding of the underworld judges, she felt she was able to support her independent behaviour with more acceptance. In one dream she visited her parents together with a man they did not approve of, indicating a beginning of separation from their values.

The special meaning of a conscious feeling function, where both the masculine and the feminine interact, is that we 'know of' the consequence of our action in relation to another. In the story of Amor and Psyche, we find this moment of inner union when Psyche does the forbidden thing and opens the beauty box when she comes back from the underworld. That surrender to the instinct of beauty activates the archetype of love itself, represented by Amor, and they are soon united at Olympus. Amor had been isolated in a room in his mother's house, but now 'suddenly' and immediately after Psyche's surrender, he was free from his mother complex and acted with responsibility and love. The point is that Psyche opened the beauty box knowing that her relationship with Amor would be healed from her action. From a rational point of view she seemed to regress in that moment of surrender, because she chose death, passivity and depression. In reality she surrendered to the *relationship* and made a conscious ego-cide. In the story of Inanna, this is the role of Geshtinanna. She also chose death as an irrational act of love for her brother. It is only rational through the function of feeling and when it happens at the right moment, not before and not too late, but in that very moment when the sacrifice touches the other's soul and makes the relationship stronger. When a woman surrenders to the unconscious as an act of love for her partner, she must choose her man carefully and from her heart. If there is no love between them, or if her surrender is a trick to make him feel strong and her weak, her sacrifice will go un-noticed and she will stay invisible in the underworld.

The point in the myth is that the feminine archetype must be made whole before the initiative to heal the feeling function can be activated, because the feminine archetype has been wounded by shame.

Typology and creativity

Usually when the concept of creativity is presented, it refers to something new and to something manifesting in the physical reality. The creative outcome depends on the main function available within the creative person: thinking, sensation, intuition or feeling. As Shepherd (1993) says, creativity in science seems to be a result of thinking and sensation, while psychotherapists prefer to use feeling and intuition. I suggest original creativity to be a result of using all four psychological functions in the psyche. The creation of soul, individuality and humanity cannot depend on one way of experiencing reality with a consequent rejection of other approaches. I remember a professor who asked: if a tree is falling on an island where no people witness the incident, does the tree fall? The professor thought not!

This is why we are now taken by surprise when the invisible shame is being understood in its self-destructive function in the human psyche. We did not see it coming and ignored the signs and connections to behavioral patterns.

Summary

Individuation is a lifelong process of inner development based on the inspiration that goes with life and the relationships we have to others. When shame prevents us from knowing who we truly are, we go blindfolded through life, avoiding shame and avoiding individuation. So the process of individuation is not without shame, but shame functions as a reminder of our humble limitation in relation to the self, more than as a judgement of who we have become.

One of the greatest challenges in the individuation process is the clash between the self and social requirements of the self. I also think it has become one of the main questions clients bring to therapy after a visit in the underworld. "How can I find a place in society where I can use my potential?" "Is there something wrong with me, since I don't succeed?" This is a different shame vulnerability that follows an inner journey and therefore it must become part of a shame-healing procedure. The risk of going back to old shame patterns when 'society' rejects our talents (and our individuality) is a time when inner strength is needed in order to stay connected to our own values. We may choose a complete new direction in our working life when the self guides us. We may want to divorce our partner who has been participating in the shame pattern we lived by, because he does not want to change the set of values that he brought into the relationship. Some of our friends may also reject our changed personality, preferring the old.

These challenges indicate that an inner journey has come to its last phase.

Literature

Abramovitch, H. (2014). *Brothers and Sisters. Myth and Reality.* Texas: Texas A&M University Press.

Abt, T. (2005). *Introduction to Picture Interpretation.* Zürich: Living Human Heritage Publication.

Ayers, M. Y. (2011). *Masculine Shame: From Succubus to the Eternal Feminine.* East Sussex: Routledge.

Brown, B., Hernandez, V. R. & Villarreal, Y. (2011). Connections: A 12-session Psychoeducational Shame Resilience Curriculum. In: Dearing, R. L. and Tangney, J. P. (editor). *Shame in the Therapy Hour.* Washington: American Psychological Association.

Dissanayake, E. (2000). *Art and Intimacy.* Seattle: University of Washington Press.

Gilbert, P. (2011). Shame in Psychotherapy and the Role of Compassion Focused Therapy. In: Dearing, R. L. and Tangney, J. P. (editor). *Shame in the Therapy Hour.* Washington: American Psychological Association.

Hillman, J. (1971). The Feeling Function. In: Franz, M. V. and Hillman, J. (editor). *Jung's Typology.* Dallas: Spring Publications, Inc.

Jacobsen, T. (1976). *The Treasures of Darkness.* New Haven: Yale University Press.

Jung, C. G. & Sonu Shamdasani (2009). *The Red Book. Liber Novus.* New York: W.W. Norton & Company.

Kaufmann, G. (1996). *The Psychology of Shame.* New York: Springer Publishing Company.

Kramer, S. N. (1961). *Sumerian Mythology.* Philadelphia: University of Pennsylvania Press.

Kramer, S. N. and Wolkstein, D. (1983). *Inanna: Queen of Heaven and Earth.* New York: Harper & Row Publishers.

Perera, S. (1981). *Descent to the Goddess.* Toronto: Inner City Books.

Rosen, D. (2002). *Transforming Depression.* York Beach, ME: Nicolas-Hays, Inc.

Schwartz-Salent, N. (2007). *The Black Nightgown: The Fusional Complex and the Unlived Life.* London: Chiron Publications.

Sharp, D. (1987). *Personality Types.* Toronto: Inner City Books.

Shepherd, L. J. (1993). *Lifting the Veil.* Lincoln: iUniverse, Inc.

Skov, V. (2015). *Integrative Art Therapy and Depression.* London: Jessica Kingsley.

Stewart, H. S. (1996). The Archetypal Affects. In: Nathanson, D. L. (editor). *Knowing Feeling.* New York: W.W. Norton & Company Inc.

Tomkins, S. S. (2008). *Affect Imagery Consciousness: The Complete Edition.* New York: Springer Company.

Index

For Product Safety Concerns and Information please contact our EU
representative GPSR@taylorandfrancis.com
Taylor & Francis Verlag GmbH, Kaufingerstraße 24, 80331 München, Germany

* 9 7 8 1 1 3 8 2 0 6 7 6 2 *